Mountain Home

MOUNTAIN HOME
By
Rosemary Whitlock

Professional Research Publishing Company
Charleston • Orlando

Published by
PROFESSIONAL RESEARCH PUBLISHING COMPANY
660 W. Fairbanks Avenue
Winter Park, Florida 32789

Library of Congress Cataloging-in-Publication Data

Whitlock, Rosemary.
  Mountain Home.

  1. Whitlock,Rosemary -- Childhood and youth. 2. Virginia --
Biography. 3 Allegheny Mountains (Virginia). 4. Mountain Life
-- Allegheny Mountains. 5. Allegheny Mountains -- Social life
and customs. I. Title.
CT275.W55334A3   1987   975.5   87-6940
ISBN 0-931807-10-7

CONTENTS

1

HOME IS WHERE THE HEART IS

Papa struck a long-stemmed match against the side of the matchbox. He held the flickering yellow flame against the wick of the kerosene lamp, then carefully replaced the lamp's chimney. These activities caused me to open one eye. Papa's stern voice caused me to open the other eye. He was saying "Children, your mama has called you twice. Come to breakfast now or get a threshin'."

Fred's and my feet hit the floor simultaneously. Still yawning and rubbing our sleepy eyes, we stumbled into the warm kitchen. I poured hot water from the black iron teakettle into the gray, enameled washbasin and added a dipper of cold water from the galvanized water bucket. We washed our faces and hands and slid into place on the gray bench at the back of the table.

Mama was putting a platter of fatback, fried brown and crispy, on the table. Her face was flushed a rosyred from the heat of the cookstove. Her white apron enveloped the front of her green and black checked cotton dress. Her hands were roughened and red from the wintry outside chores, but they were beautiful hands to us, guaranteeing love and security as she filled our plates with steaming hot flapjacks.

Mama said in her soft voice, "Eat hearty now, Mr. Snowman paid us a visit last night."

Suddenly, Fred and I were wide awake. We dashed to the window to view our white world. The snow had drifted high against the fences. The stock had not ventured from the barn as yet. Except for Rover's tracks in the yard, the white blanketing effect was unbroken. Fred and I crowded close against the frosted window pane. Our breath steamed against the cold glass and began to hamper our view. We both yelled, "Yippee!", as we dashed back to the table.

Papa was spreading grape jelly over his flapjacks, which were already covered with melting, homemade butter. We watched his broad fingers manipulating the bone handled knife and waited for his dampening words. True to our thought predictions, he said, "Now, you youngsters settle down and eat hearty like your mama said. I need you to help saw up a goodly pile of stove wood before you scatter off to play."

We stacked the wood knee-high on the back porch. Fred began to empty the snow from Rover's dish and I re-entered the warm kitchen. I beat my gloved hands together as I tried to combat their feeling of numbness. My teeth chattered and I felt as though icicles were hanging from my long eyelashes. I began to wheedle Papa, "Papa, will you teach us how to track rabbits in the snow?"

Papa grinned in spite of himself and then he frowned. "You know it's not sportin' to track rabbits that way," he said.

I entreated Papa with my very best coaxing tone of voice, "But Papa, you're always teaching us about herbs and plants. You said we needed to know how to forage for food if we ever got lost in the woods. We need to know how to forage for meat, too. Don't we?"

Papa sighed and gave in. "All right," he said, "Wait until Fred comes in and thaws out, then both of you put on some dry clothes and meet me at the barn."

Deep into the woods, we stopped while we listened to Papa's instructions. "You must look at the tracks mighty carefully. After you spot a set going in the same direction, look at them real close to see if they look like they were made by the same rabbit. Some rabbits weigh more than others, so you must find a set of tracks that are the same depth in the snow. Rabbits' foot sizes vary, so you have to find a set of tracks the same size. Sometimes there are small peculiarities in the sole of one foot or the other. Those are usually caused by a birth defect or an injury. Look for them, too. When you find a set of tracks that appear to be identical, follow those."

"As soon as we find a set of identical tracks, then the rest will be easy?" Fred asked.

"No. Followin' a rabbit's tracks is tricky business. Rabbits are easily distracted and frightened, so they seldom tread a straight course. Sometimes a rabbit will just veer off his course, but sometimes the rascal will run around in circles."

Bewildered, Fred and I looked about us. We finally decided

on a set of footprints and began to follow them. We walked slowly along, bending close to the snow's broken crust. We soon discovered that Papa was right. This particular rabbit was either very playful, or very indecisive...or maybe just scared of his own shadow. He had gone every which way but straight. After we followed several of his sidetracks and a couple of his circles, we finally tracked the tricky fellow to an old, hollow log.

Papa had given us sticks to carry. He handed me his stick to hold for him while he lay down in the snow to peer into the darkness inside the log. Then standing up, he reached for his stick and whispered. "He's in there all right. I caught a glimpse of his eyes. Bud, you get into position at the other end of the log. I'll use my stick at this end to rouse him out. Now he'll come out at your end and he'll come a runnin', so you've got to be quick to get him. Hit him across the temple a quick sharp blow so he won't suffer. Do you understand me?"

"Yes, Papa," I called out softly as I ran to the other end of the log. The brown, furry bundle hurtled from the hollow log as though a demon were at his heels. I screamed.

Papa was yelling, "Hit him, hit him!" Fred was flailing his stick and waving his arms and the frightened little rabbit turned and darted back into the hole in the log.

"Why didn't you hit him?" Papa asked.

"I couldn't, Papa. He looked so scared and little and I just couldn't," I answered.

"I'll flush him one more time and this time you'd better kill him, because this is your last chance," Papa said.

I got into position. My feet were spread-eagled for the sake of balance. My arms were outstretched, holding the stick aloft. I was ready to crown that fellow the second he stuck his head out. Papa flushed him again and I just stood there and watched as he ran off through the snow and disappeared over the hill.

That night at supper, Papa told Mama, "I want to tell you about the great rabbit hunt!" He proceeded to do so and ended by saying, "I hope I'm never lost in the snow with Bud...weak, hungry, in need of rabbit stew, because I'll starve to death."

"Well you don't like rabbit stew anyway, so there was no reason to kill him," I said.

In following winters, Fred and I sometimes tracked rabbits in the snow, but only for the skill involved in the search. We never again carried a stick to use as a club.

The day following what Papa had termed the great rabbit hunt, I was content to play quietly indoors. I colored the black and white pictures in the Love Story magazines Carrie had left behind. I held the crayon colored sheets against the window pane and placed a sheet of white paper over the colored picture. I carefully traced the pictured outline on the blank paper as the light, shining through the window pane, revealed the outline of the picture. I soon had numerous spanking new pictures to color.

I cut figures from the Sears, Roebuck And Co., Catalog. They became my paper dolls. It was great fun to choose names for my new family. I used my shoebox for an automobile. I allowed Fred to do all the driving of the makeshift automobile. That was the only way I could persuade him to play with paper dolls.

The next day, I was ill with tonsilitis. Mama said it was because I had stayed out in the snow and had gotten so wet tracking rabbits. I developed tonsilitis very often, no matter what kind of weather we were having, so she was probably just being a mama when she said that. She boiled onions and brought me a cup of hot liquid from them. I couldn't speak above a whisper, but I did whisper a vehement protest. I shook my head vigorously, which made my throat hurt even more. I clamped my teeth together. All to no avail. When all was said and done, I still had to drink the pungent onion juice.

By the next afternoon the sun was shining warmly. The melting snow made busy sounds as I watched and listened through the kitchen window. It dripped in rivulets from the eaves of the house. The icicles crashed against the frozen mounds of snow where we had heaped it as we shoveled a path to the cellar. Little mounds of snow would suddenly release the trees' branches from the snow's icy grip, and then soft, rustling sounds could be heard as though the branches had audibly sighed in relief. Water ran across the various paths and Papa's galoshes made slushing sounds as he carried more wood to the back porch. A large sheet of snow slid from the roof and showered to the ground.

"Mama, have you ever noticed how silently the snow falls from the clouds and how noisily it melts away beneath the sunshine?" I asked.

Mama looked up from her sewing, "Yes," she answered absent-mindedly. "Bud, look at these pretty scraps of material from the dress I'm makin' for Mitty. Do you want to learn how to make a dress for your doll? This material with its tiny pink flowers against the lighter pink background makes it look just perfect for a doll's dress. I've got some leftover white lace that you can use to trim the neckline.''

That sounded like it might be fun, so I seated myself on the floor at Mama's feet. I watched as she assembled all the articles I would need.

Mama cut a paper pattern using another doll dress as a model. She handed me the pattern and I pinned it to the material. I cut out the skirt, bodice, two little pockets and sleeves. I cut each of these separately.

I wet the thread with the tip of my tongue and guided the thread through the eye of the needle. Mama showed me how to allow a margin for the seams. I basted the pieces together and tried the dress on my doll. Mama showed me how to make the necessary adjustments to form a good fit. It was nearly time for supper preparations when I finally completed the dress by sewing the snap fastener to the neck opening. I tried my finished product on my Annabelle. The white lace was a little puckered in some places. The waist was loose fitting and one pocket was higher than the other.

"I don't like it," I said. "It's nice workmanship for your first dress and besides, it wouldn't take very long to remedy the mistakes you're pointin' out," Mama said.

I tried to snap the neckline fastener and the snap was set back too far. That was the last straw as far as I was concerned. I caught hold of the little dress on each side of the neck opening and ripped the dress apart.

Mama interlaced her work worn fingers and her thumbs began to circle around and around each other. She always did this unconsciously whenever she became ill at ease or agitated. Her soft brown eyes grew stern. Her soft voice grew even sterner as she said. "That was the worst exhibition of temper I've ever seen. You've got to learn to control your temper, Bud. Anger can only be justified if the result of the anger is to do or say somethin' to try and right a wrong. What you did just now was simply destructive. It's not the first time you've let your temper get the best of you. There is an old saying that a stitch in time saves nine. Therefore, I think the next thing you sew up had better be your temper. I'm goin' to start supper. As soon as you clean up the things you've strewn about, you're to come to the kitchen and peel the potatoes.'' With that final ultimatum, Mama closed

11

her sewing machine lid and departed.

I put the needle and pins in the machine cabinet's drawer and gathered up the scraps. I looked at the doll dress ripped down the front and back. I thought about all the time Mama had spent showing me how to make the little garment. She had answered my questions patiently. She had shown me how to line up the sleeve seams with the side seams. She had shown me how to measure the hem so it would hang evenly. She had shown me how to draw a basting thread around the edges of the little pockets before the final stitching to give them a ruffled appearance. I thought about how she used her less than plentiful egg sales income to purchase material and other clothing needs for us. Every scrap of material left over from our dresses was precious to her for making quilt tops. I thought about how she hadn't finished the dress for Mitty this afternoon because of pausing to help me so many times. She had tried to teach me something beneficial and I had brought it all to naught. I wondered why I could never seem to be kind, to be patient, like Mama and Papa.

2

EASTER

The sun was shining brightly on this premature spring morning. The birds were twittering cheerily as they flew from tree to tree as though trying to choose the perfect spots to build their nests.

Mama was planting tomato seeds in the long, wooden trays Papa had built for her. As she worked, Fred and I were busy putting a grain sack over Rover's head and laughing uproariously as he tried to dislodge it.

Mama said, "Since you two don't seem to have anything to do except tease Rover, I want you to go to the mailbox."

We groaned aloud. We were perfectly willing to go to the mailbox if Mama were expecting a package from Sears, Roebuck and Co., but to walk ten miles both ways just in case she might receive a letter from one or another of our relatives was not incentive enough for us.

True, we had carved out a path as the crow flies, which meant shortening the distance. Since we weren't crows, it also meant slipping and sliding over rocks and down steep hills while holding onto scrubby bushes to prevent us from falling headlong or skidding down the path on the skin of our backs. Coming back was even more of a challenge. Even on cold days we grew hot as we trudged almost straight up in places, pulling ourselves along holding onto the same scrubby bushes that had slowed our descent.

Today, we started off down the path still grumbling while Rover raced ahead, wagging his bushy tail in excitement. We took our good old time, stopping to watch the bugs and worms doing whatever they were doing. We watched Rover chase squirrels and rabbits in every direction. We threw rocks down the mountainside just to hear them plummet to some depth below us.

We finally arrived at the mailbox only to find that the mailman was running late. There were several mailboxes in a row and some of their flags were still up, meaning that he had not yet picked up the outgoing mail. We whiled away the time playing hopscotch and drawing pictures in the red clay earth, plus whatever else we thought of to do.

Fred watched Rover cavorting around and remarked, "You know, if Rover were a half smart dog we could teach him how to open the mailbox and fetch the mail. All he knows how to do is bring the cows home or chase chicken hawks away from the chickens."

"He's our good friend though, because when Mama switches us, she has to shut the door because he won't let her switch us if he can get to us," I replied.

"Yeah, I guess he's pretty smart," Fred said.

Before we had left to go to the mailbox, someone had come to the house to get Papa. He had said he needed Papa to help him with a cow who was having difficulty giving birth to her calf. We knew that when Papa was no longer needed to help the farmer with the cow, he would walk back home and the other farmer would stay with his sick cow and her newborn calf. So after the mailman finally came by, we decided to wait awhile to see if Papa would come and then walk home with him.

Just when we were about ready to give up and go on without him, we saw him trudging around the bend in the road. Papa looked pretty tired. When he got to us, we asked, "How do you feel, Papa?"

"Tolerable," he said. That was always Papa's stock answer to anyone who asked him how he felt. He'd say, "That way I'm neither braggin' nor complainin'."

"Come on Papa, let's take the shortcut home," we said.

Papa answered, "If you walk on the road at a steady gait, you will get home just as quickly as you will strugglin' up that mountainside trail. It's too steep to make good time."

"Well, you go by the road and we'll go by the shortcut," we said.

"I'll see you at the house." Papa said.

As soon as we were out of sight of the road, we broke into a run. We ran and stumbled and panted until our lungs seemed almost ready to burst. We raced on as fast as our climbing legs and reaching, pulling hands could thrust us upward. Near exhaustion, we ran out of the woods and entered the roadway. What to our unbelieving eyes did appear? There was Papa. His arms were folded across his chest. With head bowed he was walking steadily around the curve just below us. With a last burst of desperate energy, we forced our tired legs to race for home.

When Papa entered the door, Fred and I were seated on chairs in the kitchen. Sweat dampened our foreheads. Trying to quiet our heaving chests, we nonchalantly said, "Hi, Papa."

Papa grinned. His forehead was dry. His breathing was calm. "I saw you when you came racin' out of the woods just ahead of me," he said.

Mama was busily slapping bread dough from hand to hand as she flattened it into a cake shape. She glanced up and said, "Maybe what all three of you need is a set of four legs each, that is if you want to prove which is the fastest way home. Rover has been home for quite some time."

Mama awakened us at six o'clock the following morning. Papa wanted us to help him burn the brushwood. The piles of brushwood accumulated through the winter months as Papa cleared new ground. In early spring, he burned the brush before plowing and planting absorbed all his time.

There is no time of year when early morning is entirely free of fog high up in the mountains. On this particular morning, the fog was hanging thick and heavy in the air. The dampness of the fog made it an ideal morning for burning brush. It was the only kind of morning Papa would set a fire.

Even under these conditions, we each had to man a brush pile. We also had to rake around the piles frequently, shoring up the shifting brush and being alert for flying sparks. Papa said if the fires got out of hand, they could destroy the entire mountain's bounty of trees, vegetation and wildlife.

The multicolored flames with their bright hues of orange, yellow, blue and red, illuminated the foggy dimness of the early dawn. The heat of the flames added warmth to the chilliness of the damp air surrounding us.

I drank in the impressions of these mornings. The sound of the awakening farm jealously held on to realism while the drifting, misty fog shrouding the mountain top gave a vision of otherworldliness. The morning was indescribably beautiful as the spiraling flames soared upward, flirting with the now rising sun.

We saw Mama come out of the house and walk across the

barnyard to the chicken house. When she opened the door, the chickens crowded past her. They began to set up a fuss and retreat toward the chicken house as the now nearly burned out brush fires sent clouds of thick smoke over the barnyard. Mama shooed the chickens along by flapping her red-checked apron at them.

Mama had such a conglomeration of chickens. There were the Dominicks with their gray checked feathers, fat bodies and yellow legs. There were the Plymouth Rocks with their gray and bluish-black feathers and medium-sized bodies. There were Rhode Island Reds, heavy and plump with reddish-brown feathers and black fantails. There were the Buff Orpingtons and the White Orpingtons.

Added to these were the slender and sassy White Leghorns. Last, but not (implied by their demeanor) least, were the tiny Bantams. All of these busy, strutting, well-fed hens produced for us eggs of different colors and sizes according to the breed of hen. From high places, the proud roosters crowed the good news of their hens' bounty.

The Rhode Island Red hens were the best mother hens. They became mean and protective when they hatched a brood of chicks. I've seem them fly right up into the face of Prince or Lady because they were afraid these huge animals might step on one of their fearless chicks. Mama kept the wings cropped short on all of her hens, but they could still fly high enough to reach the lowered face of Prince or Lady.

Mama's favorite kinds of hens for cooking were the fat Buff or White Orpingtons. Needless to say Fred, Len and I strenuously objected to any breed of hen ending up on our table as fried chicken. We considered the chickens our friends.

We watched Mama on this particular morning as we stood guard over the brushwood. We saw her stoop over and catch hold of a Buff Orpington. We shuddered as she headed for the chopping block. We turned away and became very busy shoring up the fires so as not to watch the cold-blooded murder of the Buff.

The busy days of early spring flew by and soon it was Easter. Now Easter morning was celebrated at our house with The Great Egg Race. This was the special morning when Mama laid aside her thriftiness concerning excessive use of eggs. She also laid aside her motherly concern for us in the matter of our overloading our stomachs. She allowed us to eat all the eggs we could consume on Easter morning.

Papa tried to hide it behind a frown, but he was just as excited as we were. Fred and I eagerly set the table for our Easter feast while Mama brought up from the cellar a large bowl filled to the brim with white eggs and brown eggs.

From the gray, enameled coffee pot came the aroma of bubbling, hot coffee. From the warming oven came the tantalizing odor of country fried ham, ready and waiting to be served. A tall pitcher of fresh, sweet milk was placed near the center of the table.

In a short while, Mama began to place platters of fried eggs, scrambled eggs and boiled eggs on the table. Fred and I were glad of our open-mindedness concerning the consumption of hens' eggs.

We looked at Papa expectantly. We were waiting for the signal.

Papa's Sunday-morning-clean-shaven face broke into a smile. He lifted his fork and said, "Go!"

The race was on between him, Fred and myself, to see which one could eat the most eggs. Fred and I skipped the ham and took only a few sips of milk from our tall glasses.

We were determined every Easter morning for at least one of us to eat more eggs than Papa. We had never won a contest yet and today was no exception. We gave up and sat back with a groan, holding our stomachs.

Papa threw back his head with its shock of beautiful, white, wavy hair and laughed his deep, rumbling, rare laugh. He was still the champion egg eater thoroughly enjoying his victory!

The rest of the family began to arrive soon after breakfast. Lawrence drove up first, beeping his car horn and grinning as always. When Lawrence stopped the car, Elena slid out, holding Betty in her arms while Lawrence held the car door open for her.

Elena looked every inch the young matron in her navy dress. The dress sported stylish tucks across the breast and a wide, tailored, white pique bow at the throat relieved the severity of the dark navy color. Perched atop her salt and pepper hair was a white, bowl-shaped hat adorned with navy veiling. Her feet were encased in conservative, white pumps.

As we stood, admiring her Easter finery, Elena called out a cheery good morning and turned back toward the open car door. She said in a soft, yet firm voice, "Len, come on now."

Len slowly emerged and stood silently beside the car. His

hands were jammed into his trouser pockets and a scowl lay across his face. Mama patted his blond curls, but he didn't respond to her with his usual hug.

Elena said, "He's sulking because I made him wear his knickerbockers. He wanted to wear overalls."

Fred sidled up close to Len as a kindred spirit. He, too, had wanted to wear overalls, but Mama had told him he must wear his dress knickers because it was Easter Sunday.

The knickers were loose fitting and gathered in just below the knee with either elastic or a knitted cuff. One or both trouser legs were constantly sliding down and stopping at different levels. The boys' socks were ankle length, which left a portion of their legs bare. Consequently, both boys thought the knickers were not only aggravating, but babyish as well. They sulked every time they were forced to wear them.

Clarence drove in with Dorothea, Tommy and Frances a short while after Lawrence had arrived.

Dorothea had met Clarence just a few months after she and Frank had gotten a divorce. Clarence was tall and slender. He had pale blond hair and china blue eyes. His physical appearance was just the opposite of Frank's.

Clarence ran a shoe repair shop in Covington and Dorothea had met him when she had taken a pair of shoes in for repair. There had been no other customers at the time and Clarence had introduced himself and had drawn Dorothea into conversation. When Dorothea had returned a few days later to pick up her shoes, Clarence had asked her for a date. Their romance had blossomed quickly and they had gotten married just a few weeks past.

Clarence drove a Model A Touring car and we heard the sounds of its air horns from far down the mountain road. Clarence kept those air horns so shiny that we could see our faces reflected in them when he drove up to the gate. The black curtains were drawn back today because the weather was so warm, and Tommy was extending his arms to me through the opening before Clarence had fully stopped the car's motion.

Dorothea seemed to have resigned herself to the fact of little Eddie's death and today she was her normally exuberant self. Her infectious laughter rang out as she jumped from the car, talking a mile a minute.

Dorothea looked pretty in her Easter finery. Her white, shark-skin skirt swished around her shapely legs. Her white, slim-lined jacket emphasized her tiny waist. Her curly hair made a frame for her white pillbox hat. Her red painted toenails peeked from her white, open-toed shoes. The tips of her very high heels made little holes in the path as she fairly danced toward the house.

Frances' outfit made a beautiful contrast for Dorothea's totally white one. Frances' dress was a deep violet color. It had a deep V-neck and the taffeta lining beneath the full skirt made a swishing sound as she pirouetted. In her slim hand, she carried a violet colored straw hat with purple veiling. Tiny, pale pink roses marched around the hat where the wide brim met the hat's crown. Her white gloves, carried loosely in her hand, made a striking appearance against the violet and purple hat. Her toenails, painted pink, peeped from her white strapped, high-heeled shoes. A small, white purse was tucked under her arm.

Rover barked his message that another car was coming. This time it was Lewis with Carrie and Ronnie. Carrie was all decked out for Easter, too. She wore a long-jacketed, yellow suit. A white Polo coat was thrown across her arm. A flopping, wide-brimmed, yellow hat adorned her black, shoulder length hair. The hat's wide brim, dipping over her forehead, accentuated her tanned skin and high cheekbones.

Mama, dressed in her blue-checked gingham housedress and her black, Natural Bridge shoes, and I, dressed in my green-checked gingham dress and brown oxfords, admired their pretty outfits. The navy, white, yellow and violet colors of their clothing made a vibrant splash against the backdrop of the greening mountains.

Carrie reached back into the car and brought forth a box with several round holes in it. She handed the box to Fred and me. We lifted the lid and gazed into the box with wondering eyes. A furry white rabbit gazed back at us from curious, pink eyes. We immediately dubbed him, Pinky, because of his eyes.

Carried laughed as she said, "I thought you two might like to have a real Easter bunny."

Papa said, "Put him in the chicken coop until tomorrow, then I'll help you gather up some wire and wood scraps so you can build a hutch for him."

Mama and the girls placed a bountiful dinner on the table at noon. Papa ate heartily. Fred and I gingerly picked at our food because of our overabundance of eggs at breakfast.

Frances and Dorothea were chattering like magpies about a

19

new dance craze called The Big Apple. Neither one of the girls could explain why it was so named. The Big Apple was a swing-off from the square dance, the Charleston, and several other dances, combining parts from each. They changed the subject when Carrie made a remark about a movie she had seen recently. The kitchen seemed alive with voices as everyone joined in and the conversation began to jump from one subject to another.

Later on in the afternoon, Fred and I recovered sufficiently from breakfast to join in the big Easter egg hunt, using eggs Mama had helped us color.

As the sun began to wane, the wind grew chilly, so everyone went indoors to chat. Before long the girls began to take turns reminiscing and laughing uproariously at some of their memories.

Elena started the ball rolling by saying. "Carrie, do you remember the time you tried to threaten Mama when you were eleven years old? Remember how rebellious you were for several days? You teased the rest of us unmercifully. You kept talking back to Papa and refusing to help Mama?"

Carrie answered, "How could I forget? Mama decided to take a firm stand. She switched my legs until they throbbed. I grew so angry at the idea of being spanked when I was eleven years old that I told Mama I was going to run away from home. Was I ever deflated when Mama answered, 'Joy go with thee and peace behind thee'."

Dorothea said, "I remember when Carrie made her first bra out of yellow cotton. She didn't have a pattern and one cup turned out larger than the other. Her bust was so small, neither cup fit anyway and I surely didn't help matters when I tried to comfort her by pointing that out to her."

Amidst the laughter that followed, Frances remembered the tenseness of a ballgame at Longdale. She said, "Remember how we always had to use a stick cut from a sturdy sapling for a bat? The bases were loaded and Dorothea was at bat. We were all screaming excitedly, "Hit it, hit it!" Dorothea spat on her hands. She dug her heels into the turf. She wiggled her hips, swung at the ball like the mighty Casey and the stickbat broke!"

Deftly changing the subject, Dorothea asked, "Remember our Loop the Hoops?"

"Oh yes, they were fun," Frances said. "We used a wire bent in a semicircle at one end for a guide. We could hook it under a metal rim taken from a wooden barrel, and roll the hoops up and down steep hills and through uneven fields. It took a lot of practice to learn to keep the metal hoops upright using only a wire loop as a guide.''

"Oh, we were experts when it came to making do with whatever was at hand," Elena said. "Remember our fancy toothbrushes? We cut twigs of green wood and roughed up one end and then we put baking soda on the roughened end. After we brushed our teeth, we threw the toothbrush away.!''

Carrie said, "I remember a tale on Harry that wasn't funny at the time, but somehow it seems funny now.''

"I bet I know. You're thinking about the time Harry tangled with the revenuers," Elena said.

"Yes," Carrie answered. "It happened when Harry became so despondent because he couldn't get a job to help the family. Some grown men, who were mixed up in transporting 'White Lightnin', approached Harry. They knew the revenuers were close to discovering where they hid their filled jugs. They asked Harry if he could hide the jugs at our house.

"The men told Harry that since Mr. Clark was a respected man in the community, the revenuers would never think of looking there. Their plan ran into a snag though when Harry asked Papa for permission to hide their jugs.

"Papa said emphatically, 'No. Son, what those men are doin' is against the law. You're not to take any part in it.'

'But Papa, they promised to pay me well and you know we need the money. We don't even have enough to live on,' Harry protested.

"Papa said, 'But me no buts, son. We don't need the money that bad. If we can't manage to stay alive honestly, then at least we'll know we starved to death honestly.'

"Harry disobeyed Papa. He sneaked off and met the men a few nights later. They brought the jugs to our house and quietly hid them under the front porch. The next afternoon, the revenuers came to our house. They told Mama they wanted to talk to Harry and did she know if he had hidden any 'White Lightnin' on the premises? Mama didn't know what was going on for sure, but she was scared because of Harry's previous conversation with Papa. Mama fidgeted with the corner of her white apron as she answered in the negative. The revenuers observed Mama's uncertainty and they began to search the house. I sneaked out of the house and ran as fast as I could over the hill to where Harry was checking his rabbit traps. Unknown to me, one of the revenuers saw me leave and followed me. Harry looked up when I yelled at him. He saw the revenuer coming.

"The revenuer raised his gun and ordered Harry to stand still. Instead, Harry began to back away. The revenuer charged up the hill, and with his eyes on Harry, he didn't see the rabbit trap. The revenuer's foot got caught in the trap and as he pitched forward, his gun went off. At the sound of that shot, Harry sailed up into the air and hit the ground running. Harry leapt down the hill like a jack rabbit. He came to a halt when he got to the train tracks because a train engine was slowly backing several train cars to connect with another line of train cars.

"Meanwhile, the revenuer, having regained his feet if not his dignity, was catching up to Harry. When Harry looked back and saw him, Harry dove under one of the slowly moving train cars. I stood at the top of the hill, gasping in horror. The train's engineer looked horrified, too, as he tried to bring the engine to a stop. The revenuer waited until the engine had stopped. He ran on toward the river, having crossed the tracks between the engine and the cars. When he saw Harry halfway across the river, swimming like a professional, he gave up and turned back.

"Harry told me later that by the time he had swum to the far side of the river in his sodden clothes, he was so cold he thought he had escaped the revenuer only to take pneumonia and die.

"The revenuers did catch up with him later and he still had to spend three days in jail. The judge let him go because of his youth and because of the perfected enticement of the moonshiners."

On and on they talked, laughing and reminiscing until the small children grew tired and sleepy. They all bade their farewells and then one car after another disappeared into the darkness.

Easter day was drawing to a close and Mama said, "Time to get ready for bed, children. Tomorrow is a work day."

Her soft black hair gathered into its bun at the nape of her neck seemed to shimmer with highlights in the light from the lamp. Her soft brown eyes were smiling as she tucked the covers around Mitty. How she had loved Easter Sunday, when all of her children had come home.

3

CHORES

Mama went with Fred and me one beautifully sunny afternoon to search for her beloved teaberries. Teaberries grew in plentiful patches on the mountain so the search was always a rewarding one.

Mitty didn't go with us. Papa was feeling really ill with a head cold, so he told Mama that he would take care of Mitty at the house.

Mama cautioned us to watch out for snakes. King snakes are related to blacksnakes and they love to eat ripe berries. King snakes are generally considered harmless to man, but Mama and Papa didn't know that.

King snakes feed on other snakes. They also feed on small animals and rodents. The king snake coils around its prey and squeezes until its prey dies of suffocation. Mama and Papa had been taught all their lives that if a king snake were to become frightened and feel threatened by a human being, the snake would coil around a human being also. Their fear of the king snake was very real and they taught us to be just as wary of it as we were of poisonous snakes.

We were quite some distance from the house when we came across a very large patch of teaberries. Mama began picking the tiny, pink berries and dropping them into the pail she carried. Fred and I were picking the berries just as industriously as she, but very few were finding their way into our pails.

Suddenly, Mama straightened up and said, "Stand still. There's a king snake right over there." We stood motionless for a moment. The snake seemed to watch us but remained where he lay.

Mama said, "Back away slowly. Don't make any sudden motions."

23

We began to step backward very slowly. Our eyes were glued to the snake. Then Fred stepped on a rock and it threw him off balance. He dropped his pail and his arms flew outward as he tried to recover his stance. The snake slithered toward us and we turned and ran as fast as our legs would carry us. The king snake was slithering right behind us.

Mama caught up with us and screamed out in a loud tone of voice, "Go that way." Fred and I took off in the direction she had pointed. I glanced over my shoulder and there went Mama sailing off in another direction. We ran on, lickety-split for a short distance and then realized that the snake was no longer following us. We stopped.

We spied Mama running in a wide circle around the teaberry patch. She came around to where we stood and said, "Let's go home."

As we walked, I pondered on the chase and felt hurt that Mama had abandoned us. Finally I could stand it no longer. "Mama, why did you run away from us when we needed you?" I asked.

Mama answered, "Because I knew we could not outrun the snake. My only hope of protectin' you two was to take a chance on gettin' the snake to follow me. Thank goodness he got so confused, he just quit chasin' everybody. You see, Bud, if a body comes to a fork in the road, standin' there spittin' on the ground won't tell him which way to go. He's got to choose which way he thinks is the right one."

I was silent the rest of the way home. Mama hadn't come right out and said so, but I knew what she had done. By screaming out so loudly as she turned to run in an opposite direction, she had hoped to divert the snake's attention to herself. She had chosen to give her life, if necessary, in order to save ours.

There are two types of wild lettuce that grow on the mountain, and this same spring, we learned the hard way how to tell the difference between the two. Mama explained to us that the bitter variety was a slightly darker green and the leaves had fewer indentations around the edges than the sweet variety had. Then she sent us off to gather wild lettuce in a field high above the orchard. We came home from that expeditious gathering with an overflowing bucket and almost all of the lettuce proved to be the bitter kind.

Mama went with us the next time we gathered lettuce. We

asked her if this or that plant was the sweet or bitter kind and she would answer, "Taste it and see." It didn't take too many tastes of the bitter kind for us to learn to look at it and see a shade's difference in its color and a slight difference in its leaf pattern.

We looked forward to the springtime suppers with the wild lettuce as the main dish. We cut up the lettuce on our individual plates and added boiled Irish potatoes. Next we added small green onions and red radishes from Mama's vegetable garden. We sprinkled on vinegar, black pepper, salt, and hot meat drippings as garnishes. It was a dish fit for a king. Fried fatback, buttered corn bread and fresh buttermilk completed our meal.

After supper on one such occasion, Papa leaned back from the table and began to fill his pipe with tobacco. He said, "That was a mighty fine meal, Dora. You make a fine pone of corn bread. Sometimes I wish we still had a fireplace so you could make us some hoecakes like you used to. Sometimes I kind of crave a hoecake. I guess it's because that's the kind of bread we ate when we were growin' up." Papa puffed on his pipe thoughtfully.

"Yes, I expect that's it," Mama said. "Seems like the way a body remembers food tastin' in their younger days makes it seem like it was the best food there ever could be."

"Papa, why did a hoecake taste differently from corn bread?" I asked.

Papa's gnarled hand cradled the bowl of his pipe as he puffed a series of smoke rings into the air. I knew he was trying to garner his thoughts before he tried to explain to me, in his slow drawl, why a hoecake was different.

"I guess that was before your time bein' as you're amongst the last of the lot," he said. "When your Mama and I were first married, the womenfolk still cooked over fireplaces. We had what was called a Dutch Oven. It was made of black cast iron same as the skillets your Mama uses now, but it had a real long handle and a lid with a stand-up rim.

"Dora, and both our mamas before her, would pull some of the hot coals and ashes out onto the soapstone hearth. The Dutch Oven could be heatin' there while your Mama mixed up the corn meal with some bakin' soda, bakin' powder, salt, hog lard and thick buttermilk. Then she'd pour the mixture into the heated Dutch Oven and put the lid on tight. She'd pull hot coals under and around the pot and heap some of the hot coals and ashes on

25

top of the lid. The stand-up rim kept the coals from slidin' off the top and the hoecake would bake slowly until done.

"Sometimes she added cracklin' bits to the corn meal mixture and made cracklin' hoecakes. The hoecakes were kind of moist and finer textured than corn bread. Corn bread, baked in an oven, is baked without a lid and at a higher degree of heat."

He tamped more tobacco into his now half-empty pipe and struck a country match on the leg of his thick denim overalls. After he had puffed the fresh tobacco into burning properly, he resumed his reverie.

"We had a squirrel pot, too. It had three very short legs, and a balloon shaped bowl, and the same kind of lid and long handle as the Dutch Oven. When I'd come back from squirrel huntin' with a couple of squirrels, your mama would ready them and make squirrel stew in that pot. Now, you talkin' about some powerful good eatin'. If you could just try a hunk of that hoecake dipped in the broth of that squirrel stew, you would know what I'm talkin' about. You youngsters just don't know what you've missed, bein' born in these modern times."

I wasn't at all sure I agreed with Papa about what constituted, "powerful good eatin'." Nevertheless, Fred and I both loved to urge Papa on with questions in order to get him started on stories like this of long ago. Mama was more apt to come right to the point of a story and get on with it. But once we got Papa started, we didn't even have to say anything. He would lean back in his chair and ramble on and on...

The month of May was soon upon us and the chores of spring increased.

The corn we planted each spring provided feed for the hogs and chickens in the coming winter months. Papa took some of the corn to the mill in the autumn to be ground into meal for baking bread. Some of the corn would be sold. The fodder would be used to feed the cows. Therefore, we were very busy as we tended field after field of white corn. The corn rows were so long we couldn't see from one end to the other after the corn grew high. The tasks of thinning the corn, leaving two stalks to each hill, and chopping the eager weeds from between the rows were arduous chores.

Fred was a silver-tongued liar and actor when it came to getting out of work. He would place his hand on his forehead and clutch his stomach with the other hand. He'd bend over almost double and grown like a dying goof-off.

Papa would ask, "What's the matter with you, son?"

Fred's answer, "I'm sick, Papa. My head hurts and my stomach hurts. I think the heat has just about done me in."

Then Papa would say, "Find a shady spot and lie down. You probably need to rest awhile."

As I worked my way to the end of a long row, there would be Fred lolling in the shade of a big oak tree. He'd laugh and taunt, "Look at you. Your face is beet red and you can't see for the sweat dripping down. You sure are dumb to work like that."

I'd stick out my tongue at him in fury and reply, "Somebody has to help Papa."

"I know that. You'll help so why should I get all hot and tired, too? I'll see you when you get back to this end of the next row. Bye now. Be sure you do a good job."

When I worked my way back to that end again, Fred would lift the water jug and ask, "Do you want a drink of water before you start back? Is that why you keep sticking your tongue out at me, because you're thirsty?"

"You just wait, lazybones,I'll get even." Papa's big boots that I had to wear in the field wobbled around on my tired feet as I tried to chase him to get the water jug.

When Papa came to that end of the field, Fred managed to look sad and sickly. He'd rub his stomach with his hands and with closed eyes mumble, "I still don't feel good, Papa."

Oh, how many times through the hot summer did Fred get out of work that way?! Each day in the cornfield, I thought the time would never come when Papa would look up at the lowering sun and say, "It's nigh onto five o'clock. When we reach the end of this row, we'll call it a day."

Fred and I usually rode on Prince's broad back as Papa walked slowly alongside. When we started up the road on the homeward stretch, my heart always gladdened at the sight of home. The small, white, frame house was built in the shape of the capital letter L. Crisp, white curtains hung at the windows. Within the wire enclosed yard, Mama's flowers were a riot of color.

Rover, in anticipation of supper, usually arrived at the house far ahead of us. He waited near the back porch, wagging his bushy, tan and white tail in greeting. Lady and Jersey stood near the woodpile waiting to be milked, their udders hanging low and heavy with the day's offerings. The chickens were gathered near the chicken house. The fluffy biddies were gathered around their mothers' feet. They looked so cute as they milled around, cheeping out their baby messages.

I couldn't see Mama, but I knew she was bustling back and forth between the table and the hot cookstove. By the time we washed the dirt from our hands and faces and took our seats at the table, Mama's busy hands had laden the table with good things to eat.

The kitchen window in this house was built low to the ground as the window in the Longdale house had been. I had resumed my old habit of running in through the open window when I was in a hurry. I didn't think Mama would realize I was no longer using the window so much as a quick access route as I was an escape route from Fred.

Fred was a quiet, slow-moving, bashful lad. He was slow to anger, but once aroused, there was no reasoning with him. When I teased him unmercifully, as I frequently did, I found it best just to get out of his way when he reached his limit of endurance.

I could always get a head start and escape him by running in through the open kitchen window. Fred didn't dare try to get even with me once we were in the presence of Mama. Therefore, I was having a lot of fun at Fred's expense this spring until the problem of houseflies ruined my strategy.

Houseflies were a serious problem during warm weather on the farm. One female housefly can lay one hundred and twenty eggs at a time. Each summer, a multitude of female flies lays several batches of eggs. When these billions of eggs hatch out the following spring, that spells trouble. These hordes of flies are real pests when the windows and doors have no screens, especially on a farm.

Mama talked to Mr. Trumbolte one warm spring day about the problem. He said he would provide the screen wire and the necessary boards and nails if Papa would build the window screens and screen in the back porch.

Mama was very pleased when the screening was completed, but not me. I soon learned that screened windows were not only a hindrance to the houseflies, but to me as well.

In my haste to escape Fred, I was prone to forget all about the new screen on the kitchen window. I slammed into the screen

28

full force on several occasions.

A few bloody noses, plus a final warning from Papa the last time he had to repair the screen, taught me my lesson. I could not escape to the sanctuary of Mama's kitchen anymore.

It was then I found out that, as usual, Mama had known what was going on all the time.

She said, "I notice Fred can catch up with you now that you have to take time to go around to the door and open it before you come in. I think it serves you right, missy. Maybe now you'll learn to quit teasin' him."

Papa didn't need Prince with the work at hand sometimes, and on those days, he let Prince roam at will. Prince seemed very much like Fred and me except that he was a horse. How he loved his free days, just as we did ours. Prince would run with his beautiful flowing mane streaming in the wind his own swift movements created. He would roll over and over on the grassy slopes. Then, leaping to his feet, he would fling his head high and whinnie as with joy overflowing. His favorite place to roam was in the field high above the orchard.

After supper on Prince's free days, Papa would go into the yard and call, "Come on, Prince. Come on home, sweetheart."

Mama sometimes fussed at Papa about that term of endearment. "I don't see why you call that wild horse sweetheart. You never call me sweetheart, Frank Clark," she said.

Papa said, "Now, Dora, you watch. When I call him sweetheart, he always comes a runnin'." Papa cupped his hands around his mouth and called out, "Hey, Prince." Prince raised his head, his reddish-brown sides gleaming in the light of the setting sun.

"Come on home, sweetheart," Papa called.

Prince reared up, his slender forelegs arched in front of him, then he came racing down the hillside.

Papa threw back his head and laughed. "I'll call you sweetheart, too, Dora, just as soon as you learn to come a runnin' like Prince does," Papa said.

"Ah sugar," Mama said as she settled her apron and turned toward the door.

Papa chuckled as he set off to meet Prince at the barn. Mama's dislike and distrust of Prince went beyond Papa's teasing though. She was firmly convinced that Prince was too young and too high-spirited for a workhorse.

We spent the next several days making chicken coops. Mama had so many hens setting, there weren't enough coops to go around. Papa helped us gather the lumber, handsaws, hammers, nails and a can of green pain into a work area. He helped us build the first coop. With many words of advice, he taught us as we went along with the construction.

"Decide on the size you want first and then do your measurin' and cuttin'. Don't try to force the saw by pushin' down on it. Draw the saw back and forth with a steady motion and let it do the cuttin'. That's why it's called a saw. Hold your hammer handle near the end of the handle. Never hold it near the hammerhead because you can't put enough force behind the blow. You'll only peck at the nail until you worry it into the wood," Papa said.

When we finished the first coop, he showed us how to stir the paint until its components were thoroughly mixed. He showed us how to paint with even strokes of the brush. We found out we were pretty fair hands at painting because we had painted the old unpainted barn with water and brushes a million times just for fun. After we had finished painting the chicken coop and left it to dry, Papa said, "Now that you two know how to build a chicken coop, I want each of you to build another one apiece. You don't need me now. I'm going to the cornfield to work."

We were busy as two beavers on our new project when Mama called to us soon after the midday meal.

She said, "Your Papa forgot his jug of water. Take it to him and don't dally along the way."

We filled the jug from the water bucket. The water in the bucket was already warm from the heat of the day. Papa had taught us never to drink cold water pumped fresh from the cistern or to drink from a cold running stream when our bodies were overheated and perspiring. He said the sudden drop in the body's heat caused by the cold liquid could cause stomach cramps or nausea.

Fred held the jug and I poured water into it from the dipper. We wanted to make sure that one of us didn't do any more work than the other.

Mama watched us. She sighed as she said, "I guess it's another one of those days from the looks of things."

When we reached the field, Papa stopped digging and leaned on his hoe handle. He pulled his red bandana handkerchief from the back pocket of his bib overalls and mopped his wet brow. He took off his straw hat and fanned himself with it. His beautiful white hair lay matted and yellowish with perspiration against his head. Papa said, "I'm glad your Mama sent the water along. You two are a sight for sore eyes. How are you comin' along with the chicken coops?"

"Just fine," we said. "Can we build some more tomorrow?"

"We'll see. I'll check on your work this evenin'. If you're doin' a good job, you can build some more coops tomorrow." Papa said.

"Yippee!" we yelled. We raced toward home. For once we agreed on something. Building chicken coops won hands down over working in the hot cornfields.

We sawed and hammered to our hearts' content the next day. The only disruption was keeping an eye on Mitty. We put her in the sandbox and let her pour sand over her head so she wasn't much trouble. Mama was busy making dish towels, which was why we had to watch Mitty.

Mama used the unbleached cotton sacks the flour had been packed in at the flour mill. After the sacks were emptied, she cut away the bulky, sewn seams and using her sewing machine, she sewed flat seams instead. She boiled the dish towels in the iron kettle filled with water and lye to bleach the towels as white as snow, almost.

We finished our chicken coops and painted them. We left them to dry that evening while we went walking through the orchard with Papa to inspect the young oat grasses which were thriving.

We came across a blacksnake with its sides bulging. Papa grabbed a rock and hurled it at the snake's head. Fred and I were grabbing up more rocks to hand to Papa. He killed the snake and then, using a large pocketknife, he cut the snake open near the bulge. A frog hopped out of the snake's open belly.

Fred and I screamed and started to run. Papa called to us to come back. We came back to stand beside him. We protested what we had seen by saying, "Papa that snake ate the poor frog while it was still alive. That was a horrible thing to do."

Papa said, "Spiders catch flies in their webs when the flies are still alive. Frogs eat bugs when the bugs are still alive. Snakes eat frogs alive. So it goes and it's not as cruel as it seems. If one thing didn't eat another, the world would become plagued with pests and all the vegetation would be destroyed."

"It's still cruel, Papa, to eat a living thing," we said.

"Animals don't have a soul or a conscience as we do to help them decide between right and wrong," Papa said. Papa looked at us and he could see we were still not convinced, so he went on talking. "Some animals kill their prey after they swallow it and others kill their prey before they eat it. They all kill for the same reason. To survive. They forage and kill each other and we, in turn, kill many of them for food. It's the order of the universe. It has its beneficial properties as well as its destructive ones."

Papa was hunkered down and his grey eyes looked serious as he looked at us. He picked up a stick and with it, he slowly drew circles in the plowed earth. He drew the outline of a whale. Then he began to tell us the Bible story of Jonah and the whale. He told us that the whale had swallowed Jonah and three days later, he had spit Jonah upon the sand.

"Now Jonah was still alive. He got a second chance at life just as that frog got a second chance just now," Papa said. "This snake didn't get a second chance. Remember that and do the best you can with your first chance at life. You may not get a second chance. The Lord wasn't finished with this frog, but he was finished with this snake." Papa rose to his feet and walked on through the orchard to continue his inspection of the young stand of oat grasses.

Mama chose a Tuesday when Papa was caught up enough with the crops to help her wash the quilts. Fred and I were kept busy pumping water to fill the tubs for each quilt. Mama scrubbed the large, bulky quilts on the washboard, but she needed Papa to help her wring the water from them. She would grasp one end of a quilt and he would grasp the other end. Turning their bodies in opposite circles, lifting their arms up, over and outwards, the quilt twisted between them. In this manner, they managed to squeeze a lot of water from the layers of materials. it also took both of them to lift the sodden quilts over a pair of clotheslines to dry. The drying time usually took the better part of two sunshiny days.

After the midday dinner, Papa told us to churn the milk because Mama's arms were so tired from washing the quilts. Fred and I sat at two separate wooden churns filled with clabbered milk. Grasping the wooden handle for each churn, we pushed each wooden paddle up and down. The thicker the milk became the harder it was to push the paddle through it. We hoped the butter would gather to the top of the milk by some kind of quick magic. It didn't. We stopped often to lift the rounded lids and peep inside to see how much butter had gathered. Mama grumbled that we could churn in half the amount of time if we didn't pause so often to peep.

When we finally finished, she skimmed the butter from the top of the thickened buttermilk. She rinsed the butter in cold water to remove any remaining milk. She added salt and worked the butter with a wooden paddle to rid it completely of liquids and at the same time mix in the salt. Then she put mounds of butter in a wooden butter press to form the butter into a uniform one pound measure. The press' disc had the imprint of a large daisy, surrounded by little daisies. She pushed the patterned disc downward to push the butter out. When the rounded mound plopped onto the saucer, we could see the imprint of the daisies. The buttermilk was transferred into earthen crocks and the finished products were stored in the cool, damp cellar.

One sultry, spring afternoon, the storm clouds that had been gathering all morning suddenly closed out the patches of blue sky completely. The rains came quickly in a drenching downpour.

A mother hen had ventured quite a distance from the chicken coops with her brood of days-old chicks. Another hen had rejected her chicks, so Mama had given those chicks to this good mother hen also. The hen squatted and spread her wings. She clucked in alarmed tones to gather her chicks and her adopted chicks beneath her sheltering wings. Her efforts were to no avail. The hard rain washed over the ground, rocking the hen with its driving force. She had far too many chicks to cover them adequately in such a storm.

Mama called to us frantically to come and help. We gathered up the sodden balls of baby chicks and Mama made a bowl of her apron by holding the corners. We piled the chicks in the apron as quickly as we could. Mama carried them to the house while the mother hen pecked at her ankles in protest. Mama carefully placed the limp little bundles on the open oven door. The chicks were still and silent.

Fred and I began to cry. "Mama, it's no use. They're dead," we said.

"Shush," Mama said as she fetched an old baby blanket from the trunk. She gently spread the thin blanket over the pitiful forms.

She stood silently by the stove. We drug our arms across our wet faces where our teardrops and the raindrops had mingled.

After what seemed an eternity the blanket moved slightly. We heard a faint cheep, cheep. Gradually the blanket seemed to come alive with movement and sound as the chicks revived. Mama found a crate and placed the warm blanket in it. She lifted the chicks and placed them in the crate. We sat back and watched with joy as the chicks' baby fuzz began to fluff out. The house was filled with the sound of cheeping chicks.

The rain had ended as suddenly as it had begun. As soon as Mama was sure the chicks were as good as new, she picked up the crate and went outside where the mother hen was waiting at the door of the screened-in porch. Ordinarily the chickens were not allowed to enter the yard, but Mama had let the mother hen follow us as far as the door. The hen ran along beside Mama, squawking loudly as Mama marched through the gateway. Mama stopped when she reached the row of chicken coops and set the crate down on the ground. She tilted it over slowly and let the chicks run out. Inside one of the coops, the hen, clucking gently now, gathered her chicks to her.

As we returned to the house, Fred and I walked close to Mama. In unison we said, "Mama, you're the best Mama in the whole wide world."

Papa had cleared one corner in the barnloft by moving the hay away from it so I could have that space for a playhouse during the winter months. Now that summertime was nearing, I decided to move.

Papa had cleared off a hillside within sight of the house. There was a tree that was so bent and deformed from the crowding of stronger trees that we had felt sorry for it and had asked Papa to leave it free and clear. We named the tree Crooked Jake, and as far as we were concerned, Crooked Jake was another of our friends.

I decided that the shady spot right beneath Crooked Jake was the ideal place to build my summer playhouse. We designed and built an open air playhouse upon the ground. We used sticks and rocks to designate outer walls and inner rooms. Then came moving day and we trudged back and forth with Fred's wagon, hauling my accumulation of odds and ends to the new house.

Last of all I fetched my beloved Annabelle. I rode in the wagon with her and Fred chauffeured. We pretended that we had a long way to go to reach the new playhouse. Fred pulled the wagon up the upper road that rose higher than the plane our house was situated on. Fred made me get out of the wagon before he had pulled it very far and Annabelle rode alone. He and I took turns pulling the wagon the rest of the way up.

The ride down was exhilarating. The wagon hurtled along at a breakneck speed. The wind grabbed at our hair. It roared in our ears and stung our eyes until everything became a blur. We rocketed along bouncing up from the seat as we shot over the bumpy places. I hung onto Annabelle with one hand and onto the straps of Fred's overalls with the other.

Fred hung onto the wagon's tongue, guiding by instinct often because he could not see where he was going. It took a lot of skill because he never once wrecked. Or maybe it wasn't skill. Maybe it was a mama's prayers and her God up above having mercy on two disobedient children. This wasn't the first time we had hurtled down the steep road, although Mama had cautioned us many times not to do so.

4

DECISIONS, DECISIONS

School closed in late June. Lawrence and Elena brought Len to the farm for his summer visit. I had steadfastly refused to return to Craigsville and finish my spring term in school. Mama was already voicing concern about the beginning of school this coming autumn and what arrangements she could make so both Fred and I could attend. Fred was nine years old and he had never had the opportunity to begin school at all because of the school's distance from the farm. Mama spoke of her worry often those first few days of Len's visit.

Len and I blocked out Mama's reiteration about school as we waited impatiently for Fred to get well from his head cold. Mama was doctoring his cold with her homemade remedies. She was mainly using roots from the sassafras tree. She boiled the roots in sweetened water and set the mixture aside to steep for awhile. Fred had to drink several cups of the sassafras tea each day. The beverage was supposed to help cure the cold.

In a few days he felt much better and he, Len and I explored the many treasures nature affords. We swung from grapevines and climbed high up in towering trees. We searched for abandoned birds' nests and scaled rocky ledges. We gathered armfuls of wild flowers and mountain ferns to take to Mama.

We walked through Mama's garden whenever we grew hungry between meals. We pulled from the vines, red tomatoes, or orange tomatoes, or yellow tomatoes, according to the variety of tomato vine. We rubbed soil from the tomatoes with our hands, which we thought was sufficient cleaning. We broke open the tomatoes and ate them with the breath of warm sun still upon them.

Mama went about her work almost at a run. She had closed her sewing machine for the summer. The lid was adorned with a hand- embroidered scarf and a kerosene lamp. To her busy schedule of housework and outside chores, she added garden work and canning. She canned such a wide variety of fruits and vegetables that canning became an everyday chore also, except on Sunday. I watched her as she scalded already clean Mason jars until her hands turned beet red from the boiling water. I watched her stir the steaming vegetables cooking in large kettles. I watched as her fingers became stained from the juices of many fruits. I watched her face turn flaming red from the heat as she stoked up an already blazing fire. Often she would pause and lift up the corner of her apron to wipe the perspiration from her face. Mama never complained of being exhausted, but surely she must have been.

The air had become almost brittle with heat. We longed for some good, steady rains, but no rain fell at all for several weeks. The cattle were coming in to the emergency watering troughs every day. There were only a few small streams on the mountain except for the large water vein and reservoir that supplied water to the town of Covington. The few small streams dried up easily unless the rainfall was plentiful.

A very deep well had been dug and a series of wooden troughs led from it. The troughs were used to water Mr. Trumbolte's cattle in dry spells. It was our job to pump enough water to fill those troughs each day when needful. How we hated to fill them each morning only to have the many cattle come down from the wooded regions in late afternoon and drink until they emptied the troughs. Then we had to go back in the sultry heat of the evening to pump the troughs full again.

Papa frowned when we grumbled. "I can't rightly recall any chore you children don't hate, to hear you tell it, so that is of no matter. Just keep on pumpin'," he said.

One hot steamy day, Fred and Len had to go to the fields to help Papa, but Mama kept me at the house to help her. I helped her with various chores during the morning hours. After lunch I churned the clabbered milk. I watched her press the butter into its pretty yellow mounds with the imprint of daisies on top. While she dipped the buttermilk into crocks and washed up the churn and utensils, I sat in a chair near the window and read a chapter in a book. Mama called me to carry the crocks to the cellar. It was so hot and I resented being called from my book just when my interest in it was high.

Mama warned me, "Stop pokin' along, Bud. You've got other things to do."

Another batch of freshly canned vegetables had to be carried to the cellar also. Mama helped me carry those, walking along behind me with an armful. I walked a little slower each trip to show my resentment. Mama finally reached the end of her patience with me and told me to set the jars upon the cistern wall.

"Go fetch me a switch," Mama said.

She had many times told us that whenever we became muleheaded, she would warn us as long as we heeded the warnings and mended our ways. If we continued to misbehave after several warnings, we were spanked. I had been disobedient on several occasions of late and now I had pushed my luck too far. I brought the switch to her, my face looking like a thundercloud. How I loathed the indignity of providing my own switch. I would soon be twelve years old. I felt I was too old to be punished like a child.

I fed my resentment for awhile. I decided to pretend to run away from home. That would serve Mama justly for switching my legs. She would be sorry when she thought I was gone forever.

I sneaked my way from the house and darted along from this bush to that until I was hidden from view by the corner of the big red barn. I braced my legs and hands on the side of a large, black oak tree. Reaching as far around the tree as I could, I pushed my way upward by pushing with my bare feet against the rough bark and inching my body upward. When I had squirreled my way up to the branches, I began to use the limbs as steps. I situated myself very high up in the towering tree. From there, I could see the house and surrounding area. I made myself comfortable on a large limb and leaned back against the broad trunk of the tree.

Now all I had to do was to sit back, watch and wait for the commotion when Mama realized I was missing. I anticipated her horror. Mama would run alongside the orchard fence, jerking Mitty right off her little feet as she hastily pulled her along by the hand. Mama would return with Papa and the boys from the cornfield and they would search in vain for me. Mama would hold her apron over her face and sob into it as she told Papa that it was all her fault. She would tell him how I had worked and that she had spanked me because she was tired and irritable. She would rock her body back and forth as though in pain. She would say over and over that if only I would come home, she would tell me how sorry she was for having switched me.

I watched Mama as she went back and forth carrying the remaining jars to the cellar. After awhile she came out of the house again and pumped two buckets of water from the cistern. She came out again to gather an armful of wood from the woodpile. She came out once in a while to check on Mitty and to remind her not to unlatch the gate. All of these were chores I was supposed to have done today. Mama needed to make her blackberry jelly. Making blackberry jelly was a drawn out process, which was the main reason she had kept me at the house to do the smaller tasks.

I was beginning to feel impatient. Why was it taking her so long to discover I was gone.

Papa and the boys came in from the field after five o'clock. The boys went on to the house and Papa led Prince to the barn.

Mama came out into the yard and called loudly to Papa, "Supper will be a little late, Frank. You can take your time about curryin' and feedin' Prince."

"Alright, Dora," Papa answered.

She called again, loudly, "I hope you're hungry tonight. I cooked a pot of navy beans and a pot of corn on the cob. I'm goin' to slice up a mixture of orange and red tomatoes as soon as I fix the biscuits. I didn't have time to make the blackberry jelly, but I made a family-style blackberry pie for dessert."

I wondered why she was talking so loudly. Papa had never had any trouble with his hearing. I wished I hadn't heard. I had nearly tumbled from the tree when she had talked about the navy beans and corn on the cob. My stomach just about caved in when she told him about the blackberry pie.

Papa finished up and went on to the house for supper. After awhile they all went in and out of the house as they took care of the evening chores. Mama gave Lady and Jersey a few oat grasses to munch on while she milked. She could milk with the speed of lightning. The cows stomped their feet and swished their tails in protest whenever Papa milked though, because he was a lot slower. Papa fed the hogs and helped the boys carry wood to stack on the back porch. The boys fed the chickens and gathered the eggs.

After the chores were finished, I could hear Fred and Len giggling and whooping it up in the back yard as they played with Rover. I knew Mama and Papa would be sitting on the front porch. Papa would be rocking and puffing on his pipe as Mama rocked alongside him. They would be discussing the routine events of today and making plans for tomorrow. I could not understand why she still had not missed me. When was she going to realize I had run away?

I saw the lights come on in the house and I knew it was eight o'clock and they were preparing for bed. Eight o'clock was the inflexible bedtime hour unless one of us was ill and Mama had to stay up later to care for us. Saturday night was the only exception to the rule.

Before very long I saw the light from the lantern come bobbing along out the path toward the outhouse. I knew Papa was carrying the lantern because the light's beam would have been closer to the ground if Fred or Len were carrying it. Mama always held the lantern up in front of her, but Papa carried it in his left hand, hanging loosely at his side. I watched the light bob down the path and back again.

All was quiet, except for a rustling sound here and there as an animal or fowl resettled itself. Somewhere in the distance I heard a hoot owl's mournful cry. It wasn't really so very late to be outside on a hot, summer night. I tried to draw comfort from that thought. Nonetheless, I felt terribly alone and I was starving to death. The very thought of that blackberry pie with its crunchy, brown crust sprinkled with sugar and spices made my mouth water. I had shifted my position on the limb many times throughout the afternoon, but my whole being felt cramped. It seemed like I had been perched in that huge, old black oak tree forever. Oh, for a slice of that pie.

In the shadowy darkness, I began my descent down the long length of the tree. I skinned my leg on a jagged piece of a previously broken limb. As I dropped to the ground, I felt a wet tongue against my leg. I shrank back until I realized it was Rover. I hugged him and buried my face in his fluffy fur. Rover walked with me to the back porch and stood there wagging his tail as I opened the door.

I walked into the lighted kitchen and closed the door behind me. Mama was still up although it was past bedtime. She was sitting in a chair near the window, sewing a patch on the knee of a pair of overalls. She looked up as though this were a normal hour for me to come home.

"The beans are on the back burner and the biscuits are in

the warmin' oven. Do you want somethin' to eat? Oh, there's a bowl of berry pie in the warmin' oven, too.''

I burst into tears of anger and hurt and frustration. ''Mama, you don't even care about me,'' I sobbed. ''You didn't even know I was missing.''

Mama kept on sewing, pushing the needle in and pulling it out through the heavy denim. The silver colored thimble on her forefinger glimmered in the light from the lamp. She answered in her soft, unruffled voice, ''I saw you when you ran away. I saw you climb the tree near the old barn. I have kept a close eye on your whereabouts ever since. Besides, Rover has been hangin' around that tree most all evenin'.''

Shamefacedly, I filled my plate and sat down at the table. I knew I should tell Mama I was sorry, but I didn't say it. I felt like the little paper sack must feel that Papa brought from town each week with our ten cents worth of candy in it. After we ate the candy, one or the other of us would blow the little bag full of air and twist the top shut. We would smack it sharply on the bottom and the little bag's show-off size would collapse with a bang.

Mrs. Trumbolte toured the farm with Mr. Trumbolte the next day. On previous occasions she had chosen what vegetables she wanted and had taken them with her, but she was in a hurry to return to town today. She said she was expecting guests from Washington, D.C. She must return to town in time to meet the incoming train. In the light of this expediency, she asked Papa if he would deliver the fresh foodstuff to her home tomorrow.

Papa said, ''Yes, ma'am, I surely will.''

Papa loaded the wagon with fresh vegetables from the garden bright and early. He also placed a crock of butter and a crock of cottage cheese in a corner of the wagon's bed. Mama handed him a box that was filled with layers of eggs. She had packed straw around and in between the eggs to cushion them. Papa placed the box on the wagon seat. He could hold onto the box when the wagon jostled over rough spots in the road during the trip.

Papa brought Prince from the barn. He had already put the harness on Prince and now he hitched Prince to the wagon. He climbed up onto the wagon's seat and picked up the reins. Mama stepped back from the wagon and stood waving. Her upturned face was shaded from the sun by the wide brim of her pink bonnet.

"I'll stop at the mailbox and check for mail on my way home, Dora," Papa said.

"I'm hopin' to receive a letter from your brother, Henry, and his wife, Nancy. Accordin' to their last letter, Nancy hasn't been feelin' well for some time."

Papa nodded his head as he gave a flick to the reins. He clicked his tongue as he directed Prince to, "Gitty up."

He returned home just before supper. We listened wide-eyed as he told us of the beautiful home he had just visited. We lingered at the supper table longer than usual as the story slowly unfolded. Papa talked slowly by nature and he seemed to relish making any story a drawn-out affair by habit. Papa said, "The house is mighty big. It is constructed partly of white painted boards and partly of red bricks. It has long verandas supported by tall white columns. The huge lawn looks like it's covered in velvet instead of grass. The shrubs and flowers are hybrid plants and a sight to see, Dora."

"Did you have any trouble followin' Mrs. Trumbolte's directions, Frank?"

"No, but I would have if she hadn't given me explicit directions. There is a long windin' road to the house with a sign that marks it as bein' a private road. Did you know there are several estates not too far from Covington and most of those places look a lot alike with windin' roads and everything? I guess wealthy people live just about alike, same as poor folks do or townsfolk do," Papa said.

By this time towheaded Len had propped both elbows on the table and was resting his chin on his hands. His blue eyes were watching Papa's face impatiently. Fred's dark brown eyes met my gray green ones. I drummed my fingers on the table the way Papa did. Fred dipped his head to keep from giggling when Mama shook her head at me.

Papa continued absent-mindedly drumming his fingers upon the table. He said, "I drove the wagon up to the side porch and walked up to the door and knocked. A maid, dressed in a dark-colored uniform with a little, white, frilly apron and a little, white cap, opened the door. I wish you could have seen that apron, Dora. It was about as big as a man's handkerchief and the cap on her head was of even less use to her. The maid drew herself up tall, like she was the queen herself. She said, 'Please state your business, sir.'

"I have brought some vegetables for the lady of the house," I said.

Papa poured himself another glass of milk and then told us the maid's answer. "All trades people and delivery boys must go to the back door. The housekeeper will greet you there. She is in charge of pickup and deliveries."

Mama entwined her fingers and began to roll her thumbs around and around each other. "That was an unneighborly thing for her to say to you, Frank." Mama's voice trembled as she spoke these words.

Papa said, "Now don't go gettin' all upset, Dora. Mrs. Trumbolte must have been comin' that way. Anyhow, she overheard the maid and came on to the door herself. She told the maid, 'This is Mr. Clark. He manages one of our farms for us. He is not a delivery boy. I asked him to stop by with some fresh vegetables for us and he has been gracious enough to do so'."

"That was a hateful, mean old maid," I said.

"Bud! How many times have I told you that if you can't say anything good about a person, then don't say anything at all. Never call anybody hurtful names. No person is all bad, so look for the good and talk about that. The maid was only doin' her job. I was bringin' vegetables, you know," Papa said.

Mama got up and began to clear the table. "What did you do then, Frank? Did you take the wagon around to the back door?" she asked.

Papa smiled, the permanently deep furrows between his brows smoothed out a little as he said, "Why no, Mrs. Trumbolte came out to the wagon and carried the crock of butter into the house herself. Then I carried the vegetables and the eggs down a long hallway to a large pantry. Mrs. Trumbolte told me to set everything down there and the cook would see to its proper placement later. When I finished, Mrs. Trumbolte invited me to stay and have a cup of coffee with her. She said her guests had gone off horseback ridin'.

"Her kitchen was nice, Dora. I wish you could have seen it. There's a little room off the kitchen that she calls a breakfast nook. The walls are painted a pale yellow. There's a big window in one wall and you can look out and see her rose garden. A table covered with a green linen tablecloth, sets in front of the window. When we entered the room, a maid was placin' a pretty vase filled with yellow and white roses on the table. There's a picture on the wall of a yellow-haired girl, skippin' through a field of clover. A maid that was dressed just like the one that had opened the door served us coffee and chocolate cake.

"There we sat, Mrs. Trumbolte dressed real nice in a sleeveless, white linen dress and me clad in my overalls. We chatted a long time. She sure is a gracious lady."

By the time Papa finished telling us about his experience, Mama and I had the table cleared and the dishes washed. It was time to do the nightly chores.

Papa went back at various times to the big house to drop off vegetables or fruit. He went to the back door after that first time. The gracious lady always invited him in for refreshments and a chat in the cheerful breakfast nook.

Mr. Trumbolte came up to the farm a few days after Papa had talked to Mrs. Trumbolte. He stopped at our mailbox on his way up and brought our mail. There was a package from Sears, Roebuck and Co. It was my new shoes.

Mama had ordered me a pair of brown oxfords in anticipation of autumn. She always ordered items a little earlier than they would be needed in case they needed to be exchanged. She always measured our feet on the size chart provided in the catalog. This precaution didn't insure a proper fit. This was going to be one of those times for an exchange. I knew that as soon as I tried on the shiny, new shoes. Mama had never failed to check the size and fit when we tried on new shoes before, but this time she didn't.

She was listening intently to what Mr. Trumbolte had to say. He said, "My wife informed me that she and Mr. Clark were talking several days ago about the school problem for your children. I understand that Mr. Clark told Mrs. Trumbolte of your concern about living such a distance from a school. I have a vacant building in a little settlement called Rich Patch. As you know, its only a few miles from here. I want you to go and look the building over and see what you think of its potentiality as housing for the school term. A bus comes to the settlement to pick up the school children each school day.

"After you look at the building, if you think you can work things out, you can live in it rent free. You can live there with the children during the school term and Mr. Clark can remain here. You can come back to the farm each weekend to help him out. Think it over, Mrs.Clark, and let me know what you decide."

The very next day, Mama finished her morning chores as quickly as possible. She made plans for Papa to keep Mitty. She said we could walk to Rich Patch with her.

"Can I wear my new shoes, Mama?" I asked.

"Are you sure those shoes are long enough? Perhaps I had better check the size before you wear them." Mama said.

I didn't tell her that my toes touched the front of the shoes. I wanted to believe that the shoes were long enough. It always took from two to four weeks to return merchandise to Chicago for an exchange and receive merchandise back again. I wouldn't have to wait for autumn. I could wear the pretty, new shoes on this special occasion if I kept this pair. Mama was waiting for an answer.

"I'm sure. They're the right size," I said.

The three of us ran on well ahead of Mama as she walked at a fast pace toward the settlement. She had dressed us up as though it was Sunday. Despite their protests, Fred and Len wore their grey-checked knickers and white, long sleeve shirts. I wore my Sunday dress. It was a pale blue, voile dress. It had a very wide, rounded collar, trimmed in white lace. It had short, puffed sleeves and a wide, wide sash that tied in a big bow at my back. The skirt was gathered at the waist. The thin material swirled out over my starched petticoat. The skirt hung to the calves of my skinny legs and its hem was bordered with white lace.

Fred said the brown oxfords looked dumb with such a frilly dress. I didn't care. The oxfords were new and I wanted to wear them today.

The building Mama was to look at had been used for a store at one time. It still had a large potbellied heater in it. It also had a long counter and a row of shelves on the wall behind the counter. Mama spent several hours looking around, measuring the floor space and thinking.

We played around outside of the building and met some of the boys and girls who lived nearby. We thought it would be nice to live here this winter and have playmates again. Len was envious of the thought that Fred and I would get to live in a store building instead of a house.

Mama finished looking around and we started the long walk home.

My left big toe had been throbbing for quite some time. We hadn't gone very far back toward home when Mama said, "Are

45

your feet hurtin'? You seem to be limpin'.''

"My feet feel fine, Mama," I said. I crossed my fingers when I said it so it would be a white lie instead of a black lie. I gritted my teeth and walked steadily onward. I was determined not to limp. The terrible pains shooting through my big toes seemed to beat out their own rhythm as I walked.

Halfway home, Mama told me to sit down and pull off my shoes. As the pressure was released by removing the shoes, the pain became white hot. Mama looked at my inflamed toes.

"You will probably lose the left toenail. I can't send the shoes back for a larger size now that you have worn them. I'll have to see if Frank can put them on the shoe stretchers and stretch them. If he can't I will have to save up enough extra eggs to market, to pay for another pair of shoes. In that case, there will be no eggs for breakfast for anyone until I sell enough eggs to pay for the other shoes. I trusted you to tell me the truth.''

Once again, I was learning the hard way.

They sat in their rocking chairs on the front porch that night, discussing the pros and cons of the building. Papa stroked the banjo strings softly as he listened to Mama.

"The buildin' seems to be in pretty good repair, Frank. I've been ponderin' on whether we could work out most of the problems. We could divide the cookin' utensils and bedclothes, but we don't have enough bedsteads and bedticks for two homes.'' Mama said.

Papa continued tightening the banjo strings. Cocking his head to one side, his finger and thumb plucked against the third string and he listened to the sound.

"Is there a cookstove in the store buildin', Dora?'' he asked.

"There's a big heater. I think I could get by usin' it to cook on. I could bake enough bread while I was here on the weekends, to take back to do us durin' the week,'' Mama said.

"I guess we had better start sawin' extra wood now, to haul down there,'' Papa said.

"We would need a gracious plenty to heat two homes,'' Mama said. She looked worried. She folded her hands and slowly twirled her thumbs. She pondered for a moment and began to speak again, "I could buy several yards of unbleached cotton to make a wide curtain. I could use a length of rope as a curtain rod to stretch from one wall across to the other wall. The curtain would act as a partition and keep most of the heat in the kitchen

46

area. That would save on firewood.''

They sat for awhile, lost in their own thoughts. Their silence made nature's sounds more noticeable. I became aware of the calls of the bobwhites and the throaty croaking of the frogs. I listened to the shrill sounds of the katydids as they tried to override the whirring sounds of the nightjars. Added to these, came the chilling scream of a bobcat. From somewhere up on the ridge came the lonesome hoot of an owl. These were the natural music and songs of the mountains.

''Papa, you used to tell us that the bobwhite was a braggart because he always talked about himself. You said the whippoorwill was an agitator because he always tried to get a fight started. Do you remember?'' I asked.

''I surely do remember,'' Papa said.

''There must be a million katydids out tonight. Is there a mountain legend about the katydids?'' I asked.

Papa puffed on his pipe as he gathered his thoughts. In a short while, he began to speak. ''The story goes that long, long ago there was a rich man livin' high up on a lonely hill. He was lonely except for his only daughter. She was beautiful, sweet and shy, and he guarded her jealous-like.

''Their home was a mansion surrounded by pretty gardens. A well-trod path found its way through a rose garden and ended at a white gate. Near the gate stood a grove of mighty fine trees. The trees harbored the pale green katydids.Mr. Katydid can make the shrill sound that sounds like a chant by rubbin' his wing covers together. Mrs. Katydid can't produce the sound, which seems kind of odd since most of the females I know are always soundin' off about somethin'.

''Near those tall trees was an arched trellis filled with climbin' pink roses. Beneath this arbor there was a white bench. The rich man's daughter, Katy, often sat upon this bench. She daintily sniffed the dewy roses and gazed wistful-like down the seldom used carriage road.

''One bright mornin', a dark-eyed, handsome young man rode past. He noticed the young maiden, seated beneath the arbor of sweet smellin' roses. The next day he came that way again. He stopped his horse and carriage near the white gate and stepped from his waitin' carriage and walked to the garden gate. Katy arose from the white bench and went to meet him. He caught her little hands in his white-gloved ones. Her hands fluttered like angel's wings as he raised them to his lips in courtly greetin'. These two young people soon fell in love with each other, but trouble was brewin'.

"Katy's father returned from a long business trip and discovered the young man kissin' Katy at the garden gate. He spoke to the young man in harsh tones and drew his overprotected daughter to his side. He forbade them to see each other ever again. The father threatened to enter Katy in a private school where the young man could not find her if he ever tried to see her again.

"Many, many days passed and every evenin', Katy sat on the bench and waited. She grew quiet and sad. She watched the gate in vain. The little katydids sat restless-like in the mighty trees and watched also.

"Katy grew so despondent that she finally gave up and one evenin', she didn't go to the gate. Very late that night, as if drawn by some unseen power, Katy seemed to float down the rose scented path to the garden gate. There in the starry night was her beloved. He caught her to his breast and kissed her. They clung together. Then they heard her father's anxious voice callin' to her. The young man disappeared into the waitin' shadows for fear of her father's threat.

"Katy fled to the bench and seated herself upon it.

"Her father drew near and asked, 'Katy, have you been to the garden gate?'

'No, sir, Father,' lied sweet Katy.

'That's strange. I saw a darin' young man kissin' a fair maiden at the garden gate. Who then, did kiss the young scoundrel?' her father asked.

"The pale green insects in the mighty trees began to chant, 'Katy did! Katy she did, she did!' "

"Papa! You made that story up just now. That's not a mountain legend," I said.

Papa struck a match and puffed on the stem of his now cold pipe as he tried to relight the tobacco. In the light of the country match, I saw him smile at Mama as he answered, "Well now, if you think that story is not true, why have those little insects sat in hundreds of trees on hundreds of summer nights for hundreds of years and just kept on chantin', 'Katy did! Katy she did, she did!' "

Mama arose from her rocking chair. "Time to get ready for bed. Tomorrow is another day."

Mama went back to the settlement two or three times. Papa went with her one Sunday afternoon to look at the building. On many a night, through the remainder of the summer, they rocked side by side on the front porch and talked over the problems and the possibilities of maintaining separate dwellings.

Mama sat at the kitchen table many nights with tablet paper and pencil. With the kerosene lamp drawn near, she wrote out lists and drew diagrams. Despite the screened windows and doors, the millers encircled the lamp's globe. They often struck their dusty wings against the globe in their desire to be near the light. Teeny-tiny green bugs and teensy-tinsy black bugs would light on Mama's paper, causing her to brush at them impatiently as she tried to write.

In the daytime the farm work went on as usual, as though no great decision that would effect the rest of our lives was being thought out.

The Trumboltes came up one day to talk over the arrangements concerning school for us. Mrs. Trumbolte brought some clothing for me. She and Mama talked about how fast children outgrow clothing.

Papa and Mr. Trumbolte went to the fields and orchards to look at the crops and the stand of oat grasses. The oats were heading up nicely and Mr. Trumbolte told Papa he would send other men to help harvest the oats beginning the first of the week.

Fred and I stood near the black limousine. We shifted from one foot to the other and smiled shyly at the chauffeur. He fascinated us. We thought his uniform gave him an authoritative appearance. He stood very erect beside the opened car door as his passengers emerged. Then he shut the car's door and stationed himself near the door on the driver's side of the car. No matter how long his employers stayed, he stood right there. He never talked nor even appeared to listen to any of the conversations. He usually smiled at us though and he tipped his cap to Mama.

I thought he was very handsome in his uniform and his shiny black shoes, especially for an older man. Fred and I agreed that he must be in his late twenties. On this day in particular, it was nice that we could agree on something. We most certainly were not going to be in agreement on the circumstances of the following week.

5

CUT OATS AND COOKED OATS

I was very unhappy the following week. I was also very angry with Papa. I had assumed all spring and summer as we watched the oat grasses grow that I would get to help harvest them. I came out of the house bright and early Monday morning, dressed in Papa's baggy, bib overalls.

Papa said, "You won't need those today. You can wear a dress because you'll be helpin' Dora."

"I don't want to. I want to help with the oats," I said.

"There will be several men workin' with me. Fred can help because he's a boy, but it's no place for a lady," Papa said.

"I'm no lady," I said.

"It is improper for a young girl to be in the presence of several men unless they are relatives," Papa said.

I knew from his tone of voice and the deep frown between his brows that it would do no good to plead.

Mama didn't have to cook for the men. They brought their lunches with them in lunchboxes. Papa talked to Mama as we ate our hot, midday meal. He talked about the work and the heat. He talked about the conversations and the joking among the men. I was absolutely silent. Fred couldn't even entice me into an argument. All afternoon I pouted as I went about helping Mama.

"Mama, why did your God make me into a girl? I was not meant to be a girl," I said.

Mama looked aghast. "Rosebud! Why do you make such statements? How many times have I told you that you do not question or criticize God's wisdom? He had a purpose in choosin' you to be a girl," Mama said.

"Well I don't want to be one. My hands are big like a boy's hands and my voice is deeper than a girl's voice. So you see? He must have started out to make me a boy," I said triumphantly.

"You are never to say such things again. If you would read the Bible you would learn more about God," Mama said.

"I don't like being a girl. Girls never get to have any fun. Men never have to worry about dirty dishes. They just walk off with their hands in their pockets. Girls can't. Girls aren't supposed to jump from the barn loft. They aren't supposed to whistle or shoot marbles or go where there are lots of men. Girls just never get to do anything exciting," I said.

By the end of the week, I was totally miserable because of being penned up in the house and yard every day. The men took turns coming to the cistern in the yard to fill the water jugs. The heat was nearly unbearable and they seemed to be drinking barrels of water.

One man was a layman preacher. Every time he came for water, Mama would run outside with her Bible in her hand. Attending church from this remote farm was out of the question. Mama was thirsty for someone to discuss religious matters with. Papa had never been a church going man. He read his Bible every night, but seldom talked about what he read. Mama had been so excitied and thrilled these past few weeks. The Bible was filled with deep mysteries and seemingly impossible feats that she read about and could not understand. How she looked forward to each day now. Here was someone who could answer her eager questions.

The following week Papa talked to Mama about the preacher. He used the most gentle tone of voice I had ever heard him use with Mama or anyone else. I think he hated to say what he had to say. Papa said, "Dora, I know you don't realize how long you're delayin' the preacher when he comes for water. He is bein' payed, same as the rest of us to harvest oats. It's powerful hot in the fields and the other men are beginnin' to complain. They're sayin' that while they're wipin' sweat from their eyes, the preacher is fannin' himself in the shade. They are beginnin' to slack off in the work output. Mr. Trumbolte knows how many days it should take to finish this job. We're not goin' to finish on time because of this trouble. So either you have to stop waylayin' the preacher or I'll have to stop him from gettin' his turn to come for water. The preacher won't like that so you can see I have a problem."

Mama was very reluctant, but she promised not to talk to the preacher anymore.

Papa was beginning to feel sorry for me, too, or either Mama had talked to him. He looked across the table one night and said, "Bud, the men won't be comin' back next week. We'll finish cuttin' this week. It will take about two more weeks to finish harvestin' the hay. I think the three of us can finish haulin' it to the barns. It's mighty hard work. Do you think you can make me a good hand?"

"I know I can, Papa. I've been watching from the yard and I can do it," I said.

The following Monday morning I donned the overalls and heavy boots. I tied my bonnet under my chin. Leaving the dishes for Mama to take care of, I went off about men's important business.

The newly cut oats had a wonderfully sweet smell as the rising sun met the dew of the night. The oats lay in heaped mounds that ran the length of the field. Prince pulled the wagon between the rows, moving the wagon along a length or so at Papa's commands. Fred stood in the wagon. Papa and I pitched the hay into it and Fred packed it down. We switched work stations from time to time, but Papa had said I should start out pitching with him. He wanted to show me how to pitch skillfully.

I sunk the pitchfork deep into the pile of hay. With a confident motion of my arms and body, I swung a half-turn around from the pile of hay towards the wagon. As the hay left the pitchfork, I found out that pitching hay was not quite as effortless as it had appeared to be when I had stood in the yard and observed.

Despite Papa's instructions, within the first hour I had made a lot of mistakes. I used too little force when I pitched and the hay fell upon the ground just short of the wagon. I pitched with jerky motions, causing some of the hay to land on the side of the pile already in the wagon, only to slide off and land back on the ground. I pitched with too much force and the hay sailed clear over the wagon and landed on the ground on the other side of the wagon. I hit Fred full in the face with misdirected hay and knocked him flat on his back. He came up fussing and spitting and brushing the hay from his shiny black hair. He yelled something about dumb girls.

The higher the loaded hay became, the more I learned that I had to keep adjusting my pitch to accommodate the ever increasing height. The sun's rays beat down without mercy. Chaff flew in a dry cloud around us until the very air seemed dusty and thick. Our tongues felt as though they had been ironed dry. When we took the first load to the barn, I found I had still more to learn.

Papa said, "Now, Bud, this is yet a horse of another color."

I soon found out why as I stood on the wagon piled high with shifting hay. Trying to pitch the hay high into the air and through a barnloft door was anything but easy to do. Papa showed me how to stand with my feet placed wide apart. He showed me how to use my back, shoulder and arm muscles to throw the hay high into the air with a motion that would arch the hay toward and through the opening.

I swung with all my might. My feet shot out from under me and I landed on my back in the hay. The hay showered down upon me. I scrambled to my feet while Fred leaned out of the barnloft door, laughing uproariously. I pitched a forkful of hay high into the air and watched as it paused right in front of the loft door. It did not arch itself to enter, but fell straight down past my wondering eyes to land with a plop upon the ground. I looked down at the sad little heap. I pitched another forkful. Wonder of wonders, it sailed proudly through the doorway and hit the unbelieving Fred smack in the face.

I worked so hard and fast that Papa threatened to send me to the house. I guess I was trying to prove to Papa and perhaps to Mama's God also that I could harvest hay as good as any man.

We entered the house one evening as hungry as three bears. Mama had not started supper. The long, kitchen table was covered with rows and rows of Mason jars filled with a mixture of corn and tomatoes. The rich red color of the tomatoes and the golden yellow of the corn made a cheerful picture. The hot liquid was still bubbling slightly in the jars. Mama's face looked drawn and tired. Her eyes showed the strain of worry.

Mama said, "I have thought things out seven ways for Sunday, Frank, and there's just no way we can move to the settlement." Mama was busy cleaning up the kitchen as she talked.

Papa puffed on his pipe and ran his hand through his wavy white hair as he listened to Mama's decisive tone of voice. "But, Dora, what else can we do? We've got to get the children in school."

"We're between a rock and a hard place and there is only one thing we can do. We'll have to teach them the best we can right here at home. We have no other choice."

53

"I can get by alone here in the winter time," Papa said.

"You can't possibly handle the farm work, the chores and the cookin' all by yourself. You might get by in the dead of winter, but not in the autumn and spring. There is just no way to work it out for you to live here and us there," Mama said.

"How can we teach the children?" Papa asked.

"I'm goin' to talk to the girls about it Sunday if they come home. I need to find out if they can help with some books for Bud. You can help Bud as she already has a start and I will work with Fred. It's goin' to be mighty hard not knowin' the proper way to teach. The Lord only knows how we'll even find the time every day," Mama said.

"Now, Dora, don't go borrowin' worry. We'll manage," Papa said."

Fred and I looked at each other and waited. We just knew Mama was going to say it. She did. "We'll make do the best we can."

Early Sunday morning the rest of the family began to arrive, car by car, as though they knew they were supposed to come home. Lawrence and Elena came with their children. Young Betty looked cute. Her dark brown hair accented her yellow, ruffled dress and white shoes. Len was excited to be back. Elena had taken him home with her a few weeks earlier amid his protests that summer was not over. Lewis and Carrie came and brought their curly haired Ronnie with his friendly, impish grin and winning ways. Clarence drove in with his air horns heralding their arrival. Tommy came bouncing out of the car. His dark brown eyes were shining and his chubby arms outstretched as he ran to Mama. Dorothea alighted from the car, looking small and chic in a sleeveless, white dress, accented by a wide, red belt. Frances followed her, dressed in a pink and white, candy-striped, sun-back dress. A solid colored pink bolero covered her sun tanned shoulders and back. The dress accented her slim figure and afforded her the illusion of being taller than she was. The blistering heat of the day made the bolero an unnecessary item, but Frances did not remove it in deference to Papa's decorous dress code.

After dinner everyone took chairs into the yard to escape the heat of the kitchen. Seated in the shade of the trees, they talked and fanned themselves. The fans opened up like accordions and written upon them were the compliments of a funeral home. The women fanned their moist faces and then used the fans to tap at their arms and legs to shoo the flies away. Along with the buzzing of the flies, the motion of the fans seemed almost rhythmical.

Gene had come up with Lawrence. Papa seated himself next to them and they began to tune up their instruments. They always made such a production out of tuning up. I sometimes thought they liked that part better than playing music. Gene plucked each guitar string. He tightened one and loosened another until the guitar sounded out my-dog-has-fleas, which proved it was now in tune.

Lawrence drew the bow across the fiddle strings. He tucked the fiddle under his chin and plunked the strings with his fingers. He rubbed the resin stick down the length of the bow. Then he seesawed the bow across the strings until he heard the sound he was listening for. Fred and I had killed a rattlesnake and saved the rattle for Lawrence to put in his fiddle. He held the fiddle out from his chin and shook it to reassure us that the prized rattle was within the body of the fiddle.

Papa plinked and plunked the banjo strings. He tightened and loosened strings and struck a chord or two.

They each cocked their heads to one side and listened to the combined sounds of the instruments. Then they had to tap their feet and strum and plunk and seesaw while they tried to decide on a song to play.

The women finally decreed that the men had derived enough pleasure from the production of tuning up. They began to plead that it was time for a song.Feeling sufficiently gratified by the coaxing voices, they stormed into the music with a rousing rendition of "I'm Goin' Up Shootin' Creek" They followed that with "She'll Be Comin' 'Round The Mountain." and "Shoo Fly." They slowed their pace with "I'll Take You Home, Kathleen," and once there, they dumped the hapless "Kathleen" for the mournful "Clementine."

As the afternoon wore on the music became fragmented. The heat and exertion had taken their toll on the musicians' enthusiasm. As the music began to draw to a close, Mama began to tell the girls of her plan to teach us at home. They promised to bring reading material for me.

Carrie's tall, shapely form arose from her chair. She came over and sat down beside me on the lower step. She gathered the skirt of her navy and white polka dotted dress around her knees. She folded her arms across her knees to anchor the skirt. The wide white collar of the dress accented her soft, black hair and called attention to her slender face. Her hazel eyes danced merrily as she asked the other girls, "Do you all remember the ordeal I went through when I tried to teach Bud the alphabet?"

The girls threw up their hands and chorused, "How could we forget? We thought you were going to kill Bud before she learned the letter S."

Clarence and Lewis said, "That was before our time. What happened?"

That was all the encouragement Carrie needed to launch her tale of woe. "Bud was five years old and I decided to teach her the alphabet. She caught on real fast and it wasn't very long until we reached the letter S. Somehow Bud could not remember that letter. I had her repeat the letter after me over and over. Nothing worked. I was ready to pull my hair out by the roots. The other girls would sneak through the room afraid of being sought after to help.

"I grew desperate enough to try anything and did so," Carrie lamented. "I told Bud to picture a snake and how they usually sort of curved like an S. Bud was familiar with snakes and she nodded her heard vigorously. I told her to think about that until the next day at lesson time."

Lewis grinned his wide grin and asked, "Did she remember?"

Carrie clasped her slender hands to her breast and said, "Oh yes! She remembered all right. When we got to the S, she hesitated a moment and then triumphantly shouted, 'Snake'!"

Clarence and Lewis tried to subdue their laughter.

Dorothea threw back her curly head and gleefully urged, "You can't stop now. Tell them about your next brilliant idea."

Carrie said, "After a few days of snake for an answer, I asked Bud if she remembered the sign on the highway that we had often shot at with our gravel shooters. She said she did. I told her that the symbol was made in an S shape, meaning that the curve was dangerous, therefore the sign meant an S curve was just ahead. The next day when Bud got to the S, she said snake and I shook my head, no. Bud hesitated, then with a gleam of relief in her eyes, she said, 'S curve'. After several days, she finally learned to drop the word, curve, and say a simple, uncomplicated S."

Elena's jolly laughter sounded as she said, "And now, Mama,

you have just had your first lesson on the trials and triumphs of being a home school teacher. If you need anymore help, just call on Carrie.''

Once Mama settled on a course of action there was no such thing as putting off until tomorrow what could be done today. Bright and early Monday morning, she told Papa to hitch up Prince to the wagon. She had hurried with the chores and changed her clothes. She had put on the thin voile dress with the lavender flowers and tiny, green leaf design. This was a dress she saved for special occasions and we called it her town dress. She donned her shiny Natural Bridge shoes. She put on her white bonnet with its overlay of thin voile materials. We watched her as she tied two, ribboned bands of voile under her chin. Mama was almost forty-three years old. She weighed about one hundred thirty-five pounds, which was kind of plump for her five-feet-two-inch height. She was a pretty lady, especially when she dressed up. She told us to be good and she would try to hurry home from town. She took Mitty with her.

By the time the rattling sounds of the wagon wheels had faded away, we thought we had been good long enough. We chose a hen we thought looked kind of skinny. We fed her all the corn she wanted. She ate until her craw was so full and heavy that every time she tried to walk, her craw dragged along the ground. Several times she fell down. We stared at her in fascination and fear. How in the world would we explain her appearance to Mama? What in the world would happen to us when Mama saw her hen? We decided to deposit her inside the chicken house where the other chickens could not bother her and hope for a miracle.

We confiscated lots of Mama's graded-for-market eggs and I boiled those for our dinner. While we ate, Len and I teamed up and blamed the hen's condition on Fred. We argued about that until time to do the dishes. Then the fickle Len decided to switch sides and team up with Fred. Leaving me to tidy up the kitchen, Len and Fred went off over the hill with their arms across each other's shoulders. Huh, I thought to myself. They think they're so smart. Just wait until Mama finds out it was their idea to feed her hen all she could eat.

Mama would never let me bake sweets because I didn't want to stick with her tried-and-true recipes. She always said she could not afford the sugar for the experimental baking I wanted to do. I got out her Rumford Cook Book and munched on a salted, green apple while I read recipes. Mama didn't allow us to prop our feet on the rungs of the chairs. She said it scratched the paint. Mama wasn't here today. I propped my feet on the chair's rungs. The elevation brought my knees up into just the right position to hold the cookbook at a good reading level.

I came across a recipe for oatmeal sticks that called for only one tablespoon of sugar. Surely Mama wouldn't begrudge that little old bit of sugar. The recipe called for three cups of flour and one-half cup of oatmeal, plus some other ingredients. That didn't sound like enough oatmeal to me. I added a little more. The instructions said to mix all the ingredients together, forming a ball of dough. The instructions said to roll bits of the dough between one's fingers to form pencil-size sticks.

Before I began to roll the sticks, I looked at the ball of dough in dismay. It looked like such a little bit. I put the same amount of ingredients together again. I mixed the two batches together. It still didn't look like very much so I added two more batches.

By the time I had kneaded all four batches together into one big ball, Fred and Len had returned. When they saw what I was doing, they grew friendly once more. They wanted to make sure they got their share of the goodies. They fetched wood for me and built up the fire in the cookstove. They watched while I made little, doughy oatmeal sticks. After awhile, I rolled little, limb-size sticks. After I had accumulated quite a stack, I began to roll little logs.

Finally Len and Fred said, "Boy, you sure are in trouble. We're going for a walk until Mama gets home. If you need more wood for the fire, you can get it."

The baked sticks were heaped high upon the table. I wished that I might never see another stick for as long as I lived. I was so tired and it was getting late. I knew Mama and Papa would surely come soon because it was nearing suppertime. I got out some clean dish towels and wrapped bundle after bundle of the oatmeal sticks. I hid some of the bundles on the bottom shelf of the safe. I hid some in the pantry and some on a shelf on the back porch. I left one heaping platterful in the center of the table.

When Mama came in she stopped short and looked at the baked goodies. She said, "You shouldn't have made sweets without my permission. They seem a might dry tastin' to me. How much sugar did you you use?" I told her that I had used four tablespoonfuls. She tasted another one and said, "That should be a gracious plenty of sugar for this amount. It's odd. They should taste sweeter and not so dry.''

After supper, Mama served my new dessert.

Mitty took one bite of her stick and handed it back to Mama.

Fred and Len ate one each and said, ''We don't' like them.''

Papa ate two. He looked at Mama and said, ''Dora, what makes these little things taste so dry?''

Mama said, ''They are very dry. Bud, you must have used too much of somethin'. Don't try to make cookies again when I'm not here because I don't think you followed the recipe exactly. Thank goodness there is only one platterful.''

Fred looked puzzled. He said, ''I don't know how Bud could have eaten so many before supper. She had heaps more than this platterful.''

Len nodded his head in agreement as he looked at me in amazement.

Mama looked at me too and then she got up from the table and began to search. No one said anything as she placed pile after pile of oatmeal sticks on the table. Papa looked like he felt kind of sorry for me, but he didn't say a word. Len and Fred sort of scrunched over close together. Len's curly, pale blond hair almost mingled with Fred's smooth, black hair. One pair of dark brown eyes and one pair of inquisitive blue ones watched Mama interestedly.

Mama said, ''We'll eat as many as we can during the next few days. The rest we'll have to feed to the hogs. They need fattenin' up. There must be hundreds of these sticks. Is this all there is, Bud?''

''I think so, Mama,'' I answered weakly.

6

AUTUMN

Papa finished unloading the wagon. He brought in the new, fall and winter edition of the Sears, Roebuck and Co., Catalog. He had picked it up from the mailbox on his way home. The catalog was one of the most necessary and versatile items in our home. It was our General Store. It was also our New York Designer Salon from which we could view the most stylish attire. It was the great Wish Book in which we could see and long for the many things we could not have. It was the source of my paper doll family. Two or three catalogs stacked in a kitchen chair became the booster seat for a recent high chair graduate. Some of the outgoing catalogs were relocated in the outhouse. The softer, black and white pages were a popular and coveted necessity there. The pages that were in color were somewhat stiffer. Woe unto the one, who upon a visit to the outhouse, discovered that the last of the black and white pages was gone.

Papa also brought home a book he had purchased in town. The book was titled *Progress In Spelling For Grades I to VI.* The book was written by Ernest Horn and Ernest J. Ashbaugh. Mama figured that both Fred and I could use it for our spelling and grammar lessons. We were both disappointed that Mama had decided against moving to the settlement.

Fred had talked excitedly about the prospect of attending public school. He had bombarded me with questions about the inside layout of a schoolhouse, its rules and its school teachers. He had looked at me with his dark brown eyes shining like deep, clear pools. As I viewed the fervency in his eyes and heard the desire in his voice, I was ashamed that I had not been more sympathetic. I had looked forward to having playmates again. I still wanted to learn, but I was still somewhat leary of school. Fred had looked forward to playmates also, but much more to school itself.

He had said, "Here I am, nine years old, and I've never seen the inside of a schoolhouse. I've wished and wished I could find out what school is really like. I want to learn." Fred was usually a reticent person. Somehow I had never realized until now, how much he longed to go to school. He didn't let Mama know, but I knew how he had sobbed with disappointment when she had made her decision not to move.

We started home school sessions immediately. Mama worked with both of us from one to two hours in the afternoons. After the evening chores were finished, she worked with Fred on math and Papa worked with me.

From the first night, Papa and I were caught up in dispute. No matter what kind of math problem we worked on, we argued constantly. In division, he didn't mark off the problems in the way I was familiar with. I didn't understand his steps and he didn't understand the steps I had been taught. When my total was incorrect, he couldn't explain my error using my steps and I could not comprehend his steps if he reworked the problem by converting it to his method. Papa snorted that it didn't matter how the problem was worked if the answer was correct. I mumbled that my answer would still be graded as wrong in a public school if the method was wrong. He stated that I was the most hard headed youngun' he had ever seen. I protested that if I learned by his outdated method I might as well not learn at all for all the good it would ever do me.

Mama was near despair. She was getting further behind with her regular work load because she had to count the lesson time into her already too full schedule. Mama tried to intercede between Papa and me. Papa had a better education in math than she, so she believed he was better qualified to help me. Fred was learning fast and well in the afternoon sessions, but the night sessions were confusing to him because of Papa's and my disagreements.

I was unhappy all the time. The math work was stirring up troubled waters again. I felt chagrined that Papa was not pleased with me. Most of the correction chores seemed to fall to Mama. I took it for granted that there were times when she was not pleased with my behavior. Most of the time Papa approved of me because Mama either had not burdened him with the knowledge of my untowardness or he knew she was in the process of taking care of it. Now it was up to him and somehow it wasn't working out. Before the winter was quite over, Papa and I both were procrastinating more and more often on math lessons.

The girls were still bringing me lots of books. Regretfully, none of us realized how important reading the right kind of literature was for study purposes. None of us were acquainted with the fact that the county library would have proved very helpful. The girls were living in suburban areas made up of young couples with young children. The busy, young mothers were caught up in the now popular form of relaxation, which consisted of quickie reading material. These were romance magazines, published once a month under many names. I learned next to nothing of or about important events, famous people or required subject matter.

I did read everything the girls brought to me and not just because of the stories' plots. I sought to learn word by word. For instance, Lewis and Lawrence were discussing something about a pathway between the Atlantic and Pacific Oceans. Trying to impress them with my knowledge I blurted out, "I know all about that. It's called the Pa'nama Kan'l." Amidst the laughter, Lawrence asked, "Mrs. Clark, are you sure you are not using the Lil' Abner series for Bud's grammar lessons?"

Although I desperately needed the working skills a formal education could have afforded, I did learn other important things from reading fictional magazine stories. I learned about the variances and the similarities of people's mental and emotional makeups. I learned how to search below the apparent for understanding in a variety of personality types. I learned not to judge others on the grounds that none of us are capable of being perfect. I learned to temper criticism with mercy. I learned to rejoice in another's accomplishments. I learned that in order to achieve any degree of understanding of another's circumstances, one must listen to another's total being. I learned that one cannot fully know another person unless one has actually walked in his/her moccasins. I learned that until one learns to observe how well worn another person's moccasins appear to be, does one know the other person well enough to offer one's hand in friendship and understanding.

At last came the busyness of spring and with it, the cessation of school lessons. Spring bustled into summer and the summer flew by on winged feet, or so it seemed. Before we were ready for it, autumn was upon us again.

The county fair came to Covington in late September. The last night of the fair was always on a Saturday. All week Papa could talk of nothing else.He looked forward to attending the fair on Saturday night. This would be his third year to attend. How Fred and I longed to go with him.

Mama said, "You are not to let your Papa know how much you want to see the fair. It would cost too much for the three of you to attend. He works very hard all year and never does anything for pleasure except for playin' his banjo. This is his only extravagance and he has more than earned this one night of excitement."

On the Saturday afternoon of the fair, he would break his ironclad rule of shaving only on Sunday morning. We derived a lot of pleasure out of watching him shave because he was so excited he tried to whistle at the same time.

Mama brushed and aired his black vested suit. She brought it in from the clothesline and laid it upon the bed along with his black tie. She placed his freshly laundered white shirt and white long johns beside the suit.

We were all waiting eagerly to view the transformation when he emerged from the bedroom with his black hat in his hand. We thought he looked so handsome in his serge suit with his gold watch chain dangling across his vest. His white hair lay in rippling waves. His slender frame was erect as he smiled down at us. Somehow he gave the appearance of an excited little boy and we were glad for him that he could go to the fair.

I watched Mama as she straightened his tie. There was a faraway look in her eyes and a smile upon her lips. I wondered if she was remembering the gay young man she had fallen in love with on a Saturday night so long ago.

Papa went straight down over the side of the mountain as the crow flies. Had Papa walked on the road, he would have walked about twenty miles to get to the fairgrounds. His shortcut had to be worse than our shortcut to the mailbox, but neither Fred nor I mentioned that. Papa left before dark. After the darkness of night had descended, we went out and stood near a drop-off point where Papa had begun his descent. Far in the distance, we could see the glittering, festive lights and sometimes it seemed as though we also heard the rollicking music from the fairgrounds. Rover always left with Papa, but he always came back long before

Papa. I guess he was torn between whom he should be protecting.

Sunday morning, we dallied longer than usual at the breakfast table. We were like a bunch of eager beavers, waiting to hear about Papa's Saturday night. We listened for many days as he reiterated the news and we did not grow weary of hearing it. Papa didn't spend any money on his trips to the fair except for his gate ticket. He didn't eat, ride or participate at the game booths. He didn't enter the tents for the side shows. He did observe the games and he watched the introduction to the girlie shows as the girls appeared on the outer platform. He grinned rather devilishly as he told Mama about the girls' painted faces, swaying bodies and glittery costumes.

He told Fred, Mitty and me about the squeals and screams of the children and young people as they clung tightly to the hand grips on the daring rides. He told of people's excitement at the game booths as they strove to beat the odds against winning. He told us about the fluffy cotton candy and the crunchy candied apples. He talked about the tantalizing aroma of the hot dogs and hamburgers. He wasn't really interested in those things, but he knew we were, so he spent some of his special evening observing those things along the midway.

We could tell from his comments where he had spent most of his time. His hands, browned from many days of sun and wind and roughened from toil, gestured enthusiastically as he talked to Mama. He told her of the prize winning stock, the prize winning produce and the prize winning canned goods.

He described the women's handmade items on display. There were quilts with intricate patterns. There were scarves of every shape and size with fine embroidered designs. There were also tiny, white garments for babies made with very fine stitchery. Also on display were knitted sweaters and bootees of baby pink and baby blue colors. There were sunbonnets and aprons, some of them very fancy. Papa's gruff voice sort of stumbled along as he tried to describe these 'women's work' things. He relaxed as he went on to describe woven baskets and other things he was more familiar with. Soon it was time to put aside the magic of the fair and begin preparing for the fall roundup.

Our fall roundups on the farm weren't anything like the western roundups I had read so much about. They were hard work, though. Mr. Trumbolte's cattle roamed over the mountain range year-round. In the springtime, Papa had to search far and wide for the newborn calves so he would have a comparison figure for the total number of calves to be rounded up in autumn.

In the autumn, we found the cattle in the most unbelievable places. We went down into fissures so nearly inaccessible we had to tie a rope around a tree or a sturdy bush, then we looped the other end around our waists and lowered ourselves down into the sheltered depths. Sometimes I just stood in the depths in stunned amazement. How in the world did a great big cow get into these fissures when I had to inch my way down a rope to do so?

We climbed steeps that caused our lungs to feel as though they might burst as we gasped for air from exertion. We scrambled our way through tangled brush and vines. We slid. We fell. We progressed sideways, bent over and flat on our backsides. We became bruised, scratched, stiff and sore. Fred and I loved every minute of it. In spite of our aching muscles, each new morning we jumped out of bed like spring chickens because Papa had said if we weren't ready to go by seven a.m., he would leave us behind.

The cattle were from different breeds and some of them were mixed breeds. We could identify cows by their markings and also by the peculiar habits some of them developed. Like Old Rogue for instance. We had long ago learned to recognize her the minute we saw her. I could be halfway down a rope, carefully bracing my feet against a rocky cavity as I slowly descended, only to spy Old Rogue hiding in the bushes in the ravine. I would scoot back up in half the amount of time it had taken me to descend. She was a red cow with sawed-off horns. There were others that fit that general description, but Old Rogue had a little white star shape near her right eye and an out-to-get-you look in her eyes. We were thankful Papa had sawed her horns to a short length because she would butt anyone in the drop of an eyelash.

Rover was an expert at flushing cows and calves. Even the bulls minded Rover. His keen senses of smell and hearing were invaluable aids. When the cows were stubborn about moving, he would nip at their tails and they would move pronto. The spring-born calves were old enough now to be taken to a farm with cultivated pastures and fattened to be sold as young beef. Our job was to round them up, separate them from their mamas, and pen the calves inside a fenced pasture until we had penned the total number of calves. Then Mr. Trumbolte would come and look them over. He would decide which ones he wanted to retain for breeders. These would be turned loose again to roam the mountain.

The separation procedure was the sad part of roundup. The mamas often became frightened and bewildered as we drove their calves from them. It usually took them several days to discover where their calves were being held captive. The cows showed up, a few more each day, until the hillside was filled. Day and night, the plaintive sounds of cows bawling and calves bleating drummed against our ears.

I recalled what a thrill it had been in the spring and early summer to discover the calves. Some of them would still be wet as their new mamas gently bathed them. Some had stood on wobbly legs, leaning against their new mamas for support. Some were seen butting their small heads against each other in a frolicsome way. Others had been running and playing almost like children. Their soft, fuzzy faces with their beautiful markings, variant colorings and soulful looking eyes caused me to fall in love with each little calf.

Now they were too big and clumsy to be babies but too gangly to be full-grown. Yet, they were being forcefully removed from their loved ones as though it were of no consequence. They were animals, but their hearts were breaking. It was hard for me to reconcile the order of the universe with mercy. Even after the calves were gone from the mountain, the cows continued their mournful lowing. After many days, they gave up hope. Accepting what they could not change, they wandered back into the far reaches of the mountain.

Autumn left its night-latch off and November sneaked in its back door. The cold wind whistled around the corners of the little, white house. The wood fires in the cookstove and the King heater roared and crackled and snapped with warmth. Fred and I stayed in the house most of the time because of the strong, cold wind. Papa brought Mama a new ball of twine he had purchased from Barr Toppham's five-ten, fifteen cents to a dollar store. Mama gave Fred and me each a length of the white twine to occupy us. We spent a lot of time making Jacob's Ladders. When Mama had first taught us how to make Jacob's Ladders with twine, she had also told us the Bible story from the book of Genesis about Jacob's dream. Jacob had dreamed he saw a ladder that stretched from the earth to heaven and the ladder was occupied by busy angels. As our busy fingers manipulated the twine, I asked Mama to tell me again the story of Jacob's Ladder.

Mama answered, "I used to tell you Bible stories when you were too young to read, but now you are old enough to read them yourself."

"But Mama," I began and she interrupted, "I know. You're goin' to protest as usual that the Bible is too hard to understand. The Bible is the best teachin' book there is. It not only teaches you about God, it's a book of geography and history. It teaches you how to trace your ancestral roots back to the beginnin' of time."

"History is not my favorite subject," I said.

"The book has even more. You can read beautiful poetry from its pages and fables also. You are always after me to tell you stories. This book has lots of parables in it. You read those romance stories by the hour and this book tells the greatest love story ever told," Mama said.

Mama looked at me thoughtfully as she sat in her rocking chair. She was busily rolling one thumb around the other. She asked, "Do you believe the dawn will break in the mornin'?"

"Yes, Mama," I said.

"Why do you believe that?" she asked.

"I just do. I guess I have faith that it will. It takes faith to believe a thing like that," I said.

"The Bible can teach you why you have faith. It tells about people who have faith and people who don't. It's filled with mysteries too, like the one about the grave of Moses bein' hidden. It's bedtime now. Go fetch the gowns and you can put yours on in here by the fire while I help Mitty put hers on. That bedroom is mighty cold tonight," Mama said as she rose to chunk down the fire.

I smiled as I went into the icy cold bedroom to fetch the flannel nightgowns. Mama had told me a story in spite of her firm intentions not to. She had told me a story about a story.

Frost had fallen in lacy patterns on all the growing things that had fought so valiantly in their attempt to withstand the frost's destructiveness. Flower blossoms bowed their brown heads as though in shame of their newly drab colors. The naked trees seemed to shiver in the cold winds.

Mama called to us one day as we stood watching Papa put new shoes on Prince. We answered Mama by calling out that we would be there in just a minute. Papa held Prince's hoof up between his knees. He held the horseshoe firmly in place against Prince's hoof with his right hand. With swift sure strokes of the hammer he held in his left hand, he hammered the nail into Prince's hoof to secure the new horseshoe. Papa was ambidextrous, so it didn't really matter which hand he used for what. In a short while, Mama called again.

We answered, "Just a minute, Mama."

We were interested in what Papa was saying to us. "Prince is real easy to shoe. He stands mighty patient. Most any horse will be patient unless he is an awfully cantankerous critter. Now you take a mule. Now there's a sassy, unreasonable cuss for you. Lots of times, a man has to tie a mule up short to put shoes on him and he will still wear you to a frazzle. Never did like a mule myself, but some folks do."

Mama called again and this time the tone of her voice brooked anymore 'just a minute' answers. We ran up the steps and opened the screened door. She was waiting for us on the back porch. She handed us two galvanized pails and told us she wanted us to gather wild grapes. "I want to make some homemade grape wine for Christmas," she said.

It was no problem to find wild grapes as they were plentiful. Off we went up the mountainside. It was a beautiful day. The sun was shining brightly and the wind was very nippy. The air exhilarated Rover with his thick coat of wavy hair and he ran and barked exuberantly. His plumy tail waved like a banner as he chased little gray squirrels up the trees and little brown rabbits under the bushes.

We swung our empty buckets in wide arcs. We ran and shouted for the sheer joy of being alive. The leaves crunched beneath our feet. They drew us like a magnet. We tumbled down into their golden, red, yellow and orange glory. We buried each other alive underneath deep piles of leaves and laughed uproariously when Rover found us.

The grapes hung in heavy abundance from the sagging vines. The tiny purple clusters of grapes were sweet from the frost's ripening effect upon them. It was hard to pick and not eat, so we ate about as many as we dropped into the buckets.

The nippy breeze began to grow chillier as the afternoon lengthened. We ducked down into a ditch that ran along the roadside beneath a sloping bank. The bank blocked the wind and the leaf filled ditch was snug and warm. Rover had long since disappeared. Fred and I lost track of time as we sat and talked about what we would like to do, where we would like to go, what we would like to be when we grew up.

Then we heard a sound like a woman screaming. It sounded like it was coming from right over our heads. Mama had warned us if we ever heard a bobcat scream when we were off somewhere alone, to come home immediately. We looked at each other apprehensively. We didn't quite know what we should do because we hadn't finished gathering grapes. The bobcat screamed again as though in fury. We dropped the buckets and ran like lightning down the steep road.

We burst through the doorway gasping for breath. "What on earth is the matter?" Mama asked.

"Mama, we heard a bobcat screaming like it was right behind us and we came home like you said to do," I gasped out.

Fred said, "Yeah, we sure did run lickety-split."

"I'm glad you did. Where are the buckets?" Mama asked.

"We left them. Will you ask Papa to go get them?" we asked.

Mama said, "Never mind. He's busy. I'll go back with you tomorrow to get them."

The following afternoon, Mama came out into the yard pulling her old, brown work coat on as she walked. "Let's go fetch the buckets before time to start supper preparations," she said.

We trotted along chattering to Mama as we walked. Mama was short, but she always walked briskly as though in a hurry. In fact, she did everything that way, thoroughly but quickly. She was slowing from the steep climb, though, by the time we reached the vicinity of the grapevines.

"My sakes, you two went off a mighty long ways just to find some grapes. No wonder you heard a bobcat nearby," she said.

We looked at Mama anxiously. We enjoyed the rare times when Mama could go with us for long walks. We hoped she wasn't growing impatient. She was probably wondering if she had allowed enough time. The days were much shorter now.

"We're almost there, Mama," Fred said.

We arrived at the spot where we had been picking shortly afterwards. Our buckets were sitting helter-skelter in the ditch just as we had left them. Mama picked up the buckets, half full of grapes. She stood looking around near her feet. There were no grapes on the colorful leaves because there hadn't been enough grapes in the buckets to spill out when they had tilted to the side.

Mama said, "What did you two spend the better part of the day doin'? Don't tell me it was pickin' grapes."

That night, we devoured bubbling hot potato soup with slices of onions and bits of red hot pepper mixed in with the other ingredients. We ate biscuits dripping with melted butter. We drank cups of steaming hot tomato juice.

Papa asked, "Did you two get enough grapes to make a crock of wine or will you have to pick again?"

Mama answered for us, "They didn't pick anywhere near enough grapes, but they won't be pickin' anymore this year."

A glass of the mild red wine, served with homemade sugar cookies, was our special treat for Christmas. Needless to say, from the tone of Mama's voice, there would be no wine in our house for Christmas this year.

November sped on. We helped Papa cut many trees. Prince pulled them to the woodpile where we sawed them into firewood. We split the pine trees into kindling. We carried wood continuously from the stacks at the woodpile to the back porch where we stacked a row of wood ceiling-high. Mama carried it from there as she needed it and fed it into the stove. She called them hungry stoves. Papa said they surely must be because it took us working as a relay team to feed them. When the snows began to come, we sawed wood by the hour. It became a nearly full time job. Fred and I took turns. While one of us helped Papa, the other one went into the house to thaw out.

Mama would help us pull the cold, soggy wet gloves from our stiffened hands. She pulled off our galoshes and the snow encrusted, thick woolen socks that had been pulled over our shoes. Then she helped us pull off our shoes and another pair of socks. We soaked our numbed hands in a pan of lukewarm water. When the blood began to circulate freely once more, the pain in our fingers was almost unbearable. We alternated between groans and tears, and we sighed with relief when the pain gradually subsided.

Fred and I counted our turns in the house with jealous accuracy. Somehow I never wondered, as I would in later years, why Papa never took turns going into the house to get warm. He never complained about the cold as we did. Surely his hands and feet must have ached with the icy cold just as ours did.

It was butchering time. The days and nights would remain

very cold from the end of November through the end of February. Cold weather was a must for butchering because of a lack of any other type of refrigeration.

Naturally Fred and I disliked butchering time very much. The baby piglets were so cute in early spring as they squealed and romped and tumbled around. We loved to watch them line up against their mothers to nurse. They looked like little round wieners all in a row.

When they grew old enough to be weaned and to venture farther away, Papa would put rings in their noses. The rings were clamped through the gristly portion of their noses to prevent them from rooting their way out under the fence. Papa would clamp the ring into each little nose with a quick snap. Each little pig squealed with fright and confusion as the ring pierced the gristle. Each time, Fred and I winced in commiseration. By the time they needed the rings, we had learned to know each little pig as an individual. We named them such ingenious names as Black, Spot, Porky, Runt and so on.

Papa always said, every spring, "I've told you both, over and over, don't make pals out of the farm animals. When your Mama cooks the meat, neither of you wants to eat it. You know they're here to be used for food."

We always ignored his warnings and kept right on running and romping with our various animal friends and calling them by name.

Lawrence and Elena always came to spend the night before butchering day so Lawrence could help Papa, and Elena could help Mama with the long day's work ahead. Lawrence was the only son-in- law who Papa decreed had the skilled accuracy necessary to shoot hogs. One shot brought quick, painless death if the bullet entered the hog dead center between the eyes. Fred and I stayed in the house. This was one time of the year we wanted no part of the events taking place outside.

Though wild horses couldn't have dragged us outside, the warm kitchen was a gruesome place to be also. Mama and Elena were bustling around like bees in a beehive. They began to set out huge pots and pans. They laid out sharp knives that Papa had whetted on the grindstone. They heated tubs of water. They repeatedly urged us to hurry with our breakfast so they could clear the table and we could go pump more water. The lamp lit kitchen sounded homey with Mama's and Elena's words tumbling over each others. They always chattered as though there were never enough time to say everything they wanted to say.

Mitty was showing Betty how to play 'Pat-a-cake.' She was also showing her how to play 'This little pig went to market.' We shuddered at the last one. I rebuked Mitty by saying, "Mitty, stop playing that silly game."

Elena bent over the table as she wiped the oilcloth clean with a dishcloth. Her hair was parted on the side and it hung straight against her head in a cropped style. Her hair was graying early like Papa's had, but, unlike Papa's, the texture of her hair was changing. It was becoming stiff and unruly. The gray had more of a yellowish tinge. Her teeth were nearly perfect though. They looked like a row of white pearls, making her full-lipped, friendly smile strikingly beautiful. Her burgundy colored dress swished around her pretty legs as she hurried to and fro from the pantry to the table, setting out supplies. Neither Mama nor Elena had their minds on what they were doing. They were talking excitedly about the baby Elena was expecting in February and the one Carrie was expecting in April.

I looked toward the window and shuddered. Against the backdrop of gray dawn, I could make out the trees' silhouettes, which meant it was light enough for Lawrence to take aim with the rifle. Fred and I were silent. We knew this was Prissy's last day. We had named her Prissy because of the white hair that lay like a band across her front legs just above her feet. It gave her an appearance of stepping daintily about the barnyard. Even Mama and Elena paused in their chatter when we heard the sharp crack of the rifle's firing pen as it struck against the bullet.

I knew what would follow next because I had been on the scene one time when hogs were being butchered. In my mind's eyes, I could see the effect of the speeding bullet as it entered Prissy's head right between her eyes. The moment she fell to the floor of the pen, Papa would leap over the side of the pen to kneel beside her. The sharp blade of the knife would flash as his hand plunged forward in a sweeping motion to slit her throat. Much as we dreaded it, we knew we must go and help Papa and Lawrence now.

By the time we got there the hog no longer looked like Prissy. We could kind of shut our minds to the fact that it was she. Papa and Lawrence had poured tubs of boiling water over her and we had to help clean her down to the hide. The stench of scalded hair filled our nostrils. The freezing winds of below zero temperature stung our eyes and chapped our wet hands. Papa and Lawrence were talking in practical tones of the work yet ahead and in anticipatory tones of the fresh pork liver smothered in onions and gravy that would grace the supper table tonight.

The hog had to be suspended from a crossbar in the twenty below zero temperature. The icy cold air would take the heat from the hog's body very quickly, By dusk, there were hams and side meat and shoulders, salted down and wrapped in cheesecloth. Long after dark, the men would be busy hanging the meat suspended from wire hooks, from the rafters of the corncrib. The wire hooks would prevent mice or rats from getting to the meat.

The only pause in the long day of rushing footsteps and busy hands was suppertime. Everyone dropped wearily into their chairs and hungrily passed the prepared food. The tantalizing aroma of liver and onions filled the warm, crowded kitchen. A large bowl was heaped high with a snowy mound of whipped potatoes. Near to it stood the butter dish with its mound of pale yellow butter, dressed up with its daisy imprint from the butter press. A basket was filled with hot, fluffy biscuits. Cups of bright red, steaming hot tomato juice sat near each plate. Mama poured coffee from the gray enameled coffeepot for the adults while Elena poured sweet milk from the pitcher for us. Fred, Len and I dipped gravy over the hot biscuits we had placed on our plates, but we avoided the liver like the plague.

After supper, Elena and Lawrence gathered up their sleepy Betty and tired Len and wearily headed for Lowmoor and home. Mama gave them some of the fresh meat to take with them. Mama and Papa continued working for several more weary hours. Butchering time required several extra long days of concentrated work with extra short nights of bone weary rest.

Fred and I were tied up most of the second day turning the handle on the meat grinder. Mama fed pieces of meat into the grinder and it squirmed its way out through the grinder's plate looking like a lot of worms.

Mama grew sharp as she rebuked me, "Stop callin' that meat worms. You know full well it is trimmin's from the hams, shoulders and middlin' meat."

I wrinkled my nose at it. "It looks like worms the way it wriggles through the chopper plate. That's why I don't like sausage,'' I said.

Mama worked the salt, black pepper and the sage in with the meat, kneading the mixture with her fingers as she would have kneaded dough. She taste tested the mixture and said, ''It is good sausage.''

A few nights later, she fried some fresh tenderloin for supper. Fred and I grew callous and closed our minds to the thoughts of Prissy. We loved tenderloin.

Boy-oh-boy! After all the meat was worked up thus and so into this and that, came the day even Mama must have hated if she would have admitted it. This was the day she rendered the lard. She partially filled pan after pan with bits of fat, trimmed from around the hog's intestines, heart, etc. She slid the pans into the hot oven. The sounds of the meat as it sizzled and popped filled the house. The aroma was pungently repugnant. The fat pieces dissolved into grease. The rind trimmings fried into crispy pieces of browned rind. The rinds were now called cracklings and would be delicious cooked in corn bread, which would in turn be called cracklin' bread. She poured the hot grease into metal buckets which had clamps on the lids and wire handles. The cooled grease solidified and thereafter was called lard.

The day she made lye soap from hog fat and Red Devil Lye was another unpleasant day. As I stirred the stinky mess for Mama, I said, ''I hate this day.''

Mama clucked her tongue at me like a mother hen with an erring chick. ''Rosebud, the Bible says we are to be glad and rejoice in each and every day because it is a day that the Lord has made. I guess you will have to learn that lesson the hard way, too, just like you do most everything else. You could save yourself a lot of pain and grief if you were not so hardheaded about things.''

''But who wants to spend whole days making stinky lard and stinky lye soap?'' I said.

''If we had no lard, we would have nothin' to make our food crisp or to keep fried foods from stickin' to the pan. If we had no lye soap, we would have nothin' to bleach our white clothes with,'' Mama said.

''Yes, ma'am,'' I said.

Fred and I tried to block the offending scent from our conscious minds and therefore our nostrils, by counting the days remaining until Christmas. We had loved all the Christmases we could remember and had always looked forward to the next one coming. I had no foreboding that I would turn the Christmas now approaching into a disastrous one for Fred.

7

WHO AM I?

Mama was so busy these days she didn't have time to answer our never ending questions. School lessons had to be put aside as she prepared for the coming holiday. Any other time she would have been glad to have us so interested in staying in the house to help her. Ordinarily, we would have chosen helping Papa as the most interesting thing to do. Now that she would rather have us outside, Mama told Papa that she couldn't stir us out of the house with a stick.

Mama roared through the house like a flash of fire. She washed the windows so shining clean the sunlight seemed to sparkle upon the glass. The white cotton marquisette curtains hung in starched folds against the ivory-colored, cellulose, window shades. The wooden floors were scrubbed almost white. The kitchen linoleum gleamed as the sun's rays danced across its red and white freshness. She polished the cooking range with stove polish until it shone. She polished the King heater, too, but the roaring fires required for these cold, blustery days burned the polish off quickly. Unlike the cooking range, the King heater was a thin metal. Like the apple-red cheeks on a chubby lad, the heater's glowing red sides shined through again.

Mama hung the heavy quilts on the clothesline to absorb the cold, fresh air as the wintry winds slapped at their colorful brightness. Mama firmly believed that everything in her home must be as sparkling clean as cleaning aids and hard work could achieve for the Christmas holidays.

By this time we could hardly contain our excitement because she was starting the decorations. She hung a red wreath with a large green bow in every shining window. Carefully, she unrolled the crepe paper streamers. Her shoes, with their sewing machine treadle design, gleamed as she climbed up and down the ladder.

She tacked one end of the bright red streamers into the corner up near the ceiling. She moved the ladder and tacked the other end of the crepe streamer to the corner diagonally across the room. Mama pulled the green crepe streamer across to the opposite two corners.

We held our breath as she unfolded the big, crepe paper bell from its accordion flatness. Holding the shaped bell aloft, she directed me as to where to place the ladder in the exact center of the room. Mama climbed up and tacked the Christmas bell in the center of the ceiling where the red and green streamers crisscrossed. We clapped our hands and squealed in delight as Mama released the bright red bell to swing gently to-and-fro.

We always anticipated the hanging of the bell even more than the Christmas tree decorating. Maybe it was because the beaverboard walls could not be painted and the brightness of the red and green streamers and the big red bell gave a gladsome look to the otherwise rather dark room.

We fairly danced out of bed each morning as the baking of Christmas goodies began. Fred, Mitty and I were never hungry at mealtimes these days. We were constantly busy, running our fingers around the insides of sticky bowls or scraping the last vestige of batter from the bottom of the bowls with spoons. This routine was what we called "licking the bowl clean."

We hung over the sides of the table with our elbows braced upon it and our faces resting in our hands as we watched Mama. She measured ingredients by adding a tad of this, a dash of that and a sprinkle of the other. She sifted and beat and stirred. She threw caution to the winds and used lots of sugar and eggs. We pleaded for lumps of brown sugar and got them with no hesitancy on Mama's part. We stood at her elbow like a pack of waiting vultures as she scooped the lightly browned sugar cookies from the baking tins. We practically hypnotized a few cookies into crumbling so we could eat them while they were still warm from the oven.

Mama said, "A body would think you children never had anything to eat. Do you think you can get out from under my feet long enough to fetch some firewood?"

Mama's face was flushed from the heat of the stove. She hummed off-key as she rushed about to the pantry, to the cellar and about the kitchen. When Papa came in for dinner one day, she said to him, "I declare, I can't move these days without

77

steppin' on the heads, hands and feet of three children.'' She smiled when she said it though. I think she did kind of wish we would go off to play because she had so much to do and was so pressed for time. At the same time, I think she was glad we didn't want to because children are kind of what Christmas is all about. The real spirit of Christmas had begun with the baby Jesus being born and lying in a manger. Not that I was giving much thought to that wonderful event this Christmas season.

Santa Claus was very much on my mind this year. We believed in Santa Claus with his red suit and white beard. We believed he swooped down from the North Pole on the eve of Christmas with a sack full of toys and goodies for all the good little boys and girls. We believed that he came down the fireplace chimney without being burned. If one had no fireplace, why then he made himself very, very small and squeezed in through the keyhole. We believed that Santa Claus ate the slice of black walnut cake and drank the glass of milk left beneath the Christmas tree for him. We believed he had a list of good and bad children and we always tried to be extra good at Christmas time. We believed all these things and more because Mama and Papa had told us all about Santa.

This year, I kept pushing to the back of my mind a sense of fear, doubt and unhappiness. There were vague rumblings of things seen or overheard in other years. Things such as being told to stay out of the barn loft during the Christmas season and other oddities like Papa not needing our help to unload the wagon during this season were beginning to take on a new meaning. Resolutely I shoved the thoughts aside.

Eventually, Mama had one afternoon to settle her nerves and garner her thoughts without us underfoot. The moment she told Papa, ''I'm ready for the tree now, Frank,'' we were ready and eager to leave the aromatic enticements of the kitchen for yet another kind of treat. We even bundled Mitty up in her coat and leggings and took her with us without grumbling. Rover yipped his happiness that we were outside again by racing around our feet as we walked through the woods. Papa was smiling as he strode along beside us. Although he always said all the hullabaloo about Christmas was nonsense, he enjoyed it, too.

The sky was cloudy and the cold air nipped at our faces. When we stood still and listened, the tall pines seemed to be whispering to each other. A light smattering of snowflakes was falling about us, drifting down among the trees in helter-skelter fashion. Mitty held out her little hands as she tried to capture the errant flakes.

Papa let us choose the young pine. We took our time making the momentous decision. We finally chose a full-branched one that looked tall enough to touch the eight foot high ceiling in our living room. Papa cut it down with his double-bit axe. We carried the tree back to the house. We tried to keep it free of the ground by lifting the weight of it as much as possible. We didn't want the needles to be scraped loose.

Mama met us at the gate. We had to wait until she looked it over and gave her official approval. Then Papa helped us situate the tree in a corner of the living room. He anchored the tree in a bucket with rocks and sand. The reason for anchoring the tree in a bucket was to provide a means of keeping the cut end of the tree watered. The tree must be kept as fresh as possible until the second day of January. One must never take down the Christmas tree until after New Year's Day in order to bring forward the good luck of the passing year into the new one. This was one superstition Mama clung to tenaciously.

Mama brought out the cotton batting and we pulled small portions from it and shaped the pieces into little balls. We put these on the tree to simulate snowballs. It was difficult to secure them on a pine tree. Papa would never agree to using a cedar tree because cedars were not plentiful on the mountain. Mama carefully unwrapped her few ornaments and we placed them on the tree. It wasn't a fancy looking Christmas tree, but we loved it. We could remember Christmases when there had been no tree at all.

The next morning, Mama said, "Frank, I need some supplies from town so I can complete my bakin'."

"I can't possibly go today. I've got to fix the fence. Old Rogue butted it down in one place up on top of the hill. I found it just a little while ago. That's why I came back just now, to get some tools. If I don't get it repaired mighty quick, Lady and Jersey will find the broken spot and be gone. Then we'd have to go find them. I've also got to repair the pigpen where that fool hog knocked the bars loose," Papa said.

"Fred is old enough to look after Mitty. I'll take Bud with me and we'll walk to town. The two of us can carry back what few things I need," Mama said.

"Are you sure you can't wait? That's a mighty long walk

to town and back, especially if you carry parcels back up the mountain,'' Papa said.

"It might do me good to stretch my legs in a long walk,'' Mama said. "I'm gettin' too fat from workin' in the house and takin' short steps.'' Papa grinned, "Ah shucks, I wouldn't say that. You're just pleasin'ly plump.''

Mama blushed like a schoolgirl and said, "Now get along with you, Frank. You mustn't say things like that.''

Mama and I dressed for town. When I thought we were ready to leave, I put on my stylish, brown coat with its little fur collar, a hand-me-down from Mrs. Trumbolte's daughter. I grew hot and headachy while Mama stood at the door in her worn, brown coat and repeated her string of instructions to Fred. Then she gave Papa a string of instructions. They followed us to the yard gate. They waited patiently as we started off down the road with Mama calling out further instructions over her shoulder.

We walked briskly along the dirt road. We talked about Christmas and hoped it would snow, but not too deep for cars to still make it up the mountain road. We wanted the rest of the family to be home by Christmas morning. My feeling of unhappiness returned as we spoke of Christmas morning. Finally I asked the question I dreaded to ask but knew I must. "Mama, there is no Santa Clause, is there?''

Mama looked startled. "What do you mean exactly?'' she asked.

"You might as well tell me the truth,'' I said. My heart was pleading, "Please tell me I'm wrong, please tell me there is a Santa Claus.''

Mama answered slowly as though searching for the right words. "Santa Claus is the excitement and the mystery of Christmas. He is real for children as long as they believe in him. You are growin' up. There will be no Santa Claus in a red suit anymore for you. He can always be real for you in another sense. The sense that it means the spirit of love and of sharin' and of givin'. Do you understand what I'm sayin', Bud?''

"Yes, Mama,'' I said.

"Well then, I guess you are pretty well grown-up. You must not tell Fred. He is still young enough to enjoy the fantasy of Santa Claus bringin' gifts from the North Pole. You must promise me that this will be our secret. If you spoil his fun, you'll bear the consequences,'' Mama said.

"I promise not to tell Fred," I answered.

As we walked on, I felt very mature in my new knowledge. Mama was talking to me as an equal. I was elated because I had grown up in a matter of minutes and had left my childhood behind yon curve. We walked on in silence, each lost in our own thoughts until we reached the town proper.

When we started up Main Street, Mama said, "I'll give you some money and you can go shoppin' in other stores while I'm buyin' my supplies in the grocery store. I want you to pick out a present for yourself. We'll keep it hidden away until Christmas Eve. Then I'll put it under the Christmas tree for Christmas mornin'. It will be your special present for a grown-up girl."

"Thank you, Mama," I said. I took the proffered money and fairly skipped up the street. I looked at many items as I went from store to store. I chose a fat, squatty book titled, *Snow White and the Seven Dwarfs*.

On the morning of Christmas Eve, Mama put a ham in the oven to bake. She began mixing ingredients to make five milk custard pies. We watched her dextrously separate eggs by pouring the yolk back and forth between the portions of halved egg shell. We watched in fascination as her nimble fingers grasped a common table fork and with seemingly effortless ease, she whipped the egg whites into softly peaked meringue for the pies. She stored the completed pies in the cold cellar.

Fred and I gladly turned the crank on the meat grinder as Mama fed fresh coconut meat into it. I nearly died with covetous hunger pangs as the coconut's snowy, sweet goodness fell in moist flakes through the chopper plate. She did give us a little of the coconut milk to drink, but she had to save most of it to use in the coconut cake. When the baked layers were tiered and hidden beneath a white mound of coconut, it, too, was taken to the cellar. It proudly occupied its place on the shelf beside the custard pies, which had been topped off with toasted coconut.

Mama sent us outside to crack walnuts for the fudge she planned to make. Fred chattered excitedly about Santa Claus as we worked. My feelings of being grown-up vanished. My heart cried hot, painful tears. With this feeling, came full awareness that my faith in the whole world had crashed down around my ears. My mama had let me believe in a Santa Claus that could come through keyholes. She was the one person in the world I had believed I could trust to tell me the truth, always, under any circumstances. Mama was my idol, the person I longed to be like. She was the goal I reached for and could never attain.

I looked at Fred's happy face and felt alone in my misery. The more he talked, the more resentful I became. It just wasn't fair. Fred was talking about the walnut cake. He was wondering why Santa liked it instead of the fresh coconut cake year after year.

I could stand it no longer. I blurted out, "It's because Papa eats the cake every year. Santa can't come through a keyhole either. There is no Santa Claus. Mama told me so."

Fred's eyes looked stormy as he said, "You lie."

"I do not lie. Go ask Mama if you don't believe me."

He yelled out, "There is a Santa Claus because Mama says there is."

"Yesterday, when we went to town, Mama let me choose my own present for her to put under the tree for me. Surely you don't really believe a Santa Claus could buy presents for millions of children every Christmas," I said in a superior tone of voice.

Tears welled up in his brown eyes as he said, "You lie. I'll tell Mama on you."

I grew alarmed when I saw how upset he had become. "You just better not tell Mama. She'll skin me alive and I'll get you good," I threatened.

All afternoon, Fred looked wan. Tears filled his eyes easily. He helped in a listless way whenever Mama told him to do something, but there was no show of interest in the preparations surrounding him. I tried to disappear into a cane-bottomed chair near the window. I kept my head down as I read a love story as though my life depended upon the story.

Mama kept glancing at Fred with a worried expression on her face. She asked him several times if he felt ill.

Fred's eyes watered as he said, "No, Mama. I'm not sick."

I breathed a sigh of relief. I scrunched down a little more as he looked at me with the hurt of the world mirrored in his soft brown eyes. I wished I had never been born. Mama finally grew insistent that Fred tell her what was wrong or she would call Papa to the house.

Fred burst into a torrent of tears as he said, "Bud told me there's no Santa Claus."

Mama straightened up. There was disappointment in her eyes as she looked at me. Her work-worn hand trembled as she brushed a wayward strand of hair back from her face. She said, "You have taken the joy out of this Christmas for your younger brother. Have you already forgotten what I told you about Santa bein' the spirit of love? To break a promise is a dishonorable thing. You made a promise and you broke it.''

That night as I sat in estranged silence from Fred, I made a promise to myself. For the rest of my life I would think seriously before I made a promise to anyone, and once I made a promise I would do my utmost to keep it in honor.

After my birthday on the eighth of January, I began to pester Mama to allow me to change my name. Each time, Mama's answer was a vehement, no!

''But, Mama,'' I pleaded, ''you don't know what it's like to be named Rosebud. Kids laugh at my name and they ask me when I'm going to bloom. Grown-ups get my name all mixed up.''

''I named you Rosebud because I thought you were such a pretty baby and the name was so pretty, it suited you,'' Mama said.

''I'm twelve years old now, Mama. I'm tall and clumsy. I just can't be Rosebud all my life. What about when I'm twenty years old. I'll be an old woman named Rosebud,'' I said.

Dorothea, who was home for a visit, broke into peals of laughter.

''I don't think it's funny at all,'' I said as I stormed from the house. I slammed the door resoundingly behind me.

I heard the roar of Papa's voice. ''Rosebud, you get back in here, young lady.''

I opened the door and entered. Papa looked at me sternly. He said, ''That is no way to talk to your Mama about the name she chose for you. Now go back out and close the door quietly behind you.''

My blood boiled with helpless fury. It took all of my better judgment to shut the door quietly. I seemed to be having a lot of trouble lately with slamming doors. Every time it happened when Papa was around, I had to do the same about face.

All through the month of January, I begged to change my name. Mama turned a deaf ear. In February, Mama brought us a pack of construction paper of assorted colors. She told us we could design our valentines and write verses for them. We could hardly wait to get started. After supper, while Papa and Mama read in the living room, we spread our paper all over the big, kitchen table. We assembled our scissors, pencils and tubes of white paste within easy reach. We drew our feet up in our chairs. We sat on our feet and leaned our elbows on the oilcloth-covered table as we began to create elegant valentines.

Mama came in one night to see why we were snickering. While looking over my shoulder, she read the verse I had written on mine. "Roses are red and roses are pink, and all little rosebuds stink!" A few nights later I wrote, "When I die, bury me in a cave. Don't send rosebuds for my grave."

With hurt in her eyes Mama finally said, "You can change part of your name. You can change the Bud but not the Rose."

I began to spend a lot of time pondering different names. "Mama, after I choose something to replace the Bud, can I write to the Bureau of Vital Statistics in Richmond, and change it legally?" I asked.

Mama answered with a firm shake of her head that brooked no argument, "No. You can choose the name you want to answer to, but you cannot change it legally."

"Mama, how about Rosalee?" I asked one day.

"No. You can't drop the e from Rose," Mama said.

"How about Rosamund? How about Roslynne?" Those suggestions elicited the same answer.

"How about Roseanne?" I asked.

"That's all right if you like it," Mama said.

"How about Rosetta, or Rosemaree?" I asked. She answered by saying if either one of those suited me, she would not object.

"How about Rosemary?"

"If you like it," Mama said.

"How about Gloria or Cerise?"

"No!" Mama said, "Bud, if you think you're goin' to keep on with a bunch of names until I get so tired of listenin', I'll agree to anything, you've got another think comin'."

"Mama, you limit me no end with your rules," I stormed.

The girls finally began to entreat, "Bud, please settle on one name. Every time we come home you have a different name from the week before. We're so confused, we no longer know who you are."

I gave in and settled on Rosemary. Eventually, I even gave up pleading with Mama to let me change my name legally. I knew from her attitude that for the rest of my life, I would be Rosemary for me and Rosebud for Mama.

I didn't know who I was most of the time anyway of late and it wasn't just because of my name. I wanted to call Mama, Mom and Papa, Pop or better yet, Mother and Dad. Those were the terms my friends in town used to address their parents. Papa and Mama looked at me when I voiced my new request as though they thought I had lost my mind.

Some days, I sat in my chair near the window and looked out across the pasture. I saw the clumps of brown grass and the straggly heads of the yellow weeds in the pasture. I saw the barren tree limbs and the dull gray February sky. I saw the snow covered Allegheny Mountain Range. It seemed to shut us off from the rest of the world. I heard the whining sounds of the cold wind as it rushed around the corners of the little white house. I saw the destruction of winter's icy fingers. Those fingers had ripped away the glorious colors of autumn. On other days, I looked out that same window and I saw the clean lines of nature's unawakened beauty, like a picture of a virgin woman painted by the strokes of a brush held in the idealistic fingers of a famed artist.

I ran the gamut of emotions in so many ways. I sometimes felt thrilled with the physical hints of dawning womanhood. At other times, I just felt lumpy and dumpy and out of sorts with everybody and everything. Some days, I played with my dolls and felt perfectly at home in play. The very next day I was fiercely ashamed of the fact that I had played a silly, child's game. I wished I were a boy except I didn't want to grow a beard or have hair on my chest. I wanted to live forever and yet I wanted never to have lived at all. I liked me sometimes and sometimes I couldn't stand me.

One hour, I would feel gentle and loving. The next hour, I would cry and complain. Sometimes I worked furiously and long, helping Mama or Papa without being told or asked. Other times, they just about had to dynamite me from my state of lethargy. Sometimes I enjoyed my turns at being the brunt of sibling teasing and sometimes I believed the entire family was picking on me and did not love me at all.

I wanted a romantic boyfriend instead of boys who called me Lefty and bragged that I had a mean pitch in softball. At the same time, I wanted to act like a simpering, helpless, young lady. I would look into my mirror and the girl who stared back at me didn't know who she was or why she was.

Fred and I played in the loft of the old barn one blustery

morning. The capricious March weather seemed akin to my mood. The dashing rain slashed at the old barn. The rushing wind beat against its weathered sides as though to smash it from its very foundation.

Most of the winter's hay had already been used for feed, but there was plenty left in the loft for games of rough and tumble. We piled the hay as high as we possibly could. With a running start across the floor of the loft, we leaped as high as we could upon the stacked hay only to come cascading down the slippery, shifting heap with bits of the hay showering down upon us. We dove into the stack headfirst to see which one could make the deepest indentation.

The quicksilver sunlight peeped through the barn's cracks and was soon obscured by the return of the dashing rains. We leaned back against the hay, exhausted from our exertion and the restlessness of the weather. We chewed on straws, lost in our own thoughts.

After a while, I asked, "What do you want to be when you grow up?"

"I want to be king and sit on a throne and play a guitar," Fred said. He shifted the straw from one corner of his mouth to the other. He peeped through a crack when he heard one of the cows squishing past through the muddy barnyard. "What do you want?" he asked.

"I want to get married and I want lots of babies and I want to stand on the highest mountain top and feel the wind in my hair and I want to see the whole world," I said.

"You can come see me and you can see lots of the world and do whatever you want to do because I'll be king," Fred said.

"I only know what I want to do. I don't know what I want to be," I said.

Fred threw down his pulpy straw and selected another. "Well, I'll make you a queen if you want to be one because a king can do anything he wants in the whole wide world," Fred said expansively.

We heard Mama calling us to dinner. We climbed down the ladder and walked through the barn between the stalls. As we went out into the rain, Fred said, "Come on, I'll race you to the house. The last one there is a polecat."

So many times, so many places we had talked and dreamed of our aspirations. We changed our minds from time to time as to our ultimate goals, but our dreams of being a king and queen were the dreams we spoke of most often. That night, trying to allay my moodiness, I wrote a poem about our daydreams, the things we did and said and thought. I put the long poem away in a shoebox and went to bed not understanding why I felt so sad.

Morning dawned bright with sunshine. The strong wind whipped at the muddy ground drying the surface quickly. Fred and I raced off to play on the rocky cliffs. This was the second free day in a row for us and we didn't want to waste a minute of it.

It's amazing how many fun games prove to be boring when there are only two children to play them. Hide-and-seek is such a game. Desperation encourages ingenuity, so we devised a scheme with which to make Rover a participant in the game. We would throw a stick as far as we could send it and then say to Rover, "Go get it, boy." As Rover ran to obey, we would dash off to hide among the rocks. If Rover found me first, I'd give him a hug as he proudly wagged his plumy tail while holding the retrieved stick in his mouth. After accepting the proffered stick, I would give it back to him and say, "Good doggy, smart doggy. Take the stick to Fred." Then he would have to find Fred. If he found Fred first, Fred sent him in like manner to search for me. Sometimes one of us became the seeker, without the stick of course, so Rover could hide with the other participant.

Rover always cooperated willingly for quite some time. The only trouble with our scheme was the fact that we could never outsmart Rover except when he permitted us to do so. We could never know just when he would tire of the game and quit.

He could also be tricky. Mama said the reason was he picked up bad habits from us. He could find us almost instantly when he wanted to because of his keen sense of smell, but sometime he took his good old time about it. Sometimes we waited and waited until our legs began to cramp from being all scrunched up in our hiding places. We would rise only to discover Rover, standing on a ledge directly over our heads. He would be looking down at us waiting patiently for us to give up.

Once we concluded he must have quit the game, we would come out of hiding to look for him. At those times we always found him back at the house, either sound asleep in the shade or teasing Twinkle or eating the meat scraps Mama had given him for a special treat because she was on his side.

As she watched him gobble up his treat on one such occasion, she said, "If ever a contest is held to prove which of the three of you is the smartest, I'm bound to say that Rover will be the winner." She grinned at us and turned back toward the house.

The gustiness of several days' of winds had dried up the mud quite thoroughly. Papa prepared to leave for town early. He needed to purchase seeds for the early crops.Mama prepared to go with him. She wanted to visit Elena. Elena's baby boy, Gerald Lawrence, would soon be one month old. Mama wanted to make sure they were all doing fine.

After they had gone, Fred decided he wanted to play alone. He formed steep, curving roads in the sandpile. He took his green car and little red truck Carrie had given him. Making sounds like running motors with his tongue, he roared up and down sandy hills and slid around sandy curves as his hand propelled the little vehicles along.

I took my red and yellow jump rope to the hard-packed dirt path. I swung the rope back and forth beneath my feet in what we called, "Rocking the cradle." As I skipped the swinging rope, I chanted, "Bluebells, Cockleshells, Evy, Ivy, Over." When I got to the word, over, I began to loop the rope over my head and under my feet, counting loops as I jumped.

Sometimes I wished the other girls still lived at home. My thoughts drifted back in time. They had all been as addicted to jump rope as I was. There were many jump methods to challenge body skills. There were many chants to add to the fun. They had taught me to jump the difficult "Double Dutch" when I was six years old. We had taken turns running in and out of the twirling double lines of rope. Often, two jumpers had run in at the same time and they had jumped until one missed a beat, then that one had run out and the jumper next in line ran in. I still remembered one of the singsong chants we used when jumping "Double Dutch Hot Pepper." As I jumped my hand rope now, I began to chant the words,

> "I saw Esau kissin' Kate.
> Kate saw I saw Esau.
> In fact we all three saw.
> Here comes Ma and here comes Pa.
> Jump, jump, jump for you life.
> Jump, jump, Pa's gonna whip 'er.
> Jump, jump, jump Hot Pepper!"

88

8

THE CONTRADICTIONS OF SPRING

Clarence, Dorothea and Tommy had been staying with us since the first of February. The shoe repair shop that had employed Clarence had gone out of business. Clarence could not find a job because he wasn't trained for anything other than shoe repair. He was worried and restless. He didn't know the first thing about farming so he was of no help to Papa.

Clarence enticed Dorothea, Fred and me into helping him pass the time away by pitching horseshoes every day. Dorothea couldn't play long because she helped Mama with the housework. She was also pregnant. Fred would eventually tire of the game and go off to other pursuits. Clarence and I played on for hours at a time. Before long we grew so adept at pitching, it was nearly impossible for one of us to win against the other. Dorothea and Fred, though competent pitchers themselves, grew reluctant to play as our opponents. They didn't want us as partners either.

Because Clarence felt unhappy and useless, he smoked many, many cigarettes. He ordered some shredded tobacco from the same company where Papa ordered his leaf tobacco. Clarence also ordered a cigarette rolling machine and a bulk package of cigarette papers. The hand operated cigarette machine had a little trough into which Clarence sprinkled a small amount of tobacco. He placed one of the small, oblong tissue papers on a rubber belt just beneath the trough. When Clarence turned the handle of the cylinder, the trough emptied the tobacco along the center of the paper. A wee strip of wet sponge moistened the gummed edge of the paper. As the cylinder completed its turn, it pressed the wet, gummed edge of the paper against the far side of the now tightly rolled cigarette. The cigarette fell out into a little tray. The mechanics of this little contraption fascinated Fred and me. Clarence could roll a week's supply of cigarettes in a very short time.

Back when Frank had been married to Dorothea, he could only roll one cigarette as needed. The tobacco had been packed in a little, white cloth bag which had a yellow drawstring. Frank had carried the bag and a small packet of cigarette papers in his shirt pocket. He would sprinkle a little of the tobacco onto one of the tissue papers that he held between his fingers. After pulling the drawstring closed by catching it between his teeth, he would return the bag to his pocket. Then deftly rolling the paper around the tobacco, he would lick the gummed edge and seal the cigarette. He would pinch the ends of the loosely rolled cigarette shut to prevent spillage.

Now, with the advent of the hand operated cigarette machine such as Clarence used, we were witnessing modernization for a homemade item. Papa sat at the kitchen table one night, watching Clarence roll cigarettes with the little machine. "I never thought I'd live to see the day man would invent a thingamajig like that to roll a cigarette. Man is never satisfied," Papa said.

We liked going for long walks with Clarence and Dorothea after the evening chores were finished. With her short fingers intertwined with his long, slender fingers, they strolled along through the coolness of the early April evenings. Clarence cautioned the pregnant Dorothea to watch her step as they walked across the cattle guards.

A guard was made by digging a ditch across the road and then embedding a series of pipes across the wide ditch. The pipes were even with the road's surface. The cattle would see the ditch's depth between the separated pipes and they were afraid to cross, which fulfilled the purpose of the guard. The cattle guards did not deter exploring motorists though. There were also several gates at strategic points across the incoming roads.

Sometimes we perched atop a gate, watching and listening to nature as she closed down her day and prepared for mysterious night. Dorothea often sang love songs to Clarence on these occasions. She looked up at his tall blondness from her petite brunetteness as she sang such songs as "Harbor Lights" and "Red Sails In the Sunset." As I watched them, I wished I could hurry and grow up. I wanted to sing love songs to some handsome fellow like Dorothea did to Clarence. Maybe I would learn to carry a tune by then.

One Monday morning, Clarence kissed Dorothea good-bye

and waved good-bye to us. He was going to Charlottesville, Virginia, to hunt for work. The house seemed awfully quiet with Clarence gone. The grass lay brown and matted where the Model A Ford had been parked. The horseshoes lay still and silent around one peg. Dorothea drudged through her days. Her spontaneous laughter and quick chatter were sporadic. There was a faraway look in her eyes.

As Easter approached, Mama bustled around in a flurry of activity. She said she must get her ducks in a row so she could leave Dorothea in charge. Mama was planning on going to Craigsville to spend a week with Carrie when her baby arrived. We all went to town on the twelfth of April. Mama wanted to purchase some extra supplies in case her absence was prolonged.

As we jostled along in the wagon, Dorothea said, "Mama, I'm all grown-up and expecting a baby in August and you act as though I can't figure out what I need if you have to be away a long time."

"You're not used to makin' a little money stretch to cover a lot of things like I am," Mama said.

Dorothea laughed, "Do you want to bet?"

Mama shook her head firmly. "No. That's gamblin'," she said.

Before the wagon turned into the alley behind the A&P grocery store, I was wishing I had stayed home. I rarely came to town unless Mama walked in, which was seldom. I disliked intensely coming in on the old farm wagon. Wagons in town drew attention these days because they were no longer the accepted way to travel. I was at an age when I didn't want to do anything differently from the majority.

Papa, Mama and Dorothea sat on the board seat. Fred, Mitty and Tommy and I sat in the wagon bed behind the seat. The wagon creaked as it swayed slightly from side to side. It seemed that every head turned to watch our progress as Prince's hoofs came down on the street that was now hard-topped. Prince flung back his head and snorted. The sound of his own hoofs going clip-clop, clip-clop on the unyielding surface almost caused him to panic. Papa's calm, soothing voice held him steady as he clicked his tongue and said, "Easy, easy now, boy. There is a sweetheart."

I was relieved when Papa parked the wagon behind the store. Now I could stroll down Main Street and pretend that I was a towns person, too. No one could tell that I hadn't arrived by car or on the town bus.

Papa not only bought goods. He also sold and traded goods. He liked to dicker prices and he liked to visit with the store merchants as he took care of business. That was why it took him the greater part of the day when he went to town. There was no hurrying him.

Mama went to the dry goods store. We took the smaller children window shopping. We stopped often to chat with acquaintances we met along Main Street.

We all gathered back at the wagon at noon for lunch. I thoroughly enjoyed this part of the trip. Mama didn't pack a lunch and bring it along as she did when she and Papa or Papa alone came to town. We came along so seldom she tried to make it a special, gala event for us. She bought a loaf of presliced bakery bread, head lettuce, hook cheese and a pound of bologna. We savored every crumb.

We took for granted homemade yeast bread. We were used to leaf lettuce fresh from the garden. We grew tired of country cured Virginia ham. To eat these store purchased foods was like manna from heaven to us. Papa had brought along a sack of grain for Prince. Prince munched as contentedly on his fare as we did on ours.

A few people, taking a shortcut through the alley, slowed their steps and stared at us as though they thought an alleyway was an odd place to eat one's lunch.

After lunch we returned to Main Street. I ventured off alone after awhile. Mama had given me ten cents of her egg money to shop with. I looked around in several stores at the many, many items with a dime price mark. It was difficult to decide just what to buy. Time passed quickly. I emerged from a store and glanced beyond the row of brick buildings. I observed the lowering sun. I knew from its position against the backdrop of the sky that it was 3:00 p.m. Papa would soon be ready to leave to assure getting home in time for the evening chores. I entered a drugstore and looked around at various items. The magazine rack drew me like a magnet. In the end, I chose something to read just as I always did.

I stood near the counter waiting to pay for the magazine. I became aware of the fact that the store, which had been nearly empty of customers when I had entered it, had become quite crowded. The owner and his clerk were very busy accepting payments for chosen merchandise and exchanging pleasantries with the customers. They glanced at me as I stood quietly waiting to pay for my magazine, but they always reached for the adults' items instead of mine.

I was growing angrier by the minute. I felt time slipping from me. Papa had a very strict rule that we must be at the wagon by 3:45 p.m., and woe unto the hapless one who dared to be tardy. Worried, I shifted from one foot to the other. I could not leave without the precious magazine.

The merchants continued to reach over me to wait on the adult customers. I knew I could wait no longer. Feeling very indignant at being ignored, I turned and walked from the store with the magazine in one hand and my dime in the other. I raced up the street. I was the last one to tumble into the wagon.

That night as I sat reading a story in the magazine, I felt Mama's stern gaze directed at me. I glanced up. Mama was sitting across from me with the Bible on her lap.

"You keep payin' out hard earned money for those throw away magazines, Bud. You could learn a lot more from readin' the Bible."

"This magazine didn't cost anything," I said triumphantly.

"Just what do you mean by that, young lady?" Mama asked.

With righteous anger I told Mama how the clerks had ignored me and waited on adults, even though I had been ahead of them. I told her I had finally decided I wasn't going to beg them to take my money. Besides, I would have been late returning to the wagon had I waited any longer.

Mama and Papa sat staring at me, aghast. Very quickly I realized they didn't agree with my line of reasoning at all. Papa's wind and sun browned face had turned almost white. His gray eyes were almost closed in a deep frown. His voice was stern and cold as he said, "Young lady, you are not to read that magazine. When I return to town in two weeks, you are goin' with me. You will return the magazine, pay for it and apologize for takin' another person's property."

"I didn't steal it, Papa. He wouldn't take my money," I protested.

"It was still stealin'. The clerks may have overlooked you because you're young, but that does not excuse what you did. If you couldn't get waited on, you were supposed to return the magazine to the rack,'' Papa said.

Mama held out her hand. She said, "I'll put the magazine away until you can return it."

A few days later on Saturday afternoon, Lewis drove up. He was smiling happily. He said the fair-haired, blue-eyed Priscilla Jane had been born early that morning. He had come to fetch Mama. The date was April sixteenth, nineteen hundred and thirty-eight.

Mama laughed as she remarked, "If Priscilla could have waited until tomorrow, the Easter bunny could have brought her."

The Monday following Easter, Papa left to till a field. He said to Fred and me, "You two stay at the house and help Dorothea. She's got all the work to do with your Mama gone. She's goin' to wash clothes, so mind you help her with that. Help her look after Mitty and Tommy, too."

By nine o'clock, Fred and I had somehow ended up sitting in the living room doing nothing. Mitty and Tommy were playing in the sandpile. Dorothea was working steadily doing a dozen things at once. We weren't really supposed to be in the living room during an ordinary work day as we might dirty it up for nothing.

By ten-thirty it seemed the morning would never pass. We were bored. We were tired of being cooped up, but neither of us wanted to give up this unusual opportunity to be his/her own boss and sit in the living room. For lack of something better to do, I watched the clock hands that seemed not to move after the clock had struck once for ten-thirty.

After what seemed a long time the long hand reached the numeral nine and the short hand was almost on the numeral eleven. "It's a quarter of eleven," I said.

"It is not. It's fifteen minutes until eleven o'clock," Fred said. He had just recently learned to tell time and he thought he was an authority.

"A quarter of and fifteen until mean the same thing, dummy," I said.

"It does not. Mama taught me when the short hand is on the nine and the long hand is almost on the eleven, it's fifteen minutes until eleven o'clock." Fred said triumphantly.

"Well, it's still a quarter of," I said.

"It is not."

"It is so."

"Will both of you just hush? That's enough of that sour grapes argument," Dorothea called from the kitchen.

"Quarter of," I whispered.

"A quarter is twenty-five cents," Fred said quietly.

"But it's also a quarter of a whole dollar," I said.

"That has nothing to do with time," Fred shouted.

"It does!"

"It does not!"

Finally Fred said, "It's no use arguing with you. I don't want to talk about it anymore."

His usually soft brown eyes were stormy and almost black with fury. His arms were crossed and the muscles in his neck stood out like cords. Fred was shy, soft-spoken and slow to anger, but if pushed too far, his fury was torrential. I generally knew just when to stop teasing him. This was one of the times I misjudged.

I kept on needling. He kept on sitting, silently seething. Finally I said, "Well, you don't have to worry about it being a quarter of eleven, dummy, because it is now a quarter after eleven."

Suddenly his arm slashed out at me, barely missing as I leaped to my feet and dashed from the room. As we tore through the kitchen, Fred grabbed the broom from Dorothea's hands as she swept the floor.

Around and around the house I raced, yelling, "Stop. Don't you dare hit me."

Dorothea was right behind Fred, flailing her arms and yelling, "Fred, don't you dare."

Around and around the house the three of us went. Mitty and Tommy were jumping up and down and clapping their little hands as though they were betting on race horses in the Kentucky Derby.

All of a sudden we jerked to a stop as a thunderous voice asked, "What in tarnation is goin' on here?" Papa stood looking at us, his small frame looking as big as life as we tried to excuse what we could see was inexcusable.

He reprimanded Dorothea for not asserting her authoritative rights. He reprimanded Fred for allowing his temper to get the upper hand. He reprimanded me for being to blame in general. The generalities he applied to me included teasing, loafing and disobedience. Then he told me the same thing he and Mama always told me, which always brought a serves-you-right smirk to Fred's face. Papa said, "You are older than Fred, Rosebud, and you are supposed to set a good example for him.''

Papa took Fred back to the field with him and I was left to help Dorothea, so the rest of the day was quiet and uneventful.

I think Papa missed having Mama to sit and talk with him and share in reading the Bible with him at night. Her rocker sat next to his, quiet and empty. Dorothea was usually busy embroidering tiny designs on baby clothing or writing letters to Clarence. Somehow we all ended up sitting around in the kitchen at night where she was.

Papa began whittling out spinning tops for his grandchildren. Thus, he had carved wooden spinners for each of his children long ago. The blade of his brown, bone handled pocketknife moved slowly over a small portion of one of the empty spools which Mama had saved after using the thread from it.

Many little spinning tops, made from spools, had danced and twirled upon this very table. Sometimes they danced over the edge of the table to fall to the floor. Often they had kept on twirling as they touched the floor.

We could remember when Papa used to make us wooden whistles from chestnut shoots. The winter's rains and snows always drove some of the fallen chestnuts into the soft, moist earth. The warmth of the following spring called to the soil-covered chestnuts to reproduce and thus were born the tender shoots that made such marvelous whistles.

Papa would rub a piece of wood up and down, slowly and methodically over the young chestnut shoot until the bark had loosened from the shoot. Then the bark would slide easily from the shoot in one piece. The inner stem would be moist and sticky.

With his pocketknife, he would cut one end of the hollow stem slantwise to form a mouthpiece. He would position the blade about one third of the way down the stem. He would cut slantwise and downward into the side of the stem. Then he would cut straight across to form a little half-moon slice. With the tip of his knife, he would carefully lift out the little slice. He would cut several rounded holes near the bottom of the newly formed whistle.

The finished, sticky whistle would be laid aside to slowly dry and harden. After several weeks had elapsed, the whistle would be ready for use and the proud recipient could play it similar to the way one plays a flute.

We also had dolls formed from clothespins. Some of our other dolls were made from corn shucks. Papa had taught us how to use a thin tissue paper on a fine tooth comb and the comb became a make-shift harmonica. Papa had always seen to it that we had toys, although the toys rarely came from a store.

Mama had to return from Craigsville sooner than she had planned because of a death in the family. Aunt Nanny, Uncle William Henry Clark's wife, had been very ill for some time. On April twenty- first, she passed away. Lawrence drove to Craigsville that night to bring Mama home.

We were glad to see Mama. Dorothea and I pelted her with questions about baby Priscilla. We especially wanted to know how eighteen-month-old Ronnie was accepting her. Mama said Ronnie was so busy being an inquisitive little boy, the baby seemed to be just one more interesting object to him.

As she talked, she handed Dorothea a letter from Clarence. Mama had gotten Lawrence to stop at the mailbox and she had picked up the mail on her way home. Dorothea became her usual vivacious self as she told us about the contents of the letter. Clarence had written that he had found a job as manager of a shoe repair shop. He had rented a house in Charlottesville, Virginia. He would be driving in on Sunday, May seventh, to take Dorothea and Tommy home.

On the day following Mama's return, John Henry Clark came from Clarks Gap to fetch us. John Henry and Papa talked of many things as we rattled along the highway in John Henry's truck. They began to reminisce about how their ancestors had come to America from Ireland.

Seven or so Clark brothers, who had come over from Ireland with their parents, had settled in the Blue Ridge Mountain area. They had been drawn to the area because of its plentiful timber. Chestnut groves had stretched along the crest of the mountain as far as the eye could see. Poplar, oak, hickory and walnut trees were plentiful also.

Wild animals and wild game were in abundance. Wild berries and fruits as well as clear mountain streams made the mountain an ideal place to settle down and raise large families. Nelson H. Clark was one of the brothers to settle there. He had fought in the War of 1812. He was later granted bounty land in this area on two separate occasions because of his military service.

John Henry and Papa were two of Nelson's great-grandsons. One of Nelsons' brothers, Joe Clark, Sr., owned seventeen hundred acres of the mountain land. On and on, the brothers had spread out across what became known as Clarks Mountain.

Some of the Clarks began to marry Indians, who were also inhabitants along the range of Blue Ridge Mts. This was especially true of those residing in Amherst County. This region was sparsely populated, therefore intermarriage between Clarks and Cherokee Indians, as well as Monacan Indians, took place according to scanty courthouse records and some census records.

Mama's people, the Branhams and Willises, were of English descent, but they, too, had intermarried with Cherokee Indians.

Papa and John Henry talked on about the past and how the Clark brothers had eventually lost most of their land to a group of land swindlers. The mountain is still legally named Clarks Mountain, but actually the smaller portion known as Clarks Gap is all that remains of the land owned by Clarks.

When we arrived at Uncle Henry's, there were many relatives and friends crowded into his house. It brought back memories to Papa of the deaths of his petite mother, Margaret Tyree Clark, and of his beloved sister, Carrie. It showed in his drawn face as he shook hands with his older, half-brothers, William Henry and Luther Jackson. Awkwardly, he put his arm around the shoulders of Luther's ailing wife, Elizabeth.He turned to greet John Henry's brother, Herbert. John Henry's wife, Leann, and Herbert's wife, Lizzie, came over and began to talk to Mama. Houstan and Rosie Clark were there, too.

I ran over to Vealy Mason and she gave me a big hug. Vealy was about Elena's age. She often came for extended visits with us. She was such fun, always teasing and telling funny jokes. The Masons were relatives, too, but they had blond or red hair, such a contrast to the Clarks' dark tresses.

I didn't know Uncle Henry and Aunt Nanny's children very well, except Lilburn. Most of them were sitting together against one wall. I picked out Rebecca, Vernie, Milton, Bea and of course, Lilburn.

It didn't take us younger ones long to gravitate into a corner of our own. We were well acquainted with Bruce, one of Herbert and Lizzie's sons. We were well acquainted with Pike, Hallie and Melvin, John Henry and Leann's children. These children came to visit us often. We always had a good time together.

I overhead some of the grownups talking about how Uncle Henry and my Papa used to make caskets whenever needed. They said whenever anyone had died, one would see a man approaching Grandma Margaret's home, carrying a sapling length over his shoulder. Whenever someone died, a close relative of the deceased would cut down a young sapling. He would measure the corpse by it and then cut off the sapling at the needed length. He would then bring the sapling length to Uncle Henry so he could build a casket of the necessary length. Papa was much younger than his brother, Henry, but helping him build caskets was how Papa got his first training in carpentry.

We all gathered at the family cemetery two days later. I saw Papa standing before Carrie's tombstone. Engraved upon it were the words, "On That Bright Immortal Shore, We Shall Meet To Part No More." In nineteen hundred and twenty-one, Grandma Margaret had been buried beside Carrie and now Aunt Nanny was laid to rest just a few gravesites distance from theirs. After many tears, hugs and kisses among family members and friends, we left the cemetery to return home.

On Friday, April twenty-ninth, Papa told me to dress in something suitable for town. This was the first opportunity he had had, considering the birth of Priscilla and the death of Aunt Nanny, to take me to town to return the magazine. These past two and a half weeks had been the longest of my life because I had wished I had my humiliating task behind me. It had also been the shortest period of my life because I had dreaded the end result.

Papa and I arrived in town. Papa said, "You can take care of your business while I tend to mine."

"Go with me, Papa," I said.

"If you were old enough to take the magazine alone, I believe you are old enough to return it alone," Papa answered.

The owner of the store looked at me unsmilingly as I tried to explain what I had done. I expressed my apology to him. He took the proffered dime. He shook his head concerning the proffered magazine. He said, "You can keep the magazine. It is paid for now. I trust you have learned a lesson from this?"

"Yes, sir," I said meekly.

Papa and Mama never mentioned the incident again and neither did I.

One could tell the days were getting longer. The gay yellow of the jonquils' blooms made me think of miniature Easter bonnets on parade. The little, woods violets lifted their sweet scented heads of deep purple. The gray of winter's sky had surrendered to the azure blue of spring. Yes, spring was definitely here.

The mating season had begun. Every morning at the crack of dawn, the roosters just about lifted the rafters from the chicken house with their braggadocios crowing. There was a hen on every nest, wanting to set. Sometimes there were two hens trying to lay claim to the same nest. There was good reason why I had to put on gloves to gather the eggs. Each hen jealously guarded her daily production of an egg. They hoped to set on the eggs until they hatched. They pecked at my hands vehemently when I reached under them to remove the eggs.

Fred and I often let Pinky out of his rabbit hutch during the winter months. We had played with him so much since last Easter, he was very tame. Pinky liked to hop around in the barnyard pasture. He looked so funny with his snowy white fur and large pink eyes.

Pinky was so different from the regular barnyard creatures. They either scratched at the ground or pawed at the ground. They walked or ran on the ground. Pinky alone hopped over the ground. They all made vocal sounds, but Pinky could not. He was different in so many ways, but they had grown used to him. They accepted him as one of the barnyard family.

This beautiful spring morning we released him. We cuddled him and then we set him down in the home pasture. We watched for a while as he busily nibbled at green shoots and wiggled his ears in pleasure. Then we went off to tend to other things. We were very busy throughout the remainder of the day and gave no further thought to Pinky until it was time for the evening chores.

We looked for Pinky so we could put him back in his hutch, but we could not find him. We searched the barns and the chicken house. We searched near the hogpen and around the woodpile. We searched under the corncrib. We searched everywhere we could think to search. It grew dark and we had to give up.

Mama said, ''Springtime is matin' season. I expect Pinky has gone to the woods in search of his own species.''

''But Mama,'' I said, ''Pinky is a tame rabbit. He doesn't know how to provide for himself or how to protect himself out in the wild.''

''He may or may not survive. He was happy here for awhile. Now it's spring and he senses the call of a fellow creature. He has gone to answer that call,'' Mama replied.

We continued to watch for him and to search for him for many days, but to no avail. We never knew Pinky's fate for we never saw him again.

Even Rover seemed caught up in the magic and contradictions of spring. Through the open windows at night came his mournful sounds. For several nights Rover sat in the yard and howled at the golden moon. The moon was full and ripe. Then Rover disappeared. He came back a week later, tired and gaunt.

Spring was hard for me to understand. It seemed that the earth was not all that awakened. All of the earth's inhabitants were awakening also to a keener sense of the need for companionship. There seemed to be a new awareness of love, of birth and of growth. A sense of well-being seemed often laced with a vague feeling of discontent. A sense of happiness and a sense of loneliness seemed inseparable.

Mama was a classic example of this paradox of spring. When the three older girls came to visit, together or separately, Mama thoroughly enjoyed their visits. She admired their stylish clothing and freely told them so. It did not appear to bother her one whit that she did not have clothes like theirs. Frances' visits seemed to unsettle Mama this spring.

Nineteen-year-old Frances came quite often. Sometimes she came dressed in a fitted sweater and a gaily colored neckerchief knotted loosely at her throat. With this she wore riding breeches and knee- high boots. A roller brimmed hat rested jauntily on her shoulder- length hair to complete the ensemble.She and her group of young friends never went horseback riding, but this getup was considered ''the thing'' for any outdoor activity.

She liked jackets with action pleated backs, wide lapels and padded shoulders. The padding gave her shoulders an exaggerated, squared looked. She always chose flared or pleated skirts that accented her short stature. Sometimes she even dared to wear slacks or one-piece playsuits with tie-on skirts, which Papa strongly objected to.

One or two girl friends with their boy friends always accompanied Frances and her boy friend. A sporty roadster, or a coupe with a rumble seat would come roaring up the mountain road and slide to a stop just outside the yard gate.Frances and her friends would tumble out of the car for an afternoon visit. They always came dressed to go on from the farm to a weiner roast, a dinner, a dance, or the theater.

They would stroll about over the farmland, laughing and teasing one another. One or another would step aside and take snapshots of the others, grouped together with their arms around each other. The girls took snapshots of their boy friends stroking Prince's tawny mane. They took snapshots of their boy friends, taking turns, standing with a foot on the running board of the car. The boys snapped pictures of the girls as they took turns swinging on a gate or kneeling beside Rover. They snapped pictures of a boy and girl, paired off as sweethearts, standing beneath the spreading branches of an elm tree and gazing swooningly into each other's eyes.

As these balmy, spring afternoons dwindled toward suppertime and choretime, they would crowd back into the car and wave their merry good-byes. The sound of the car's motor would fade into the distance as they hurried on their way to exciting and carefree adventures of youth.

Mama always smiled as she stood in the yard and waved good-bye to Frances and her friends until the car disappeared from view. We could see the storm clouds brewing on this typical day as she gathered up her milk bucket to begin her evening chores. She seated herself on the little milk stool and began to milk. The thin, fast streams of pale yellow milk pinged against the sides of the milk pail with unusual force. Lady turned her head sideways until it rested against her shoulder. She looked at Mama with one unblinking eye as though to make sure it was Mama doing the milking. The force with which the milk was being dashed into the pail caused foam to gather abundantly. With each ping of milk, Mama's words of dissatisfaction tumbled out.

"Frank, do you realize that I never get to go anywhere? I have never had any leisure or any fun since I was five years old. All I ever got to do when I was growin' up was take care of Mama's babies. Since I was sixteen, all I've done is take care of my own babies. I never have anything stylish to wear. I'm just a dowdy old woman before my time." She stood up and gave Lady a whack on the rump in dismissal. Lady's head jerked around in disbelief.

Even the chickens looked at Mama askance. They fluttered their cropped wings. The hens clucked as though they were saying in chicken talk, "What has that old rooster done? He sure has gotten her feathers all ruffled up."

102

Mama handed me the milk pail. When I came back from straining the milk, she was shooing some baby chicks away from the woodpile by holding her apron by the corners and flapping it at them. Papa and Fred were sawing wood and as Mama's apron flapped, her tirade continued. It sounded almost like I had never been absent.

Mama was saying, "I never had boy friends except you. How do I know if other boys would have liked me? I didn't even get to date you except right under the eyes of my parents. I went straight from doll babies to babies. I've never been young. With one giant step, I jumped right over one phase of my life completely and it was all your fault, Frank Clark!"

She picked up the basket of eggs from where she had set it near the chopping block. She walked furiously toward the house. In a voice filled with tears, she flung sentences over her shoulder until she reached the back porch. She entered, allowing the screened door to slam behind her.

Papa always looked at us and shook his head in silent warning on these particular spring evenings. Once or twice Mama caught sight of his warning to us. Her self-pity intensified as she accused, "You can just stop warnin' the children to pay me no mind. I don't have to be humored. You're actin' like I'm slow-witted or sickly or somethin'."

Fred and I were bewildered. Whatever could be happening to our Mama this spring? It only happened when Frances had been home with her young friends. In a day or two, she would be almost back to normal, except for being a little subdued and preoccupied. Then Frances would visit again and as soon as she left, Mama would fly into her tirade again. Frances was unaware of the restlessness she caused in Mama this spring.

We felt sorry for Papa because it wasn't his fault Mama felt so unhappy. We felt hurt and sort of unwanted because she had complained about so many babies. We felt sorry for Mama, too, because she seemed to be crying inside. I felt like that sometimes, but I was going on thirteen and Mama had said that was why I felt like that. Then Papa confused me even more.

He said, "Don't feel hard toward your Mama. She don't mean the things she says when she's all teary-eyed. Your Mama is forty-four years old. She's goin' through a time of life that is mixin' up her feelin's."

"She's grown-up, Papa. Why would her feelings change

now?'' I asked.

"You and Fred are too young to understand. The heat is botherin' her this spring. She thinks she's got heart palpitations because she gets so flushed and breaks out in sweats, even at night when the air is cool. She's awful nervous these days,'' Papa said.

"Last Saturday, she was fussing at you because Frances earned wages for her work in a restaurant and could spend some of her earnings on pretty clothes for herself. She said Frances danced the nights away with a different boy every Saturday night. She said Frances was nineteen years old and still single. What did she mean? What's wrong with those things?'' I asked.

"Nothin','' Papa said.

"Why was she upset about it then?'' I asked.

"Because she never got to do those things. A body makes choices when they're young. A body is sure at the time they are the right choices, and nobody better tell a body different. Then a body comes to a point, usually in their middle years, when for a spell of time, they're not sure they made the right choices. It's then a body needs the time to come to grips with the questions. The heart usually knows the answers. It's the mind that gets unsettled for awhile. Until a body gets all the questions settled, a body's family has to be patient. It's best to leave your Mama alone. Let her talk out her doubts without arguin' back at her. It makes her mad when we don't answer her. It'll make her even madder if we do. Just leave her be,'' Papa said. He laid the crosscut saw lengthwise between the arms of the V-shaped sawhorses. Papa picked up an armful of wood and trudged imperturbably toward the house.

Fred and I gathered an armful of wood each and followed him. We stacked the wood on the back porch and went back out to sit on the steps. Dusk had erased the late afternoon's shadows. The frogs were beginning their melancholy croaking sounds of "ribbit, ribbit, ribbit.''

We looked at each other questioningly as we tried to understand all that Papa had tried to explain to us. I wasn't sure at all that I understood. All I fully understood was the fact that predictable Mama was suddenly much like unpredictable me.

9

TORRID HEAT AND LOCUSTS

Mother nature picked up her brush and painted the month of May. The sky spread a canopy of blue above the earth. The fragrant sweetness of apple blossoms permeated the air. The dogwood trees seemed adrift with their clouds of snowy white blossoms. (The dogwood tree is Virginia's chosen state tree; the blossom is its chosen state flower.) Beautiful pink and purple flowers begged redemption for their Judas trees. Morning-glories entwined the rows of fences in a rainbow of glorious colors. Tiny lady's-slippers seemed to step gingerly across a carpet of green grass. Dainty Virginia bluebells clustered upon earth's floor. The magnitude of the surrounding Allegheny Mountains, holding aloft their newborn greenery, loaned dimension to this fairyland of colors.

Smack in the middle of this picturesque setting, lay the realism of a working farm. The heat of June was fast approaching and the sheep needed to shed their winter coats of wool. Several men came from one of the other farms to help Papa with the task of shearing the sheep. Once more I was told I could not take part, just as I had been told that I could not help harvest the oats. Once more I was angry and disappointed. I wondered why all of the interesting tasks were consistently men's work?

For two days I listened to the bleating of the sheep. I watched from the yard. One by one, the sheared sheep dashed from the barn, looking like they had been caught skinny dipping. The next day I could stand it no longer. I sneaked into the upper side of the barn. I found a knothole in the dividing partition. I scrunched down until my eye was on a level with the knothole. I soon grew cramped and stiff from my uncomfortable position, but dared not move around for fear of discovery.

The sheep had to be anchored securely to prevent accidental

wounding from the sharp shears the men wielded. I could understand why the sharp shears were dangerous as one of the men moved them swiftly about the frightened sheep's wool. The sheep's head was held rigidly by a stock. One man held the sheep's forelegs and another man held the hind legs. A third man worked steadily and quickly, shearing the mounds of curly, dirty looking wool from a sheep. I watched a sheep as he strained to move from his fixed position. I observed the rippling, corded muscles of the men as they immobilized the sheep. As man pitted his strength against beast, I understood why a girl could not be competitive in this instance.

The piles of wool mounted upon the barn floor. The bleats of the sheep were loud as they were led to-and-fro. The noise and the stench of the sheep, the heat of the day, and the grunts and sweat of the men were not pleasant to hear, smell or see. It was most interesting though and I wished I could view the activities with both my eyes at once. After awhile, my eyes blurred. My back throbbed and my limbs went to sleep. I crawled stealthily away and tiptoed from the barn.

Twinkle was sunning herself upon the back porch step. I sat down beside her and stroked her gray fur. I tried to think of a way to get even with Fred because he could take part in the sheepshearing and I could not.

Papa talked about the day's work as he hungrily consumed his supper. He tilted his chair back when he had finished eating. Mama didn't like for any of us to tilt our chairs back because the chair's legs dented the linoleum. She didn't voice an objection now, I guessed because Papa looked so tired. Papa tamped tobacco into his pipe and struck a match to it. The match head blazed against the tobacco. Papa puffed on the pipe's stem until smoke spiraled upward from the pipe's bowl.

He puffed contentedly as he winked at Mama and said, "Dora, somethin' kind of odd happened today. Several times I glanced up when it was my turn to help hold a sheep's legs. When I was down on my knees like that, I thought I saw a large, greenish eye kind of glued to a knothole. I thought maybe Twinkle was tryin' to see what was goin' on.

"Then after a spell, I thought I saw a reddish eye at that same knothole. I wondered if Pinky had come back and was starin' at us. It kinda looked like Bud's green eye, but then it changed to red. Besides, she's too tall for her eye to be on a level with that knothole. Whoever it was, that eye sure did look funny a blinkin' and a blinkin' through that old knothole. I wouldn't want to think it was Rosebud's eye though, because I told her to stay away from the barn.''

Mama had an ironclad rule that we could not go barefoot until the first day of June. It might cause us to get sick to go barefoot any earlier she said. But on the first day of June, be it a cold day, a wet day or a hot day, we could shed our shoes and run free for the summer, except when we worked in the fields. The soles of our feet soon became tough as shoe leather and we could conquer any terrain. There was only one exception to our joy in going barefoot. Sometimes we misstepped when running through the cow pastures. Then one would have thought we had been mortally wounded by fresh cow chips.

I loved to wade through the fields of tall oat grasses to reach the cherry orchard above. Eating ripe, red, sour cherries with the little bubbles of morning dew still on them was nectar to my taste buds. Eggs for breakfast didn't interest me on these beautiful June mornings when I could feast upon cherries. Barefooted and wet from the dew on the oat grasses, I came back to the house in time to strain Lady's morning offering of milk.

Although Papa and Mama needed our help badly, they recognized youth's need for play and just plain loafing. Therefore, we were given frequent free days. On one such day we headed high up on the mountain range to some rocky cliffs. Although Mama forbade us to play on the cliffs, she never actually elicited a promise from us, so sometimes we sneaked and spent hours up there.

Today we climbed up the steep sides of the cliffs. When we reached the top, we stood on a sharp peak and shouted. We listened to the sound of our voices fading into the distance. We tried to write on the large rocks with the sharp edge of a little rock. We played hide-and-seek with Rover.

At noon we sat with our backs propped against a huge, rocky expanse and propped our lunch pail between. We ate flaky breakfast biscuits with fried fatback encased in them. We ate another flaky biscuit spread with country butter and homemade damson preserves for our dessert. We drank water from a gallon jug. Then we secured the jug and the metal lunch pail in a crevice.

Feeling restless and very adventuresome, we climbed up much higher than we had ever dared to climb before. We threw sticks down and watched Rover leap from one rock to another as he chased them. Lifting my arms high in sheer exuberance, I leaped across a space from one jutting cliff's edge to another. I landed on my feet, but the thin edge gave way beneath my weight.

I screamed as I fell, rolled and slid down the side of the cliff. Loosened rocks pummeled me. They seemed to roar over me. I could hear Fred screaming and Rover barking. It seemed to me that I had fallen through an eternity of time, but it couldn't have been more than mere seconds. I came to rest covered, more or less, in dirt and rocks.

I lay there moaning and groaning until Fred and Rover scrambled their way down to me. Rover reached me first and I felt him licking my hair. Fred began to lift the rocks as quickly as he could and soon I was free. He helped me sit up. I huddled over in kind of a ball, moaning from the throbbing pain.

After awhile Fred said, "Bud, can you walk? We've got to get home and let Mama help you."

I answered, "I think I can walk. My hands and arms are hurting most of all. But I can't go home. Mama will kill me when she finds out how I got hurt."

Fred said, "Oh Bud, you know doggone better than that. Mama won't kill you, 'specially when you're already hurt."

Slowly we entered the house. I had groaned and cried every slow step of the way home. Mama looked alarmed and asked what on earth had happened. Fred's words tumbled out as he told her.

Mama looked stern as she said, "Just wait until your Papa hears about this."

She was already hurrying about assembling various homemade remedies and clean white cloths. My hands were so swollen they looked like huge, unbending claws. Hurriedly, Mama told Fred, "Go gather lots of fresh mullein leaves and bring them to me as quick as you can."

While she waited for Fred to return, she carefully lifted my clothing from me and discovered that my back was badly scratched and swollen too. She poured liniment over my back and sides, then wrapped strips of white cloths around me to provide firm support. She poured tepid water over the cuts and bruises then gently coated them with a creamy, homemade salve. When Fred came back with the mullein leaves, Mama had me place my hands in a pan of cold water. She placed several layers of wide, soft, mullein leaves over my hands.

Several times a day for quite a few days, Mama would have me lie down and she would place wet mullein leaves across my back. When the mullein leaves began to dry out, she would remove them and rebind my back with fresh strips of cloth. As soon as that was taken care of, I would have to sit with my hands submerged in water and weighted down with layers of mullein leaves. Mama said they would draw the swelling out. Fred had to go out many times to gather fresh leaves. Papa helped him gather the leaves sometimes, although it was the kind of chore that was considered women's and children's work.

As soon as I began to heal, I began to fuss and wish out loud that I might never see another mullein leaf.

Fred had no pity for my predicament of being confined. When I complained of suffering and of smelling like a medicine safe, he said, "My back hurts from bending over gathering mullein leaves for you. I almost wish I hadn't dug you out from under those rocks."

I had no more recovered, except for some stiffness in my back, until the locusts began to come. For several weeks they came like swarming black clouds. Fred and I thought they looked right interesting the first few days when there were but a few. Then there were many more. We began to kill and kill and kill.

Finally Mama said in despair, "We might as well stop tryin' to kill them. The more we kill, the more comes to take their places."

Even though the sun was shining, they came in thick swarms until the days were darkened. No matter how fast we tried to scoot in and out in order to shut the door quickly, they entered the house. Mama fought a frantic battle by using more and more tight closing containers as she tried to keep them out of the foodstuffs. They crawled on the tables and over the floors. They crawled on us. We began to feel nauseated. We walked on top of them on the ground until we felt as though we could not bear the squishy sound of their bodies beneath our feet. They covered the trees and bushes, slitting the bark ruinously.

The locusts crawled on the animals. The constantly swishing tails, flapping wings and stomping feet of the animals were to no avail against the awful pests. The constant, horrible, roaring sound made by the locusts' wings never ceased, day or night. Slowly, tree after tree and bush after bush began to wither and die. The orchards were the first to go.

Sometimes I would smash the locusts with my hands and feet, crying tears of fury because of our helplessness against their destructiveness.

In a tired voice Mama said, "It does no good to kill a few when there are so many. Save your energy for things that count. We still have to prepare for winter as best we can."

We were in the process of drying green beans. We had just finished drying peaches, what few we had been able to salvage from the dying trees.

The drying process meant climbing up ladders to the rooftops to move the screened frames from east to west and west to east. The drying process had to be regulated. The single layers of vegetables or fruits had to get so much sun per day. The vegetables or fruits had to dry thoroughly from the outside in. If they dried too fast they became tough. If they dried too slowly some of them would rot. The direct heat of the noonday sun would scorch them. They must be moved to shelter when it rained. It was a job all of us must take part in, even Papa.

Fred and I disliked the job and even more so with the constant sound of the locusts. We sat down beside the tall, slender baskets filled with beans we were taking to spread on the frames. We clamped our hands tightly over our ears, but we could not shut out the roar of the locusts' built-in drums.

Mama came by carrying a basket and said, "You two had better get busy. You never want to help prepare, but you always want to eat come winter time."

The dried beans really were very tasty in the cold winter months. They were sort of tough fibered, but they had a flavor all their own and quite different from fresh green beans or canned beans.

I sat propped up against a tree trunk in the yard, forming grasshopper nests from dandelion stems. Rover was fast asleep beside me. His golden brown coat of hair shone warmly in the sun. Mitty was sitting on the back steps talking to Twinkle. Twinkle had her eyes half closed and her front paws were placed demurely in front of her. Mama was seated on a stool nearby shucking corn to cook for the midday dinner. Fred and Len had gone off someplace with their BB guns.

Rover sat up and yawned as he looked toward the road. He stood up. His collie ears pricked up. He stuck his plumy tail straight up in the air. He growled low in his throat and ran to the gate and began to bark. Someone was coming. Who could it be? Mr. Trumbolte had come up in his chauffeur-driven limousine on Monday to assess the damage the locusts were causing. He wasn't likely to come back today since this was the Wednesday following.

Mama said, "Mercy me. I dropped the dishrag this mornin', that means whoever is comin', is comin' hungry. I had better run to the garden to fetch a few more ears of corn although I've probably got a gracious plenty." Short, plump Mama stood up and shook some clinging cornsilk from her red-checked gingham apron.

When Rover heard someone coming, that meant we still had some time left to hurry and get squared away. He could pick up the sounds of a motor much sooner than we could.

After awhile, a Chevrolet Sedan driven by Lewis came into sight. We ran to meet them and Mama lifted the sleeping Priscilla from Carrie's lap. I picked up the giggling Ronnie and jumped him up and down in my arms. Fred and Len were coming down the hill beside the orchard fence, their BB rifles slung over their shoulder, trying to act like real huntsmen. Papa was coming from the cornfield. He was holding Prince's reins loosely in his hand as he came down the hillside.

Soon everyone except the baby was seated around the long wooden table Papa had built so long ago. The unexpected visit in the middle of the week was soon explained. The Chesapeake and Ohio Railroad's company policy allowed employees to pull for jobs according to their seniority. Some man had pulled by vote for Lewis' job as railroad miscellaneous clerk in Craigsville, Va. Lewis in turned had pulled another man in Lexington, for the same kind of position.

Lewis was moving Carrie to a small house just up the street from his parents' home in Clifton Forge. He didn't think the Lexington post would last long. He wanted Carrie and the children close to relatives in case they needed someone in his absence. They had driven up today to see if Mama could keep Ronnie for a few days, and they wanted me to go back with them. They needed me to help Carrie with Priscilla and with the cleaning of the house they had just rented.

We took some flowers to the cemetery one day after Carrie was nicely settled in the small rental house. Dorothea's baby,

Eddie, was buried beside our brother, Harry. Elena's baby, Lois, was buried at Harry's feet. After we had placed the flowers on their graves, we strolled on as though by mutual consent to the twin grave where two lovers had been laid to rest in nineteen hundred and seven.

The romance and the tragic ending for the two, seventeen-year- olds, had always pulled at our heartstrings whenever we thought about it, even though it had happened so long ago. The young sweethearts had tried to elope because her parents thought they were still too young for marriage.

By request of her family, the young couple had been intercepted on the Washington bound train when it stopped in Staunton. They had been sent back to Clifton Forge on passenger train No. 3. The Chief of Police met them at Clifton Forge and started them on their way home across the swinging wire bridge that spans the Jackson River. The young couple paused near the middle of the bridge and suddenly the beautiful young girl jumped over the wire railing to the murkey water below. The young man climbed over the railing and dropped to the water to rescue his sweetheart. She threw her arms around his neck and they both drowned.

The young lovers who had left for Washington with such happy hearts and high hopes were buried in identical caskets in a double grave. The young girl had been buried, dressed as a bride. One of Lewis' ancestors, E.M. Mahaney, had been one of her pallbearers. As a tribute of love, their friends gave the tall marker for their graves. Embedded in the stone is an oval picture of the young couple. Their story has often been likened to that of "Romeo and Juliet."*

When I returned home, the heat of August had us caught in its grip. On a boiling hot day, Clarence came to take Mama back with him to Charlottesville.

Clarence said, "Patricia Ann was born last night about eleven o'clock. She has my blue eyes and Dorothea's black hair. She is already just like her mother because she is very definitely making her presence known."

Mama said, "I'm already packed. I've been expectin' you

---

*For a more thorough study of this tragic, intriguing story, contact Mr. Jim Cantrell, Clifton Forge Review, Clifton Forge, Virginia.

any day. I'll be ready to go just as soon as I give Bud some last minute instructions.'' Mama had been busy doing just that for the last two weeks. Just as she had instructed Dorothea when waiting for Priscilla, now she had instructed me while waiting for Dorothea's baby. She had a much more difficult undertaking this time. Maybe she was remembering the oatmeal sticks. Anyhow she had given me so many instructions as to this and that, I was thoroughly confused. Now she wanted to give me some last minute instructions!

The first day she was gone wasn't bad at all. She had left lots of prepared food. All I had to worry about cooking was the hot bread. Mama cooked from scratch, seasoning and mixing it by pure instinct. She had tried to work out some measurements to write down for me. I soon decided Mama wouldn't have been a good cook if she had been made to cook by the measurements she had written down for me. Especially the biscuits. I made biscuits that fell apart and biscuits that were, when baked, golden yellow on the inside but still white on the outside. I made biscuits that were black on the outside when removed from the oven. I made biscuits that were too thin to cut open or too fat to want to.

Poor Papa grinned sickly. He tried to offer suggestions. ''Maybe if you used less soda, or maybe more soda, maybe more, or maybe less bakin' powder, maybe that's what you need to do to make biscuits that taste like your Mama's,'' he said. ''Don't be discouraged, Bud. You make a mighty fine biscuit to be just learnin' how. Hey, why don't you try your hand at makin' corn bread for supper tonight?''

Before Mama left, she had said, ''You can use some extra eggs, but don't be wasteful.'' She had baked a Busy Day Cake and had filled a large tin with molasses cookies. Each cooky was as large as Papa's hand. She had also made five coconut custard pies with golden meringue heaped on top. Those desserts were supposed to last us for the two weeks she would be gone. They were all gone by the end of the first week.

At the end of the first week, Papa said, ''I expect you are mighty tired of tryin' to cook. Why don't you just fix eggs and corn bread for our meals for the next few days?'' Very soon, Mama's eggs for market were gone, too. I longed to go back to helping Papa in the fields. This stuff of cooking three hot meals a day wasn't for me.

Mama had said, ''Be sure you sweep under the beds.'' I

crawled in and out from under the beds shoving boxes of stored goods, kept under there for lack of other space, to the middle of the room. I swept under the beds, but my broom handle was too long apparently, because I kept hitting other beds and the dresser and stuff. Then I shoved the boxes back under the beds, but I always had some boxes left over. When I finished and picked up the broom to sweep the middle of the room, I found that the wind from the open windows had blown all the dust balls back under the beds.

On Monday, I hadn't finished washing the clothes when Papa came home for supper. When I tried to sprinkle the clothes the next morning, they were so stiff with starch, I had to hit some of them to get them to lay flat on the table so I could dampen them. I sure was glad Mama had taken Mitty with her and I didn't have to try to iron her little dresses.

I fixed a macaroni pie for supper that night. I used too much cheese and not enough milk. It tasted kind of dry and gummy. Now I understood why Elena couldn't cook when Fred was born and she was supposed to take over the kitchen. Elena had been almost seventeen years old at the time. Mama cooked with a dash, a dab, a sprinkle, a tad, a level handful or a gracious plenty. Everything turned out tasting simply delicious when she cooked, using those so-called measurements. It wasn't an easy method for a novice cook.

Two days before Mama returned, the dishes had piled up something fierce. I never seemed to have time to finish anything. Papa left Fred behind to help me catch up on the dishes. I washed and Fred dried. The table was stacked high with dishes when we finished.

Fred said, "I'll be glad when Mama comes home. I shouldn't have to help you do girls' work. I'm not going to help put all this stuff away. I'm going outside where it's cooler."

"Ah, it will only take a minute. It's all in knowing how," I said.

Fred had placed several short stacks of plates on the table. I restacked them to make one very tall stack. Carefully, I pulled the stack to the edge of the table. I picked up the plates and balanced the heavy load in both hands. I made a couple of wary steps. I lifted one foot to make another step. The plates wobbled. They crashed to the floor. I was left standing holding about eight plates.

Fred's brown eyes were round with wonder. He crammed his slender hands into the pockets of his bib overalls as he said, "Uh oh, you're in for it now when Mama comes home."

The dinner plates had been a leftover conglomeration from many different sets. They had been the survivors of many young dishwashers. Mama probably didn't know exactly how many she had of each pattern and color I thought to myself.

I pleaded with Fred until I persuaded him to help me. We gathered up the plates that were badly smashed. We took them far into an area thick with undergrowth. We scattered the pieces by throwing them as far as we could. We came back to the house and I knelt before the bottom shelf of the safe. Fred gathered up the plates that were broken into large sections. He handed them to me and I fitted them together on the shelf, much like working a jigsaw puzzle. I stacked the plates that were merely chipped on top of the jigsaw plates. I completed the stack with unbroken plates.I made two more similar stacks on the same shelf. By the time I swept up the fragments, disposed of them and had thrown out the now cold, greasy dishwater, it was time to start supper.

The next day, Papa worked out Mama's garden and Fred and I weeded her flower beds. My eyes were drawn as though by a magnet to the hillside over which we had thrown the broken plates. I feared some of the jagged pieces might come skipping up the hillside like in a nightmare.

Mama came home the next day. I was never so glad to see her in my entire life as I was now. I was overjoyed that the management of the house could be returned to her capable hands. I had a tale of woe a mile long to share with her, not to mention the things I didn't tell her about.

"At a glance, it looks like you made do pretty good, Bud," she said. I breathed a sigh of relief.

The next day as she began to get back into harness she said, "Bud, what on earth happened to all the eggs? Surely the hens have been layin'." Later in the day she said, "Bud, I told you to sweep under the beds. There is enough dust underneath the beds to create a man." She started to cook dinner and she said, "Rosebud! What is the meanin' of all these broken plates and where are the rest of the plates?" I tried to explain. Mama said, "You should never have tried to hide them because you were afraid of bein' punished. The Bible says, 'Be sure your sins will find you out'."

With a self-righteous sigh, Fred said. "I told you you were gonna' get caught."

Mama became very busy putting up damson preserves the following Monday. Her hands had often been stained through the summer months. They had been red with cherry juice, beet juice and tomato juice. Now they were purple with damson juice.

Frances had come home for a week's visit and as she helped Mama, she said, "Mama, I need your recipe for damson preserves. I was telling a friend that you made the best damson preserves in the world. She wants your recipe."

Mama said, "Well, I stem the fruit first of all. Then I wash and drain it. I cut the damsons loose from their pits. You're already well acquainted with that step because you girls have always claimed it takes forever to pit damsons. After they're pitted, I layer the fruit and sugar in a large pot, usin' one cup of sugar for each cup of fruit until the pot is nearly full. Then I add one cup of water to the pot. Let the mixture stand for thirty minutes. When the time is up, set the pot over the heat and cook the mixture slowly, stirrin' once in awhile. When a small amount will form a steady stream from a spoon and drop into a saucer in a soft ball, it's ready. Skim off the foam and pour the fruit into jars. Your friend won't have a bit of trouble. That's all there is to fixin' damson preserves."

"My goodness," I thought as I sat with two big pans in front of me. I was slicing the clinging damsons from the pits. There was another pan beside me filled with moist stems. The table was laden with steaming hot jars Frances was gingerly lifting from a pot of boiling water. There were buckets of colored water, caused by rinsing the fruit, waiting to be emptied. Our hands were purple. The sweet, cloying smell of simmering fruit filled the still, hot air of late August. The perspiring Fred was bringing in more wood for the hungry fire. The messy Mitty was eating some of the soft-ball- stage drippings from the saucer. The sticky, purple preserves were smeared all around her mouth. They had also dripped down the front of her pink cotton dress. My goodness, I thought again. Mama had made making purple damson preserves sound so simple.

10

STORING FOOD FOR WINTER

Early this past spring Papa had told Fred and me that we could each plant a potato patch. He had said it would be our responsibility to tend the patches. Whatever amount of money we made from the sale of the potatoes would be ours to do with as we wished. We had been exuberant as we showed Papa the twin fields we had chosen.

Papa had cautioned, "Are you sure you want to plant such large patches? It will take a heap of work to tend such big crops."

"Ah, don't you worry, Papa, we'll work hard. We want to make lots of money."

So Papa and Prince prepared the fields. We took the seed potatoes Papa gave us and quartered them as we had been taught. The potatoes had so many eyes sprouting from within, it was wasteful to plant whole potatoes.

Papa and Mama believed in planting potatoes on Good Friday whenever possible to insure a bountiful harvest. They believed in planting all crops by the signs of the zodiac. There were certain signs and certain days best suited to plant root crops. There are, supposedly, about fourteen days in every twenty-eight days that are good signs for planting. The moon is another infallible sign according to Papa and Mama. For instance, one should plant corn when the moon is full. One should kill hogs during the last quarter of the moon, or when the signs are in the feet or the knees. This is believed to cause the hogs to bleed more thoroughly. Blum's Farmer's and Planter's Almanac was often referred to as the farmer's Bible. I could see why, the way Papa and Mama referred to it the year round.

Almost as though to verify my observations, Mama came out of the house with the Almanac in her hand. "This is a good day to start plantin' your potatoes," she said.

117

We dreamed big dreams as we dropped two quarters of a potato into each mounded hill. We covered them with rich soil.

We watched with avarice as tiny, green shoots began to crack from the soil and peep forth. Any potato hill that did not show forth fresh green sprouts within a reasonable length of time, we redug and replanted with more seed potatoes.

Papa's slender frame approached as we worked. He observed what we were doing. He shook his head sagely as he said, "The potatoes you just dug up was sproutin' fine and dandy. You get in too big a hurry. Haste breeds waste."

Papa's brown fingers encircled the handle of the hoe that rested on his shoulder. His blue chambray shirt sleeves were buttoned at his wrists as ever they were. I knew without a doubt that he was also wearing his long johns beneath the shirt and overalls. Papa contended that any garments that kept the cold at bay in wintertime would also serve to keep the heat at bay in summertime. He never offered an explanation of why he didn't wear his jacket in the summer though. The why of that paradox was one question I somehow knew better than to ask. Anyway, there he stood all protected from the warmth of the sun as he watched us. He shook his head again as he turned and walked away.

Soon we had twin patches of potatoes to be proud of. There was not one barren hill and the patches were weed free. Then as the novelty wore off and the days grew hotter, we got slack. Papa had to needle us several times to tend what he called our "growin' crop of weeds."

One day later on, he told us to follow him. As we stood in one of the patches, Papa said. "Both of you were offered a chance to be your own boss and to make money for yourselves. You are neglectin' your job. This is the last reminder you will get from me. From now on it's strictly up to you. Just don't ask for my help when it comes time to dig and you can't find your potatoes. Nobody ever made any money yet by goin' off and swingin' on a grapevine."

"Yes, Papa," we answered meekly. "We'll work on the patches tomorrow."

Papa turned and walked away. The straps of his bib overalls rested against the back of his sweat-soaked, blue work shirt. His size eight-and-one-half work boots left crushed weeds where he had been standing. As he disappeared over the hill, we knew his gray brows were drawn together in a deep frown of displeasure.

We couldn't work today though. This was our free day and we had some important plans. We had taken a twist of Papa's chewing tobacco and several country matches from a shelf in the pantry. Fred had hidden the stolen goods deep down in the pocket of his overalls so Papa wouldn't know he had them. I had found some cigarette papers Clarence had accidentally left behind.I had those hidden in the pocket of my blue gingham dress.

We started off toward the rocky cliffs, enjoying many side excursions and diversions along the way. We reached the cliffs and settled down on a wide rocky ledge. We removed our loot from our pockets. We knew full well that Papa never smoked his pipe unless he was in the house or yard. He exercised this precaution against the chance of causing forest fires. He always chewed tobacco away from the house. Surely a chance spark wouldn't escape the broad expanse of the rock where we were seated.

We rolled a few lumpy cigarettes. Fred tried to strike a match against the leg of his overalls as we had seem Papa do. The match wouldn't light. I grew tired of waiting for the exhibitionist to strike a light. I picked up a match and lifted my foot sideways. I tried to strike the match against the rubber sole of my scuffed brown shoe as I had seen Clarence do against the leather sole of his well shined, black shoe. We both gave up and struck the matches against the rock.

We leaned back and puffed away on lumpy cigarettes. We coughed and blinked our eyes. The cigarettes were soon gone.

We sprawled out on our stomachs on the flat expanse of rock. We had each bit off a portion of the twisted tobacco as we had watched Papa do so many times. We looked down upon the brown leaves from the locust killed trees. We chewed and we spit. We talked about the million and one things we were going to buy with the money from our potato crops. Near suppertime, we dug a hole below the cliffs and buried the spent matches and the remaining tobacco. By the time we headed for home, we didn't feel so good.

Before we had time to think about how time flies, Papa said, ''It's time to start diggin' potatoes today.'' We spent two weeks or more helping Papa and Mama dig their potatoes.

The blazing heat of the late August sun brought the blood rushing to our faces as we bent over close to the heated earth.

It felt as though my face would explode from the pressure. When I stood up the whole world seemed to turn black. The slight thudding noises from Mama's and Papa's hoes against the hardened earth, now cracking from the full potatoes, seemed to intensify the heat. The buzzing sounds of bees further added to the aggravation. They were drawn by the moisture of some fresh dug potatoes that had been cut open accidentally by searching hoes.

Mama wore one of Papa's blue bandanna handkerchiefs draped around her neck beneath the short ruffle on the neck of her bonnet. The tip of a red bandanna peeped from the left pocket of Papa's overalls. Often their drudging figures paused while they slowly straightened their aching backs. They would stand for a moment, leaning on their hoe handles as they mopped their perspiring faces with their handkerchiefs. Then they would bend forward again as their arms methodically lifted and fell to sink the hoes into the earth.

Mama and Papa dug the potatoes and piled them beside each hill. We came along behind them with buckets in our hands. We each filled a bucket and carried it to one edge of the field where stacks of bushel baskets had been deposited. Each basket would hold the contents of several bucketfuls. In this manner we filled basket after basket.

We leaned sideways from the weight of the potatoes in the buckets. By afternoon we usually dragged the buckets along leaving scraped paths on top of the sunbaked earth. The buckets banged against our legs at times and elicited exaggerated groans from us. Though the chore of gathering up the potatoes should have been the fastest of the two phases, it didn't work out that way. Papa and Mama would have to stop digging to help us catch up on the gathering.

At the end of the day Papa would leave the field and return with Prince pulling the wagon. Papa could lift the filled baskets into the bed by himself. Fred and I had to grasp a wire handle situated on each side of a basket and simultaneously lift the basket up and into the wagon bed. Mama busied herself gathering up scattered potatoes we had let roll from too full buckets. Once home we would unload the baskets from the wagon and carry them into the yard. After supper and evening chores were finished, even though the air remained hot and stuffy, Fred and I would suddenly dredge up enough energy to chase fireflies and run with Rover.

The following morning we would return to the back breaking harvesting. By ten o'clock, Fred was telling Mama he had a headache and I was telling her I had blisters on my feet. Mama just kept on digging.

Papa said, "If you two children spent half as much time workin' as you do complainin' we would have finished harvestin' these potatoes several days ago."

We had brought cornstalks from a nearby field. We used them to make a teepee for Mitty to sit under when she grew too hot in the open field. Papa told us to build two more teepees for ourselves and we could rest awhile in their shade. We sat within our teepees, sheltered from the scorching rays of the sun. I watched the bent figures of Papa and Mama as they toiled silently on. I wondered how they could keep on when we couldn't.

While they began the chore of grading their potatoes, Fred and I began to search for ours. We couldn't determine exactly where the potato hills were because the entire field was covered with matted weeds. Because we couldn't find the hills, we chopped into many potatoes, thereby rendering them unmarketable.

Fred and I met at the middle of our twin patches. I removed my bonnet to use as a fan. I knew my curly, brown hair must be a matted mess. Even though Papa's bib overalls were two sizes too large for me, the thick material still made me feel hot. His size eight-and-one-half work boots hung heavy on my feet. I looked at Fred as I fanned myself with my bonnet. I said, "I wish you hadn't kept wanting to do silly things on our free days when we should have been working these fields. Papa's potatoes were a lot less work than these weed-matted potatoes."

Fred took off his straw hat. His coal black hair was soaking wet with sweat. He dribbled some water from the water jug over his head. He flicked water from his fingers at me. "Oh yeah? You're the oldest, remember? You know doggone well Mama said you were responsible for whatever I do. You can't blame this on me," he said.

We pulled and chopped and kicked at the tall weeds and tough grasses. We argued every time we met at the middle of the patches. There was no point in making a cornstalk teepee because there was no one to dig while we rested in its shelter.

The scorching sun bore down upon us through several days

of digging and arguing. Papa came each evening with the wagon. He helped us load our potatoes.

The work of sorting and grading had to be carried on as steadily as possible. Heat gathered quickly in the heaping full baskets and in the piles of potatoes we had poured out upon the ground. Heat and sweating would rot this root vegetable very quickly.

The potatoes must be sorted according to size and defects. Empty baskets were placed in three separate rows. The larger, first grade potatoes filled one row of baskets. The medium-sized potatoes filled the second row and the smaller-sized, the third row of baskets. The potatoes that were too small for market and those with cuts from the hoe or other defects were culled for home use. Some were sun blistered, causing greenish-colored jackets, from growing too close to the soil's surface. These were culled out too, regardless of size.

The refilled baskets would be stored on the cool cellar floor until Papa could haul them to market. There were large, dirt-filled storage bins for potatoes, onions and turnips, which we would fill with root vegetables for our personal use. Before the first killing frost, the onions would be brought in and placed in the bins with their cut tops turned downward. The turnips would be gathered before the ground began to freeze.

My thoughts abruptly returned to the task at hand as I reached up a dirty hand to brush the stinging perspiration from my eyes. My hands were sticky from the whitish juices of chopped-into potatoes. Bees and flies were swarming and flitting from the potatoes to us and back again. We slapped at them futilely.

We made many trips to the cellar carrying basket after basket of potatoes. I was tempted to linger. I looked around me as I felt the touch of the captured coolness upon my sweaty skin. Wooden shelves, that Papa had built, lined one wall. Hundreds of jars of canned vegetables, fruits, jams and jellies adorned those shelves, creating a varicolored beauty. Wooden trays were filled with sun-dried vegetables and fruits. There were long table tops that held the white and brown crocks filled with sweet milk, buttermilk and clabbered milk. There were bowls filled with white or brown eggs. There were platters filled with golden mounds of daisy printed butter.

I looked at the big wooden barrel filled with sauerkraut. How well I remembered sauerkraut making day. Fred and I had carried cabbage heads and piled them very high upon a table in the yard. Mama had checked the cabbages for bugs and worms and less than perfect leaves. She had washed and cut the cabbages. The large, sharp butcher knife had made quick slicing motions through the crisp, tightly layered heads.

Mama would bend over the top and down into the barrel with first a layer of cabbage to tamp down and then a layer of salt. When short, chubby Mama was filling and tamping near the bottom of the barrel, I always watched her anxiously. Her feet, encased in her sewing machine shoes, dangled about midway of the barrel on the outside. I was always glad when she had filled the barrel past the halfway mark. Then I no longer had to fear she would tip over into the barrel of sauerkraut.

The cabbage stalks were peeled and packed in the barrel here and there all the way up. Fred and I always badgered Mama to search for them on winter days. We loved to munch on their sour crispness at snack time.

The sound of Papa's voice brought me out of my reverie. He was saying, "Why do you stand in here daydreamin', Bud? Fred is waitin' for you to help carry another basket of potatoes down here."

I left the damp coolness and the dimness of the cellar behind and returned to the heat of the day and the work at hand. When we had finished sorting our potatoes, Fred had seven and three-quarter bushels and I had seven and one-half bushels for market.

I bubbled with excitement the morning Papa hitched Prince to the wagon to take a load of potatoes to town.

"Mama, what shall I buy with my very own money?" I asked.

Mama said, "Any time you are given a chance to make up your own mind, why then no matter what suggestions I can offer, you will get whatever you are already thinkin' of. You always have in times past."

I did know what I wanted so I didn't pester Mama too much. I knew my thrifty-minded Mama would never suggest what I had in mind. I wanted some clothing like that of my girl friend, Marion.

I had quickly made friends with Marion who was my age. She lived only a few streets from Carrie in Clifton Forge. Whenever I spent a few days with Carrie, I usually spent one night with Marion. Marion lived with her family in a large two-story brick home.

I hadn't forgotten the first night I spent at her home. At bedtime we went upstairs to Marion's room to prepare for bed. Marion undressed quickly. Chattering all the while, she pulled her pretty dress up over her head. Beneath the dress she wore a pretty, pink silk underslip. She caught hold of it with both hands and it glided up over her head like sliding egg whites. Her panties and beginner bra were of pink rayon. Marion picked up her tailored, two-piece silk pajamas and her arms and legs glided into the appropriate openings. She plunked herself down in the middle of her bed with the fat pillows against her back and reached for a bright red apple from a bowl on the bedside table.

I sat in a chair as we talked and giggled. Finally she asked, "Aren't you going to get ready for bed? Mother said she would come up to chat with us awhile when she comes upstairs. She made some fudge today. We might talk her into letting us have some of it since you're my guest. She doesn't like for me to eat fudge because I'm having trouble with bumps on my face. Mother says my skin may become scarred if I don't stop eating so many sweets."

We talked about the teenage problems of being too skinny or too plump, and of being too shy or too giggly. We spoke of one's hair being too dry or too oily. We were still discussing these world shattering problems when Marion's mother came in with a dish of fudge.

Marion's mother left after awhile and still I sat curled up in the chair. Marion looked at me as though very puzzled. She said, "I'm getting sleepy. Mother will come back before long if we don't turn off the light pretty soon. She doesn't like for me to stay up late."

I didn't want to get my friend in trouble so I stood up and began to prepare for bed. I removed my dress. I removed my white cotton underslip. My white cotton bloomers bloused out around me. I had no need of a beginner bra. I reached into my paper bag and brought forth my white cotton gown. I settled it over my head and tied the self-fabric bow at my throat.

My friend spoke in envious tones, "Gee, I wish I had underclothing like yours. It looks so soft and comfortable. My silky things slip and slide one way when I move the other way. They cause me to be hotter in the summertime and colder in the wintertime."

"My mama makes my clothing on her sewing machine," I

said.

"I wish my mother could sew. That would make my clothes special," Marion said. She slid down under the store bought sheet and went to sleep, her voice drifting into a mumble and then a nothingness.

No matter, even though Marion really meant what she said, I really wanted factory-made, silk undergarments. I wanted pajamas to wear in the place of a gown. And now today, I could hardly wait for Papa to return from town.

He had taken all our potatoes on this first load. Rover heard him coming before we did. When we could pick up the rattling wagon wheels, we ran down the road to meet him. Papa was grinning so we knew he was pleased with the day's results. He had sold all of Fred's and my potatoes. As soon as he gave us our money, we ran into the house to ask Mama if we could go to town with Papa his very next trip. Mama said yes.

I had such fun shopping with my very own money. I wished now more than ever I had tended my potato patch. I would have been richer today. I was thankful for what I had though. It was much, much more than I had ever had before. I didn't dally this time at the magazine racks. I shopped for and purchased the rayon silk undergarments and the two-piece, silk pajamas I had so longed for.

As soon as we arrived at home, I jumped down from the wagon and ran to show Mama my purchases.

She said, "They are pretty. You picked good quality material, but you bought them to fit you with no margin for growth and you haven't reached your full growth yet."

"I want them to fit. I get tired of having to always grow into things and then having to wear them until I grow out of them," I answered.

"It is well and good to have things that fit you if you have plenty of them and can easily buy more as soon as you need them. When you have to make do, it's best to have some leeway. The way you've been growin' of late, you'll have to enjoy these mighty fast because they won't last you long," Mama said.

We became very busy harvesting the last of the late white corn. The yellow corn was already hanging in big bunches to finish drying. The last of the white corn was too tough to eat except as roasting ears. We no longer had a fireplace in which to roast corn in the ashes, but we thought it tasted almost as good when roasted in the oven. Mama baked the ears of corn slowly in a moderately heated oven until the kernels turned a brownish-gold. The kernels were rather tough but the flavor was delicious. It was worth the busy chewing as we worked our way from one end of the corncob to the other.

There was another method of removing kernels from corncobs that wasn't nearly as much fun. After the drying process was complete, Mama, Fred and I (Papa helped too when he could) would begin the dreaded shelling. We had shellers that fit over the thumb and helped pick the kernels loose. They worked much as a guitar pick that plucks at the guitar's strings, only we had to pluck faster. We always had blisters on our fingers in the autumn from long hours of corn shelling.

We were now in the process of filling the corncrib with more corn to be shelled at various times throughout the winter. The corncrib was built with one inch spaces between each board. It was an elongated building. the floor was about one foot above the ground. This type of construction allowed air to circulate through the corn somewhat to prevent sweating and souring of the toughened, but not yet fully dried out corn. Even with these precautions, we sometimes had to move the corn about as best we could to allow air to circulate against other portions of the heaped corn.

Field mice had a heyday in the corncrib. They had become too wise for the lure of baited traps to catch many of them. When Len spent weekends with us, Mama often sent Fred and Len to the corncrib to roust out and kill as many of the field mice as possible. I was terrified of mice, but, as usual, I hated for Fred and Len to be able to do something I couldn't do.

One weekend I promised that I would not bolt from the premises at the first sight of a mouse. Len and Fred went to the back of the corncrib. I stood near the door. I had a wide board in my hands to use as a club. They began to shuffle the corn around.

A mouse ran toward me. His beady eyes were black. His tiny feet attached to his little, black body scampered over the corn. Len and Fred were trying to maintain their footing on the rolling, shifting corn as they hurled ears of corn at the creature from their stations in the back corners of the corncrib. As the tiny, horrible creature raced up to me, I dropped the board. With my hands over my head, I ran screaming like a banshee toward the safety of the house and Mama.

I ventured out into the yard sometime later when I spied Len and Fred playing with Rover.

Len looked at me and spat upon the ground. "Girls," he said.

"Yeah. We might have known if she couldn't kill a rabbit, she couldn't kill a little old mouse either. Girls are no good for anything," Fred said.

That evening I stayed away from Fred and Len. In order to occupy myself, I pestered Papa to tell me again of the square dances at Mama's girlhood home when the frost was on the pumpkins and the corn was horse-high in the corncrib.

Papa grinned as his thoughts turned back in time. "I had some mighty fine times at Edmund and Elena Branham's house," Papa said.

"Seems like I can still see Dora when she was thirteen, sittin' on the stair steps, tappin' her bare feet to the music.

"After we married, a bunch of us used to go to her parents' home. We'd dance the night through, then we'd eat breakfast. Then we'd dance all day. That evenin', around five p.m., we'd move on to somebody else's house on the dance list. They would have supper ready for us. There would be two or three big tables loaded down with food. We could all eat supper and then we'd dance all night. We would stop dancin' long enough to eat breakfast, then dance all day and move on to another house at supper time. Goin' on day and night like that, those square dances lasted one week when the frost was on the pumpkins. They lasted three weeks at Christmastime."

"I wish I could remember seeing you and Mama dance," I said.

"Well we were still holdin' square dances and goin' to them at other people's houses after we moved to Longdale. You were still a very young lass though when we quit. By that time we had a "passel" of youngun's. Some of the youngun's were school age and it got to be too much of a problem," Papa said.

"I still wish I could remember seeing you and Mama dance together," I said wistfully.

"Now that's easy to remedy," Papa said. With those words, he grabbed Mama by the hands. He whistled a lively square dance tune as he promenaded the red-faced Mama around the room.

Mama fussed as he whirled her to a halt. "Frank Clark, we're too old for such foolishness."

Papa laughed as he said, "I'm not any older now then your parents were when I was courtin' you. Edmund and Elena Branham could do some fancy steppin' at those square dances they gave at Big Island."

One could tell autumn was definitely here. The chickens milled about the corncrib as though in anticipation of good things to come. The days were approaching when the bugs and worms would either burrow deep down in the earth or freeze. Snow would cover the now browning grass. Then the chickens would feast on bran and corn. The chickens and pigs were not the only beneficiaries. Papa also hauled some of the corn to the mill in Covington to have it ground into corn meal for our use.

The fields were dotted with fodder shocks. These would provide winter feed for the cattle. To form the shocks, we gathered the cornstalks into bundles. We crisscrossed the bundles to form huge teepees and tied them near the top with strong fodder twine. Shocks were formed in this particular manner for a purpose.

A farmer always had a good reason for doing things certain ways. If the big bundles of stalks were stacked straight up and down, the strong winter winds could force the shocks over on the ground to lie there and rot. Rain could also pour down into the straight shocks. Their compactness would hold the moisture and soon create mold within.

The rains will run off the teepee shocks because of their slanted sides. The warmth of the sun can penetrate teepee shocks and a little air can filter through them also. In fact, these shocks are so well preserved, if any are left over until the following spring, the fodder will still be good.

As we worked through the autumn days, busily forming shock after shock, it felt great to be outdoors. The air was crisp and clear, as though mysterious fingers had pried loose the imprisoning grip of summer's blazing heat. The sun stood out from the bright blue sky like a giant, golden ball. The sharp contrast seemed to confirm the popular song Gene Autry could be heard singing on our new record. In mellow tones he sang, "There's A Gold Mine In The Sky."

The sound of the locusts had ceased, but the ground was laden with their empty shells. Their winged, brownish shells clung to the furrowed bark of the trees they had destroyed. We could catch hold of the trunks of small trees and as we shook the tree, the dried shells would fall like a thick shroud around us. In unrelenting anger, Fred and I stomped on the shells.

Mama said, "It's over now. Let's be thankful the locusts won't be back here for another seventeen years and maybe not then. This species is called the seventeen years' locusts and they don't strike in the same locality more often than that."

"I bet the other grasshoppper families are ashamed that this species is one branch of grasshoppers. I like the other grasshoppers, but I shall always loathe these Cicados," I said.

Mama said, "It says in the Bible, in the book of Exodus, that God told Moses to hold out his hand with a rod in it. This brought forth the locusts to Egypt because Pharoah would not let the Israelites leave Egypt. The locusts were borne in on an east wind. The Bible says there were so many locusts, they blotted out the sun and it looked like the whole world was in darkness. The locusts plague left not one green thing. This plague was next to the last plague that God told Moses to call forth. Even destructive things serve a good purpose sometimes because it was not long until Pharoah let the Israelites go."

"God was serving a good purpose for the Israelites when He brought in the locusts. He sure didn't do the Egyptians any favors with them," I said.

"Rosebud!" Mama said. "The Egyptians were persecutin' the Israelites, who believed in God. The Egyptians didn't believe in God. They didn't want His help. Now be ashamed of yourself for makin' such a terrible remark."

The squirrels were as busy scampering about and hoarding nuts as we were at hoarding everything we could salvage after the locusts were gone. Yes, the days were growing shorter. Papa's eyes mirrored an awareness of that fact as he hurried his normally slow gait. He was trying to accomplish as much as possible before time for a killing frost. Mama was hurrying right along beside him. I wondered if they gave much thought to the long ago days when good friends and neighbors had joined together to help each other gather their harvests and then had celebrated their good fortune with a lively square dance. I wondered if they ever missed those long ago traditions as they struggled alone now to wrest a living from this newly cleared ground?

It wasn't long until Papa's tobacco arrived by mail order from a place in North Carolina. He removed a few of the tightly packed tobacco leaves from the box. The wide, dampish leaves had a very strong odor as he spread them out to inspect them. He wasn't overly interested in the tobacco at the moment though. He was in a hurry. Tonight would be the last night of the county fair for this year. We could sense the feeling of mounting excitement in Papa. He tried to act indifferent to the faint sounds of the gay music borne upward on the cool, September winds.

Mama laundered and stiffly starched Papa's white dress shirt. She brushed and aired his black, vested, wedding suit. When the shirt was dry and then redampened, she stuck her moistened finger against the surface of the flat iron to test the heat. She ironed the shirt until not one wrinkle was left. She pressed his gray tie and shined his black dress shoes.

We all went out into the yard early that evening to wave good-bye to our smiling Papa. His thin, well-dressed figure disappeared among the trees as he made his way down the steepest side of the mountain.

The warm memory of that gala closing night was still fresh upon his mind the following Monday morning as he began twisting his pungent tobacco. He seated himself in a straight backed chair out in the yard with tobacco leaves piled around his chair. He layered several of the leaves together and twisted them into a long rope. He looped the rope over his fingers to let both dangling ends meet evenly. Then he twisted the ends around each other for about two thirds of their length. This left a loop at the top. The finished twist resembled a corkscrew.

This was one autumn chore that Mama never offered to help Papa with. She disliked tobacco in any form. She had a running argument with Papa, year in and year out, about his chewing and spitting. Part of the argument always centered around her cookstove's ashes. She kept a big, gray enameled kettle with a wire handle beside the cookstove. She emptied the wood ashes from the fire into it. There must be no feeling of warmth left in the ashes when she scattered them upon the ground. A long lingering spark might ignite. Therefore, each kettleful of ashes must set for two or three days before being emptied. Mama often used part of the ashes in her flower pots.

Papa sometimes entered the house while chewing tobacco and whenever he did so, he continued chewing until he finished with it. Alas, when he needed to spit, he spat the tobacco juice in Mama's kettle of ashes. Mama's soft brown eyes would flash fire when that happened and a tirade of words would burst forth from her softly curved lips.

"Frank, you know better than to spit that nasty old tobacco juice into my clean ashes. I meant to put part of those ashes in my flower pots and now that nasty stuff will kill my flowers!"

"Ah thunder, Dora, the tobacco juice just helps settle the ashes down so they won't blow about when the door is opened."

"They don't blow about sittin' clean over in the corner beside the stove, so don't use that as an excuse. I like clean ashes. I don't see why men think they must smoke and chew anyway."

Mama's flowers always grew abundantly, but that didn't prevent the ongoing argument.

Papa grinned whenever she caught him spitting into her wood ashes. He always said, "Now, Dora, don't go gettin' your back all out of joint. That juice is what makes your plants so healthy. The blooms wouldn't be near as big and pretty with just plain white ashes to feed the plants. You ought to be thankin' me instead of fussin' about it all the time."

"Ah sugar, they grow in spite of that old tobacco juice. It's because I've got a green thumb," Mama always retorted.

Carrie and Lewis moved from Clifton Forge to Staunton, Virginia in October. Marion and I bid each other good-bye. There would be no more weekends spent at her house, but we pledged to keep in touch. I knew I would miss seeing her as I had each time I visited with Carrie.

Carrie loved living in Staunton. Their lovely, white, two-story house was situated high upon a hill. The steep, narrow street was shaded by towering black walnut trees.

Lewis and Carrie came home for a visit in November. Carrie asked, "Rosemary, do you want to go home with us for a visit?"

I grinned as I answered in the affirmative. I liked it when the girls called me by my new name. I still wished I could have chosen something quite different, but there was no doubt in my mind that even the name, Rosemary, sounded better than Rosebud.

I, too, fell in love with Staunton. I soon made a new friend, a golden-haired girl who was my age. Betsy lived a few blocks from Carrie. We had such good times visiting in each others homes and going for long walks up and down the hilly streets.

Betsy loved to roller skate. She finally persuaded me to go to the busy roller rink with her. I loved listening to the gay music and watching the skaters as they glided around the rink in time to the music. I watched them figure skate to a singer's instructions. After observing for a while, Betsy and I put on skates also.

Betsy skated out into the rink and joined the other skaters, She glided along on her skates as easily as a duck glides across a pond. I fell all over and under the ropes. I hung onto the ropes and talked to some cute boys who stopped to see if they could be of help. I never did learn to skate.

Lewis had one weekday afternoon off from work each week. On one such day, Carrie decided to meet him at the office. She dressed Ronnie in his double-breasted overcoat. She dressed Priscilla in her furry white snowsuit with its matching hat. She put Priscilla in the blue and white baby stroller. Carrie guided the stroller. I held Ronnie tightly by the hand. We descended the steep hill at a running walk.

Fellow employees enjoyed visiting with the children while Lewis finished some last minute details. When Lewis closed his desk and reached for his brown overcoat, Carrie bundled up the dark-haired Ronnie and light-haired Priscilla once again. Carrie looped her red scarf warmly at her throat and Lewis helped her don her long, brown coat. Lewis buttoned his overcoat and placed his brown felt hat atop his wavy, black hair. With the gleeful Ronnie riding upon Lewis' broad shoulder and Carrie pushing Priscilla's stroller, the little family and I bent into the face of the biting wind.

Laughing and talking we made our way to Main Street. As Christmas approached, we spent many such carefree afternoons Christmas shopping. Sometimes we went to a matinee at the theater. Carrie's favorite actor was Errol Flynn and she wanted to see every picture he starred in.

We went home for the jolly Christmas Holidays. The little white house was filled to bursting with family, good food, joyous music and voices lifted in song. I remained at home after the holidays to catch up on the home-taught lessons. The day after New Year's Day, we took down the Christmas tree. Mama still held firm in her belief that it was bad luck to remove the tree one bit sooner. After that, we settled back into the normal routine.

January eighth dawned cold and clear. Mama said, ''We're runnin' low on corn for the chickens. As soon as we finish the mornin's chores, we will spend the remainder of today shellin' corn''.

My spirits slumped. ''I don't think we should shell corn today.

This looks like a special kind of day to me,'' I hinted.

"I know what you're gettin' at. Today is your birthday. I wish you well, but it's still a workday," Mama said.

"But Mama, do you realize why today is so special? I am thirteen years old today. I don't want to spend the day shelling any old corn," I said.

"You're actin' just like you acted all last year when you were twelve years old. I don't see why today is any different in that respect. I tried to make you all's birthdays as special as I could when you were small. There is just too much work to be done to keep it up as you all become older. You're old enough now to understand that. I'm not as young as I used to be, either. I can't seem to accomplish as much in a day as I used to," Mama said.

After shelling corn for a couple of hours, I was still pouting. I couldn't understand why Mama didn't realize that today was different. I had become a teenager overnight. Why, the whole world should be shouting, "Rosemary is thirteen years old today!"

"Mama, don't you remember when you turned thirteen?" I asked.

"I surely do. I had to start puttin' my hair up in a bun. I kind of wished I didn't have to grow up because I hated puttin' my hair up every day. At the same time I wanted to grow up real fast so I could marry Frank. I know becomin' thirteen is special from other birthdays. Someday you'll think your twenty-first birthday is special," Mama said.

"But Mama," I said.

"But me no buts," Mama answered.

I tried another angle. In a positive tone of voice, I told Fred, "Mama is just trying to fool me. When she goes to the house to cook dinner, she's going to make me a cake."

Mama smiled as she answered, "Don't count your chickens before they hatch, missy. You know I don't have time to make a birthday cake. Your birthday comes at a hard time of the year for special things anyway. I remember when you were little, you always got your birthday mixed up with Christmas and New Year's."

We shelled in silence for awhile. My large bucket was filled almost to the brim with shelled corn. I began to crowd corncobs into the top layer, standing them upright.

"What are you doin'?" Mama asked.

"The corn is my birthday cake. The cobs are my candles. Hand me one more corncob, Fred. That will make thirteen," I said.

Fred giggled.

Mama said, "Ah, sugar."

We went to sleep one cold February night to the sound of rain dashing hard against the windows. I awoke once and heard the wind howling around the little, white house. I snuggled deeper into the indentation I had burrowed out in the straw tick. The thick, white cotton sheet that covered the tick was warm beneath my body. I drew the top sheet and the patchwork quilt up over my head and went back to sleep.

We awoke to find that the rain had turned to snow during the night. The land was buried under its white blanket. By midmorning, the snow had turned to driving sleet. Mama opened her sewing machine and settled down to sew. Fred and I spent the rest of the morning aggravating Mitty and the gray cat equally.

After the dinner dishes were washed, dried and put away, Mama said, "You two can go to the barn to play this afternoon."

We donned our heavy wraps and put on a pair of Papa's thick, gray socks over our shoes. We buckled our over-sized galoshes on over the socks and left the house.

We didn't go to the barn. We wandered off deep in the forest. The sleet had stopped, but its crusty layer discouraged snow games. We finally paused near a huge rock. The rock made an excellent windbreaker. We talked of many things as we stood there. We daydreamed aloud about all the things we were going to do, all the places we were going to see after we grew up. After awhile, our desultory conversation faded into silence.

I stood looking up, drinking in the beauty of our totally white world. The sleet covered snow stretched into the fathomless distance. The trees seemed encased in frozen shimmering diamonds. Even the sheltering rock was draped in robes of white. The almost white sky hovered protectively, like a gigantic angel's wing, over the white world beneath it.

As we stood there without voice, I became aware of how alive this seemingly silent world is. The burden of ice made cracking sounds as the wind's force struck at the trees it clung to. The wind seemed to howl in agony as it beat in helpless fury at the ice. Then as it paused, it seemed to whisper in caressing tones to the beauty of the glittering trees. Icicles fell with clinking sounds to the crusty layer below. As a bush tried to raise its imprisoned head, a goblet of snow would fall from it, creating a smushed sound. I became aware, as I listened to this world of ours, that the only time the world sounds silent is when we are too busy talking to listen to it.

When our feet became so cold they seemed not to be there, we headed for home. We took off our snow-crusted galoshes and peeled off our wraps. We left them on the back porch and entered the warm kitchen. Papa was seating himself in a green chair near the cookstove. We could hear the crackling sounds of the fire as it hungrily devoured the wood. Papa held out his reddened hands toward its warmth. Mama was sprinkling ashes into her flower pots. The plants filled a table near the washstand. Papa looked at us and winked as he said, "Dora, do you see that little bitty flower pot sittin' to the left of that red flower pot?"

Mama glanced down. "Yes," she answered.

"I bet I can spit from here and hit it plumb center," Papa said.

"Mama's eyes flashed. "Frank, don't you go killin' my flowers again. I just finished nursin' them back to health from the last time you spit in my ashes."

11

COMINGS AND GOINGS

March of nineteen hundred and thirty-nine came roaring across the mountain like the proverbial lion. The snow was deep and drifted high. The sound of icy cold winds whistled around the little, white house. Snow was drifted upon the window sills and foot long icicles hung from the eaves. The roaring, crackling fires belched heat up through the chimney and the icy wind slapped at the warm gray smoke as it emerged. No one ventured outside except when absolutely necessary.

Papa was seated in the corner near the kitchen stove. He had brought his shoe repairing supplies from the shed and had a pile of shoes at his side. Papa would place a shoe on the last and remove the worn-out sole from the shoe. He would carefully cut out a new leather sole, or half sole, or heel, whichever was needed. He usually held one of the small tacks between his teeth where his hand could quickly find it. Placing a tack just so against the leather, he would nail the new leather into place.

Some shoes he placed on the shoe stretcher, trying to stretch them to fit a fast growing foot for just a little while longer. With tough thread and a repair needle, he sewed up rips in the upper portions of the shoes. Papa always caused me to think of the little elf shoemaker as he sat leaning over the last with his little tack hammer in his hand.

Dorothea had come home to stay while Clarence followed his chosen trade to Knoxville, Tennessee. She, with Tommy and six- month-old Patsy, would stay with us until Clarence found suitable housing. Dorothea stood looking out through the window at the nearly unbroken whiteness that reached as far as the eye could see. The devilish winds drove at the snow, lifting the dry fluffiness of it and twirling it in little eddies.

Dorothea's small hands rested against her sides as she whirled her short stature around and lashed out at the world in general. "All we have had since I came home is snow on top of snow. Just look out there. There's not a creature in sight. What few tracks there were are covered again. I cannot stand this godforsaken place one day longer."

Papa looked up from his last, the perpetual lines between his brows deepened as his heavy brows drew together in a frown. His gray eyes looked stern as he said, "Nobody can get up here so how do you think you will leave, young lady? I think you can stand it."

Mama was kneading a big mound of yeast dough on the breadboard. Her small hands punched harder at the dough and her soft brown eyes looked worried as she looked at Dorothea and said, "I know it's hard on young folks to be isolated like this, but you've got food to eat and shelter and warmth. Count your blessin's. You can make do with what you've got."

I looked around me. The red-checked oilcloth on the table added a touch of brightness to this morning's gray-white world. The iron teakettle was making a slight whistling noise as the water boiled.

I looked at Fred stretched out full-length on the gray bench behind the table. He was playing Clementine on his jew's-harp. Mitty and Tommy were seated on the floor in front of the stove, playing with scrap pieces of new leather and teasing the sleepy, gray cat. Mama and Papa were busy doing familiar things. Patsy was seated on my lap. As her little head turned from side to side, her bright, brown eyes mirrored an interest in everything and everyone around her. I thought to myself, Dorothea misses Clarence, but her conclusion is wrong. This is not a godforsaken place.

Capricious March soon dispensed with her burden of snow and danced forth with such a marvelously lovely day that Dorothea could not resist it. Her spontaneous laughter and natural gaiety burst forth once more. She chattered brightly as she helped me split kindling with the hatchets. She reminisced of bygone days when I was yet a baby and they helped supply wood and kindling for the fireplaces.

Dorothea said, "Papa forbade us to use the double-bit axe because he believed it to be a man's axe and too dangerous for girls to use. We always had to use the single-bit axe or the hatchet when chopping."

One of the banty roosters came up and began scratching for worms near the chopping block. Dorothea absent-mindedly waved a stick of kindling at him to shoo him away as she continued speaking.

She said, "Tomboy Carrie kept wheedling Papa to let her use the double-bit and Papa kept refusing. Carrie was in a bad mood one day because she had been told to split the kindling for me. The kindling was ordinarily my job, but I was feeling puny with a cold and sore throat. Carrie finished the chore and then, to vent her resentment against both Papa and me, she chopped knotches up and down Papa's double-bit axe handle. I ran out and caught her in the act and vowed to tell Papa. Carrie called me a big tattletale and she slapped me across the face. As soon as Papa came home that evening, I ran to meet him and told him about Carrie's dastardly deeds.

"Papa picked up a switch. Then he said, 'So you like double-bits, huh? Well, Carrie, here's a single-bit for slappin' Dorothea, and here's a single-bit for choppin' on my axe handle. Now you have a double-bit!' "

Dorothea's laughter rang out afresh as she said in remembrance of that long ago time, "I never will forget the stormy look on Carrie's face when she passed me on the steps where I sat smiling in satisfaction. She stopped to rub her tingling legs. 'I'll get you back. You wait and see if I don't,' Carrie said."

"Knowing Carrie, I expect she did even the score the first chance she got," I said.

Dorothea laughed and nodded her curly head as she answered, "Several days later, we were sent to pick potato bugs from the potato vines. I noticed Carrie whispering something to Elena just before we left for the potato patch, but dumb me thought nothing of it. Well, on our way to the potato patch, Carrie and I sneaked , as always, and went swimming in our panties in the nearby creek. When we came out of the creek, we hung our wet panties on bushes to dry while we were ridding the vines of bugs. When we went back to retrieve our dry panties, Carrie's were still on the bushes just as she had left them, but mine were nowhere to be found. Of course, I had to explain to Mama why I needed fresh underwear in the middle of the day.

"For several days it seemed as though every time I came into their presence, Carrie and Elena would look at me, then at each other, and double over with laughter. There was a rather smug,

'Cat got the cream,' look on Carrie's face. I noticed also that Elena was now the proud owner of Carrie's prized, heart-shaped necklace.''

Mama brought us back to now when she came out of the house and called, "Dorothea, Patsy is up from her nap and she's hungry."

Dorothea turned toward the house singing, "Lazybones, sleepin' in the shade---,'' in her clear soprano voice.

Papa had skipped three of his usual weekly trips to town because of deep snow in early March. Mama was running low on some of her supplies. She was also yearning for the mail to be picked up. Mama was hoping for letters from the girls since they had been unable to come home in March because of the heavy snow and then the resulting muddy roads.

The strong winds and bright sunshine of this past week had dried up the mud. The roads were hard-packed again. So Papa hitched the excited Prince to the wagon and readied for the trip to town.

The young horse had been penned up in his stall during the snow. Then Papa had kept him confined this past week, pulling the manure-laden wagon to the fields. That meant Prince had been standing much of the time in harness, waiting for the cart to be loaded and unloaded. Those long work days had gotten to Prince. He was seething with pent-up energy and the desire to run free.

As I helped Papa carry the crates of eggs to the wagon, I observed this beautiful day. It caused me to think of the Biblical recording of God's creations on the third day. The Bible said that when God finished the third day he looked down upon it and saw it was good. I looked at the surrounding Allegheny Mountains. They looked very much like a herd of huge, humpbacked camels, marching proudly across the horizon. They stretched upward and onward, forming their own strength.

As I gazed at the mountain's majestic beauty there was no question in my young heart as to why Black Americans of olden days had sung the now historical state song of Virginia. It seemed I could almost hear the chorus of those long ago voices singing,
"Carry me back to old Virginny,
There's where the cotton and the corn and taters grow.
There's where the birds warble sweet in the spring-time,
There's where this old darky's heart am long'd to go.
There's where I labored all day in the cotton,

There's where I worked in the fields of yellow corn.
No place on earth do I love more sincerely,
Than old Virginny, the state where I was born.''

Fred was already planning to go to town with Papa. They both looked kind of surprised when I asked Papa if I could go, too.

Every so often, all the way down the hard-packed road, Prince would speed up or even break into a trot. Papa would tighten the reins and say, ''Whoa there, sweetheart.'' He wanted the wagon to stay as steady as possible because of the eggs he was hauling.

Rover ran along beside the wagon and into the bushes and up and down the banks. He disappeared and reappeared at will. He sniffed and wagged his tail at everything of interest to him on the ground. He barked at a buzzard circling overhead.

Rover would be commanded to stay when we reached the mailbox. Papa refused to let him go any further towards town. Rover's interpretation of the word, stay, was peculiarly his own. He knew the command to stay meant he could follow no further, which he never did, but he reserved the right to go home whenever he took a notion to.

Pulling the wagon to town hadn't taxed Prince's energy level at all. Then too, he had stood in an alley hitched to a post for most of the day, so he was just as restless going home as he had been going to town. Papa continued to talk to him in low tones, trying to soothe Prince's jumpiness.

Fred had opened the gates going to town and he did so coming back without complaint until we reached the very last gate on the way home.It was then he said, ''I've taken Bud's turns both ways. This time she can open the gate.''

I glared at him and climbed down. Fred knew how scared I was to get near Prince's head. I always had been. I began to edge past Prince.

Papa said, ''Go on, Bud. Prince wouldn't act up if he didn't sense your fear. Just don't pay him any mind and he'll stand still.''

I eased on up and just as I reached, slowly, and I hoped boldly, for the latch, Prince threw up his head, snorted loudly and pawed the ground. I screamed and jumped to one side with my hands up to protect my head.

Fred was grinning from ear to ear.

Papa was telling Prince, to ''Whoa there, Boy.'' Then Papa said, 'It's all right now, Bud. Go ahead and open the gate.''

140

I looked at Prince. It seemed he was looking straight at me with the one great big, horse's eye on the right side of his head. The gleam in his eye seemed to be saying to me, "I dare you." I stood there with my fist in my mouth, shaking my head negatively at Papa and watching Prince.

Papa frowned, but he said, "Go ahead and open the gate for her, Fred."

Fred jumped over the side of the wagon and marched to the gate. He opened it while Prince stood quietly, waiting.

Papa had stood up and was leaning forward toward the wagon's side, He had put the reins on the wagon seat and his hands were extended toward me to help me back into the wagon. I hadn't moved away from the post. It was as though my feet were rooted to the ground as Fred pulled the gate all the way open. Suddenly, Prince gave a lunge toward the opening and Papa was flung from the wagon. He landed on his knees with a thud upon the hard-packed road and then he pitched forward.

Prince stopped as suddenly as he had started. He dipped his head as much as the bridle would allow and blew with a fluttering sound as though ashamed of his disobedience.

Papa got up slowly and rubbed his knees. He leaned against the bank as though to steady himself. He brushed the dirt from his overalls and climbed back into the wagon.

He clicked his tongue at Prince, meaning, "Gitty up." Then he said to us, "Don't you children say anything about this to your Mama because I know what she'll say. She doesn't like Prince. Prince is a good horse. He's just a might coltish at times."

Papa was limping slightly the next day as we walked toward the field. We asked him about his legs. He pulled up his overall legs and showed us his knees. They were swollen and scratched and bruised. We asked him if Mama hadn't noticed his limp.

Papa grinned, "She asked me why I was limpin'. I told her I must be gettin' old."

After a few days his limp disappeared and we thought his knees were healed.

Towards the end of April, Grandma, Euna and Sam came for a visit. Grandma was preoccupied and she didn't refer to me as 'that child' except to ask what happened to, 'that child's red hair.'

Mama's lips tightened, but the tone of her voice was pleasant when she reminded Grandma that my hair was not sun-streaked red except in the summertime. Then she asked Grandma, "Did many of my acquaintances come to the spring square dance?"

Grandma said, "We didn't give the dance this year. Landsakes, your Pa is gettin' too old for that sort of thing."

Euna looked at Mama and winked.

Mama was trying to keep from laughing so she just said, "Ah sugar."

Sam lowered his big, muscular frame into Papa's rocking chair. Even when he was seated he still looked mighty tall. He crossed his legs and gave Patsy a pony ride on his size thirteen shoe. Patsy chuckled when he sang "Yankee Doodle" as he bobbed her up and down.

He handed Patsy to Dorothea and ran his fingers through his wavy, black hair as he turned to Mama. "Dora, Mama wanted to come and talk to you before she makes a decision. I want Mama and Papa to move to Washington, DC, to live with me."

Mama knew Sam had gone to Washington several months earlier and had gotten a job as a guard at a large plant there. Now she looked at him in stunned surprise at this new idea.

Sam continued, "As you know, I've been kind of looking after Mama and Papa these past few years. They aren't getting any younger, and I would feel better about them if I had them right there with me. They can't do much farming anymore and I just think it would be best all around."

Grandma fiddled with the brooch at the neckline of her gray dress. The dress was made of Rayon Crepe Romaine. Sam had bought it for her in Washington. She said, "I told Sam that I just don't know what to do. All Edmund and I have ever done is farm. I don't know as I would like livin' in the city. Besides, Euna and Eugene are still livin' at home. I don't want to go unless they can come, too."

Sam answered, "Mama, I told you they can come, too, if that's what you want. Dora, don't you think my plan is best?"

Mama said, "Sam, it's not up to me. You're the one who's been lookin' out for them, so it seems to me the decision has to be yours and theirs."

Euna plunked herself down on the company bed. The strawtick kind of caved in under her more than ample weight.

Grandma looked at Euna sternly. "Euna, you know I didn't raise you to sit on anybody's made-up bed."

I, too, was looking at Euna, admiring her audacity, because

that was Mama's ironclad rule, too.

Euna got up and changed the subject by saying, "I told Mama, I'm ready and willin' to go. Eugene says it makes no never mind to him. He says he can live one place same as he can another."

"What does Papa think about movin' away from the country to the big city?" Mama asked.

"Edmund says whatever I decide on is what we'll do," Grandma said.

I suspected that everyone already knew that anyway. They spent most of the weekend rehashing the for and against aspects of Sam's plan.

Around eight o'clock Monday morning, Sam put the suitcases in his car. He remained out in the yard talking to Papa. Dorothea replenished the fire in the cookstove to heat the big tub of water for washday. Euna was seated in the kitchen, talking to Dorothea. Mama and Grandma emerged from the bedroom and came through the living room into the kitchen.

Grandma had her hat on and was jabbing the pearl hatpin into the hat to anchor some of her thin, gray hair to the purple hat. That way the hat would remain squarely on her head, looking just as invincible as Grandma herself did. She said, "I'll write you before long, Dora, to let you know what I decide. I'll probably move to Washington so I can look after my baby boy."

Sam was the youngest child and even though his great height and great size dwarfed Grandma, she still usually referred to him as her baby. Sam had long ago resigned himself to hearing it.

Grandma said, "Come on, Euna. Landsakes, it's gettin' late."

Grandma marched out the door. Euna followed her. When Grandma put on her hat, anyone planning on going with her knew better than to delay.

That very afternoon Lawrence drove up with the bad news. Elena had been rushed to the hospital for an emergency appendectomy. Lawrence had stayed at the hospital until the operation had been successfully completed. He had come to ask Dorothea if she could come to look after the children and the house. The doctor had told him that Elena would have to remain in the hospital for about two weeks.

Dorothea agreed to go. She asked Mama if I could go, too, because it would be hard for her to care for Tommy and Patsy, as well as Len, Betty and Jerry without help. Mama said of course I could.

Poor little Jerry was barely over a year old and he couldn't understand why his mother was not there. He cried a lot those first few days. Dorothea told me to keep him occupied.

Jerry was pulling up and walking by holding onto things, but he wouldn't turn loose and walk alone. He liked for me to hold his hands and help him walk. This gave me an idea. Maybe I could teach him to walk as a 'welcome home' present for Elena.

I worked with him at various times throughout each day. At first I would stand him alone, free of furniture to grab hold of, and I would kneel a few steps in front of him. Extending my hands toward him, I would cajole the plump baby to come to me. The first few times, he would grin and plop down on his hands and knees and crawl to me. One day I convinced him he could do it by holding a cookie just beyond his reach. He took two stumbling steps and fell into my arms. The rest was fairly easy. Each day I could move back a little further from him.

Dorothea didn't seem to be aware of what I was doing. I guess she was too busy trying to cope with the responsibility of such a large household to notice that Jerry was now walking alone.

I was breathless with excitement the day Lawrence brought Elena home. He helped her into the living room and seated her in a comfortable chair. We all gathered around her in warm welcome, except Jerry, who was asleep in his upstairs crib.

Elena said, "Rosemary, go get Jerry, please. If he's asleep, bring him anyway. I can't wait to see my baby."

I re-entered the room with Jerry in my arms. Elena's pale face brightened. Her pale lips parted in a broad smile of welcome. She steadied herself by placing her hands on the arms of her chair as she rose. She held out her arms to receive Jerry.

"Wait a minute," I said.

Across the room from Elena, I steadied Jerry upon his feet. I turned him loose as Elena gasped. Jerry almost ran in his toddling gait and tumbled into her outstretched arms. Elena picked him up and sank back into the chair. She buried her face in Jerry's soft brown hair and broke into a torrent of tears.

Amidst the heartbroken sobs, we were all asking in alarm, "Elena, are you all right?"

Elena dabbed at her eyes with the big, white handkerchief Lawrence had handed to her from his coat pocket. She said in a broken voice, "I didn't get to see him take his first steps alone. I wasn't here to share his triumph."

I learned something that day. I learned that in a growing child's life, each attainment, each triumph, each goal that is reached is reached only once. I learned that the sharing of each milestone between a mother and her child is the soul of a mother's joy.

As soon as Elena regained her strength, Dorothea and I prepared to return to the mountain. Elena thanked us for our help and said she could never repay us. She told me she was sorry she had cried and spoiled my well-intended present to her. I told her I understood. We entered Lawrence's car for the trip home and Elena stood on the porch, still waving at us as we drove out of sight.

Lawrence stopped at our mail box on the way home. There was a letter from Grandma among the waiting mail. When we reached home, Lawrence and Dorothea seated themselves in kitchen chairs Mama brought outside. That way they could all enjoy the warm sunshine as they talked. I knelt upon the grass to give Rover a big hug. Lawrence handed Mama the mail and Mama read the letter from Grandma.

Grandma said they had completed their move to Washington. She said they were all settled in now and Edmund was adjusting to retirement just fine.

Grandma described the dark brown, row houses where they lived. Each apartment was one unit. The houses extended the length of a block with steps and a small stoop leading to each unit of apartments. The descending steps ended abruptly at the front sidewalk, adjoining the wide, busy street. There was a pocket-sized back yard behind each unit for a clothesline and a garbage can. There were no pets allowed. They had given their dogs, Driver and Rover, to a neighbor at Big Island. Grandma said they had electric lights in each of the four rooms and a bathroom that made up one apartment.

In reference to the bathroom, Grandma had written, "Landsakes, Dora, I've been used to goin' to the outhouses and takin' baths in a washtub all my life. I can't hardly get used to the idea of these fancied up bathrooms built right inside the house. It's not sanitary."

She said there was linoleum on every floor and that the apartment dwellers bought a liquid wax and waxed their linoleums once a week. Grandma wrote, "My, how slick and shiny our linoleums look, Dora. I advise you to get some liquid wax, too, for your kitchen linoleum."

The next day, Mama ironed. She ironed even faster than her usual swift pace. She was still talking about the contents of Grandma's letter. She stuck her left forefinger to her tongue and touched the wet finger to the flat iron. That was the way she tested the iron's heat to determine if it was too hot or not hot enough for the particular type of material she was about to iron. She was getting ready to iron a white dresser scarf. The iron made a sizzling sound as she placed her wet finger against it. That meant the iron was ready for starched, cotton goods. She set the iron down upon the iron rest and readjusted the thickly folded cloth with which she protected her hand from the heat of the iron's handle. She picked up the iron again and slapped its surface down upon one end of the dampened scarf. She began quick backward and forward motions of the iron that would not leave a wrinkle in the scarf.

As she ironed she spoke again of Grandma's advice to her. She said, "Can you imagine Mama tellin' me to buy a liquid wax and to wax my linoleum? Ah sugar. Mama is just puttin' on airs since she moved to the big city."

I tried to picture going to Grandma and Grandpa's new apartment. I tried to visualize my grandparents stepping out onto cement instead of a big, shady, wooden porch and onto a big, shady yard. There would be no Driver and Rover to wag a hound dog greeting. There would be no springhouse and no apple orchard. "Mama," I said. "It seems kind of strange to think of Big Island without Grandpa and Grandma."

Mama said, "Yes, I was just thinkin' the same thing. I keep rememberin' when they lived in Mr. and Mrs. Miles' tenant house on Battery Creek at Big Island. That was back before you were born. Mr. Miles and Mama both loved to garden. They kept up a runnin' feud, though, about the best way to raise a garden. The feud was in fun of course.

"Mr. Miles would lean on the fence in the spring and watch Mama plantin' her garden seeds.

"Mrs. Branham, you always plant your seeds by the Almanac's moon signs. Well I'm not goin' to plant my seeds on the moon. I'm goin' to plant mine in the ground," he would say to Mama.

"You go right ahead, Mr. Miles. You know best whether you want to raise a good garden or not," Mama would answer him.

"Sure enough, his garden didn't produce well at all, but Mama had an abundant garden. His butter beans fell off the vines when the hulls were only half filled with beans. Mama raised a bumper crop of butter beans and shared them with his family.

"Mama would tell him, 'I'm not one to say I told you so, but I'm glad I planted my beans by the moon's signs,' each time she took him a bucket of beans.

"Mrs. Branham, you've got to be partly witchy to grow things by the moon," he would answer.

"Mama would reply, "But this witch has butter beans!" Sometimes, she would take an empty bushel basket to his house and say, "Mr. Miles, how much are you chargin' for your butter bean hulls?"

"He would get back at her by sayin,' "Does witchy people eat nasturtiums? Is that why you planted nasturtiums all around your garden?"

"She would answer, "No, sir, Mr. Miles, I planted those nasturtiums to protect my garden from the likes of yours."

"Those two had such good times teasin' each other about their gardens. I can hardly believe it's my mama writin' me now about liquid wax. I can't picture her steppin' outside onto cement, either," Mama said.

"Is that why you always plant sunflowers around your garden every spring, because your mama planted flowers?" I asked.

"I guess so," Mama said. "I was used to Mama havin' a border of flowers around her garden. Guess a garden would look kind of unfinished to me without a flower border."

Dorothea was sweeping the kitchen floor after dinner, which was another one of Mama's ironclad rules. After each meal, day in and day out, the table must be completely cleared of everything except the kerosene lamp in the center of the table and the kitchen floor must be swept. These rules, too, were carry-overs from Grandma's teachings.

I was rocking Patsy to sleep while Dorothea swept, and as she wielded the broom near the rocking chair, I lifted my feet.

She laughed as she said, "Don't lift your feet, Rosemary. You know Mama's superstition that if anyone sweeps under a girl's feet, that girl will never get married."

As my laughter mingled with hers, we heard Rover barking his 'company is coming' bark. Then we heard the sound of air horns. Dorothea flung prudence to the winds. She flung the broom down and raced for the open door. She was waiting at the yard gate when Clarence pulled his Model A Ford to a stop.

Clarence lifted Dorothea from the ground and her little feet dangled in the air as he grasped her in a bear hug. After having kissed her soundly, he said, "I have tried very hard to find a rental house in the suburbs with a nice yard for the children, but there's none available. I had to rent an upstairs apartment in an old section of town. Don't you worry though, we'll keep looking until we find a suitable place. I couldn't stand it any longer. It's lonesome there without you and the children."

Dorothea hugged him and said, "I was lonesome, too. We'll probably have a better chance of finding a nice place with me there to help look for one."

Dorothea asked Mama if I could go with them for a visit and Mama said yes. I could hardly contain my excitement. I would soon see another state in this huge America of ours. I had never been out of the state of Virginia. I still wanted to see what was on the other side of the mountains that sheltered Virginia.

Mama kissed us all good-bye the next day and wished us a safe journey.

Dorothea laughed as she hugged Mama good-bye and said, "Mama, I declare, between us and Rosemary and the Branhams, I guess we've kept you right busy with our comings and goings this spring."

We piled into Clarence's old car. We exchanged good-byes with Papa, Mama, Fred and Mitty a few extra times, and then we set off on our way to Tennessee.

Knoxville was situated on a rather wide and flat terrain, but I soon found out that other parts of Tennessee had mountains, some of which made our Virginia mountains appear small in comparison. We all liked the beautiful and busy city of Knoxville. The Tennessians were a friendly and helpful kind of people.

Mama was right. This side of the mountain was just like the other side. A long time ago, I had asked Mama, "What does the other side of the mountain look like?"

"Looks just like this side," Mama had answered. She meant that the other side of the mountain would take whatever a person gave to it and it would give whatever a person earned or took from it.

I was beginning to get a glimmer of what she meant. I must

view my world of mountains from inward attitudes. Wherever I might be, it was up to me to choose the kind of person I wanted to be. I could build or I could destroy. I could give or I could take.

Fred Clark
"Pickin' & Singin'"

Carrie with children,
Ronnie and Priscilla
Staunton, Virginia

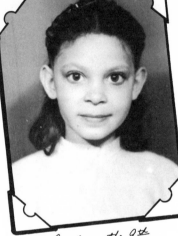

Carolyn, the 9th
child of Frank &
Dora.

May, 1940
Dora, age 45 yrs.
Daughter, Carolyn, age 9 wks (right)
Grandson, Harry, age 6 wks (left)
Notice Farm Wagon in background

Ken Whitlock

Rosemary

Dorothea and children,
Patsy and Tommy 1941
Knoxville, Tenn.

1940's
Rosemary
View of Waterfall seen
through the trees at
romantic Falling Springs, Va.

Seeing is believing,
'anklets' and saddle oxfords
worn with suits, oh, stylish.
Woe is me, skinny legs weren't.

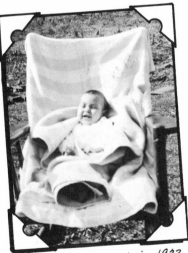

Mildred, "Mitty" in 1933
Frank had made the
rocking chair for Dora.

From left,
Rosemary
Frances
Carrie

12

WALKING CANE

Fred had celebrated his birthday on the twenty-eighth of April. When I returned from Knoxville, I found that Fred and Papa weren't getting along very well with each other. Fred was going through some kind of phase in which he wanted to sleep late every morning. He did not want to work in the fields at all. Papa tried to be firm with him. Papa left most of the discipline to Mama, but I could see he was getting aggravated in this instance. Every morning Fred would complain of a headache and Mama would say to let him sleep.

"Dora, you're spoilin' that boy," Papa said.

"Frank, you don't want him to work when he's sick. You're never mean with the children," Mama said.

"But that boy is not sick. He's lazy. Just because he's the only boy among six girls, you overprotect him."

Fred would groan and Mama would entreat, "Let him rest awhile. I'll send him along later."

One morning, Papa said, "You don't believe me, Dora, but that boy is not sick. He's puttin' on. Fred has gotten so lazy, he would be a good one to send for the doctor when the devil is sick."

Fred pulled the sheet over his head to muffle noises and went back to sleep. Papa stomped from the house in defeat.

I finished getting ready for the day's work and then I asked, "Mama, whenever I get stomach cramps, you make me drink cups and cups of boiling hot ginger tea. Why can't you give Fred ginger tea for his headaches."

"That's different," Mama said.

I heartily disliked ginger tea made from ginger roots. I was disappointed that Fred would escape drinking the tea. I was never one to want to suffer alone.

Sometimes Papa was late coming to dinner or supper. Mama was puzzled, to say the least. Papa had always been a very punctual man. Whenever Mama inquired as to his tardiness, he always attempted to give a reason. The reasons usually came out sounding more like lame excuses.

Sometimes when we were along, he would stumble and fall. He would sit awhile and try to rub his legs in an unobtrusive way. He cautioned, "Don't say anything to your Mama. I guess I'm gettin' old and clumsy. I stump my toe sometimes."

We found him seated near the shed one day. He was trimming bark from a long, sturdy oak limb. He continued working on the limb in his spare time. First he chipped away at it with his hatchet. He smoothed it with his plane. He whittled here and there on the stick with his carving knife.

We kept pestering him, "What are you making, Papa?"

He would smile and answer teasingly, "If you can't figure it out, then you don't need to know."

He soon began to soak the stick in a long trough filled with water. With the aid of a vise and rope, he started slowly curving one end of the stick. Then we figured it out.

"Papa, you're making a walking cane. Why do you want to make a walking cane?" we asked.

"One of these days, I'll be an old man. I might need three legs instead of two. By the time I need a cane, I'll be too old to carve one. I might just as well do it now while I'm still young and handsome. Huh, Dora?"

Mama had come into the shed hunting eggs from recalcitrant hens. She had paused as she overheard the conversation.

"Ah, go along with you, Frank," Mama said in answer. There was a worried look upon her face as she stepped out into the sunshine from the shadowy shed.

Lewis and Carrie came one day in June to take us to Rockbridge County to visit Papa's relatives. We left Papa, Mama, Fred and Mitty chatting with John Henry and Leann, while Lewis, Carrie and I went to visit Natural Bridge.

The bridge is fourteen miles south of Lexington. It's one of Virginia's famous natural wonders. It's also one of the most famous natural bridges in the U.S.A. The bridge is 215 feet above Cedar Creek. Scientists and geologists believe this particular bridge was formed by water eroding the limestone rock. Thomas Jefferson bought the bridge from King George III., in seventeen hundred and seventy-four.

It's cool and damp under the bridge even on the hottest days of summer. Hosts of people from all over the world have carved their names or initials into the sides of the rocky tunnel beneath the bridge. I stood there drinking in the atmosphere of this historical site. Little did I know that one day, yet future, I would make an important decision beneath this bridge that would affect the rest of my life.

The memory of that interesting trip to Natural Bridge stayed with me as summer's crops began to grow abundantly. Papa hoped to make up for last year's losses the locusts had caused. He planted even more fields this year. Mama planted a larger vegetable garden, too. Papa always plowed between the rows for her with his hand plow. She would follow along behind him, chopping the weeds from around the plants with the hoe.

Today she worked right along behind the furrows Papa was making with the plow. Papa fell down. This was the first time it had happened in Mama's presence.

She asked in alarm, "What's wrong, Frank."

"Oh, I just stumbled. Guess I'm gettin' old and clumsy, Dora," Papa said.

Papa placed his hands upon the freshly turned earth and tried to regain an upright position. He couldn't get up. Mama placed her hands underneath his armpits and tried to lift him to his feet. His legs doubled up and he sank back to the ground.

Mama gave him a drink of water from the water jug, for the lack of knowing what else to do at the moment.

Papa sat there for almost two hours. Mama stayed with him, talking in worried tones. Papa kept offering excuses for his predicament. Mama wanted Papa to see a doctor as soon as he could regain his feet and make the trip to town.

Papa shook his head emphatically. He said, "Now don't start that, Dora. You know how I feel about doctors. Seein' a doctor didn't heal my sister, Carrie. I feel fine now. I just needed to rest a bit." With those words of assurance upon his lips, Papa managed to rise to his feet.

We were just finishing the chores early one Sunday morning in July, when we noticed Rover. His ears were pricked forward. His tail was straight up. There was a low growl rumbling deep in his throat.

Papa said, "There must be somebody comin'. Rover isn't

familiar with the sound of the motor though. I can tell from the sound of his growl. He doesn't know whether to bark a welcome or a warnin'.''

After awhile we could hear the sound of a motor. "That's not one of the children comin'. It sounds like a truck motor to me," Papa said. Fred and Len nodded their heads in agreement.

It wasn't long until a pulpwood truck came into view. John Henry was driving the truck. He had Leann and Lizzie in the truck's cab with him. And lo and behold, they had built sideboards for the long truck bed and the bed was crammed full of people of all ages. Wooden kitchen chairs had been placed near the back of the cab to seat some elderly ladies and some ladies holding babies. The men and the young people were standing like canned sardines. Their arms were extended in all directions as they waved and called out excited greetings. Fred, Len and I began jumping up and down with excitement when we spied Melvin and Hallie and Bruce, as well as others near our ages.

Mama and Papa were waving and smiling at their visitors as the truck braked to a stop. I could almost see the mind's wheel spinning like crazy in Mama's head as to how to stretch that one, fat hen boiling in the pot to feed this many people.

Of course she didn't have to worry about it though, because those ladies came bounding out of that old, black pulpwood truck, all talking at once.

"Dora, we didn't have room to bring any food with us or we would have prepared plenty and you wouldn't need to worry about this surprise visit. You just show us where you keep your supplies and we'll pitch right in and help. You'll have dinner a plenty by noon.''

Those ladies marched toward the kitchen and cellar like an attacking army.

Fred, Len and I were ecstatic. There are so many fun games that can't be played without a group. We could barely contain our eagerness to get started. We had to wait though, until our mothers said the magic words, "You children, scoot. Mind you, behave yourselves.''

We played softball, leapfrog, tag and drop-the-handkerchief. We played cat-and-mouse, skip-to-my-loo and hide-and-seek. We jumped double rope on opposing teams. We were so afraid of leaving something out, we raced almost frantically from one thing to another.

By twelve noon, we didn't look anything like the same group of clean kids that had bashfully eyed each other for the first few moments of our early morning encounter. We were sweaty and dirty, our hair was tangled. Our dress sashes were dangling and some were almost ripped loose. Everyone had kicked off their Sunday shoes in order not to scuff them. The boys' shirttails were pulled half out of their knickerbockers. We made ourselves as presentable as possible and assembled in the yard to eat.

By the time dinner was ready, Lawrence and Elena had arrived with Betty and Jerry. The men had carried our long kitchen table outside. They had gathered smaller tables around it. These, as well as the back edge of the truck bed, were laden with food. Several other fat hens had followed the fate of Mama's first one into pots and then into frying pans.

Fred, Len and I didn't want any fried chicken on our plates. Even though we couldn't recognize them cut up and fried into these golden crusted, succulent pieces, we knew these former hens had to be some of our friends. We did eat the rich gravy, made with some of the chicken broth and we ate some of the steaming, fat dumplings, cooked in some of the broth. These weren't quite the same thing as eating our chicken friends, we reasoned. There was no lack of other satisfying foods to eat anyway. There was a variety of fresh vegetables, fluffy biscuits, corn bread, blackberry pies and dairy products with which to satisfy our voracious appetites.

After the meal, the men gathered in the shade of the huge oak trees. The dapper, grinning Lawrence played his guitar and Papa played his banjo. The other men grinned and tapped the toes of their low-quartered, Sunday shoes in time to the music. I heard their deep voices rumbling out the words of such songs as "Bringing In The Sheaves," "She'll Be Comin' 'Round The Mountain," "Little Brown Jug" and "Shoo Fly." They really let it roll far and wide as they sang, "Old Joe Clark." The original version of this song belonged to Atzal Music, Inc. The version our family sang included legendary verses, handed down from one generation to another.

The women were busy taking care of the chores that always follow mealtime, cleaning up, washing up and putting away. We young people took advantage of the fact that there were enough women to handle the work without our help. We raced off to play frantically fast again.

These people had made arrangements for other relatives and friends to take care of their evening chores for them. Nevertheless, farmers are used to retiring early on Sunday nights to restore their strength for Monday's work. About five p.m., everyone was gathered up and packed back into and onto the truck. Last minute messages were called out. Promises to come back soon and to write often were made as the truck's motor began to roar and rattle with sound. The truck looked like an octopus with multiple arms waving in farewell. The sound of gay voices lifted in song could still be heard as the truck disappeared from sight.

As their voices faded, we turned back from the gate to get ready for the evening's chores. When Fred, Len and I ventured into the chicken house at dusk, we found that Potsy, Checko, Bossy, Fanny and Mrs. Black, were missing from the roost poles. We were very glad that we had not eaten any chicken for dinner.

That night the memory of the gay sounds of the men singing "Old Joe Clark" came back to me. We were on the front porch enjoying a cooling breeze that had sprung up at dusk. Papa and Mama were rocking slowly to and fro in their side-by-side rocking chairs. Fred, Len, Mitty and I were seated on the front steps.

"Looks as though it might be tryin' to blow up a rain," Papa said.

"Papa, tell me again about the "Old Joe Clark" song," I said. I had heard the story many times before, but I never tired of coaxing Papa to tell me the legends of old, much to Mama's dismay. She was a futuristic type of person. Papa loved to tell the legends, so it was easy to get him started. Tonight, all it took was another, "Will you, Papa?"

"Well, the story goes that Sam Downey made up the song, 'Old Joe Clark.' Now mind you, there really was a man named Sam Downey and one of my ancestors was Joe Clark, Sr. He was called Old Joe to distinguish him from his son, Joe Clark, Jr.

"The legend goes that Sam Downey was courtin' Betsy Brown. He pledged to her that she was his one and only true love. Alas, he was also courtin' another girl secretly. When Betsy Brown found out about his philanderin' ways, she talked to a dear friend of hers, who was an upright man, Old Joe Clark. Old Joe summoned Sam Downey. He told Sam that his treatment of Betsy Brown was disrespectful. He said Sam could not continue to court both girls at the same time. He demanded that the situation be corrected by Sam at once and that he choose between the two

155

girls. Now, no one in his right mind dared buck Old Joe's code of honor.

"Sam told Old Joe that he would decide between the two girls within a few days. He promised to let Old Joe know which girl he decided upon.

"Sam was angry about having to mend his ways, but a few days later, true to his word, he gave Old Joe his answer. He chose a rather darin' way to do it. He drove past Old Joe's house drivin' a team of Guernsey mules. Sam was half drunk and he was singin' this song,

'I won't go back to Old Joe's house,
I'll tell you the reason why,
His nose is always drippin'
And his chin is never dry.

'Fare-thee-well, Old Joe Clark,
Farewell to this town.
Fare-thee-well, Old Joe Clark,
And good-bye, Betsy Brown.' "

As Papa's deep, melodious voice faded into the night, Mama arose from her rocking chair and said, "Time to get ready for bed."

We settled into our beds and gradually all became silent, except for the night chorus emanating from animals and insects. Mama thought we were sound asleep when I hard her say to Papa, "I'm glad your kinfolk came to see us, Frank, but do you know what Selentia had the nerve to ask me? She asked me how did Rosebud come to have red hair. I told her mighty quick that I did not have a redheaded daughter. I declare, I wish Rosebud would keep her bonnet on when she's in the sun. You can tell her anything over and over, but if she has already made up her mind to do it her way, it just goes in one ear and out the other."

I could almost see the smile in Papa's gray eyes when he answered, "And where do you think she got that stubborn streak?"

Papa couldn't afford any spare time in his ten to twelve hour workdays, but the trouble with his legs was increasing in frequency. The fields were beginning to show some signs of neglect. Mr. Trumbolte looked puzzled when he came up, but he didn't say very much about it. Mama began to neglect her work to help Papa catch up.

Mama was no longer the strange Mama of the past two years, who had changed with lightning speed from happy to angry to sad. She no longer arose from her bed to go outside on a winter's night because a feeling of heat was consuming her from within. She no longer turned pale and placed her hand over her racing heart. A cup of hot coffee would still bring beads of perspiration to her face, even on a cool morning, so she had learned to substitute lukewarm water for her breakfast beverage. The unexplained tears that had suddenly welled up in her soft brown eyes had ceased. Mama had learned to understand her premenopausal symptoms.

Yes, Mama had changed back to her more familiar self. She was once again secure in her choice of Papa for her life's partner. She was content with the life they had made together. She was once again our optimistic, "Do the best you can with what you have and count your blessin's" Mama.

Yet in other ways she was a different person from either of these former selves. She was quieter. When caught unawares, there was an unusual look of worry in her eyes. If Papa were late, she moved the bubbling pots away from the heat of the stove and set off to look for him. She no longer tripped easily into her pet argument about his spitting into her clean ashes. There was a softer quality to her voice when she talked to him.

There was something about August that always made Fred, Len and me ill-tempered. Len's summer vacation was drawing to a close. Len had reached his ninth birthday this past March. He asked, "Grandma, why can't I stay here and you can teach me like you do Fred and Bud?"

Mama smoothed his blond hair. She smiled into his questioning blue eyes as she said, "You will learn much more in public school. I don't have enough education, or enough time either, to do much teachin'. I wish I could figure out a way to get Bud and Fred into public school."

Her answer didn't satisfy Fred. He still resented what he felt was the inequality of circumstances. As a result, he started arguments and we couldn't quite resist the bait.

Fred was restless, too, probably because Len would soon be gone. He began going off with his BB gun, presumably hunting snakes to shoot. No one thought anything about it at first. Then one day, Papa had to take a young bull to one of the other farms and leave him.

That night Papa said, "On my way home today, I heard a snappin' sound and a cow came tearin' over the hilltop. She was bawlin' and squallin' somethin' fierce. Then I saw Fred rise up out of a gully with his BB gun aimed at the cow and his hat pushed to the back of his head. I knew right away who had flushed that cow." Papa was hanging Fred's BB gun up on the big nails that served as a gun rack. He finished telling Mama what happened.

He turned to the downcast Fred. Papa said, "Young man, that gun is to stay right there until next August. Maybe by then, you'll be old enough to know a snake from a cow."

Len and I were seated on the gray bench behind the table as we waited for supper to be served. We both tried to slide down unobtrusively until we could hide our faces in the overhang of the red checked oilcloth. We dared not let Papa hear our smothered giggles.

The oats were cut and in the loft. The beans called October beans were dried. The brittle heat continued and we grew more disgruntled. We looked longingly at the azure sky and wished aloud for rain.

Mama said, "There's a blessin' in every day if a body looks for one. I need a dry day to clean the bedticks and fill them with new straw.

This, too, was a yearly chore and one we happened to like. I don't know about Mama. She never complained of disliking certain chores as we did. Neither did she ever complain of being tired or of feeling ill. We had entered the kitchen unexpectedly at times and discovered her using some of her home remedies for herself. Had it not been for those occasions, we would have thought she was immune to illness. I often wished I was more like Mama.

The following morning dawned clear and hot. We hurried with the morning chores. We helped Mama strip the beds. Papa helped Mama carry the ticks from the crowded rooms. They manipulated the heavy, wobbly burdens through the front door. They proceeded cautiously down the five steps into the yard. Mama clipped the handsewn threads from one end of the blue and white striped, cotton ticks. The other end and both sides had been sewn on the sewing machine to insure greater seam strength. Mama and Papa went back into the house and brought out the bed springs. She washed the springs while we were supposedly emptying the ticks. She always washed the springs around on the other side of the house to prevent any wetness of the grass where she had placed the ticks.

We always took advantage of the fact that we were hidden from her view. We ran and jumped and rolled upon the ticks. It was great fun. About the time we judged she might be coming back, we settled down to work. We pulled most of the straw out through the opened end of each tick. We turned the ticks inside out and shook them to loosen any clinging straw. Little shredded pieces of straw clung to our moist skin and caused our skin to itch. Some of the straw found its way into our dampish hair.

Late in the afternoon, we helped Mama pull the washed and dried ticks from the clothesline. We pushed and punched them full of fresh straw. The ticks were so full Mama could hardly close the open ends to sew them together again. The beds smelled so clean and fresh. The odors of soap, water, air, sunshine and fresh straw mingled together. The first few nights, it was hard to keep from rolling out of bed because of the fullness and fluffiness of the ticks. It didn't take many nights for us to burrow out nice indentations in the fresh straw. That made us hotter now, but those indentations would keeps us cozy when winter came.

The days sped on and soon it was late September on a Saturday night. It was also the last night of the county fair. Papa was swinging his new cane in his hand when he disappeared down the mountainside. "I'll just carry my cane along in case of comin' upon a snake," Papa said.

Mama allowed us to stay up on Papa's fair night. This was a special treat for us. The clock hands marched on. We grew tired of playing. Fred began to yawn uncontrollably.

Mama said, "I think it's time you two went to bed."

"Let us stay up a little while longer," Fred begged.

Mama's darning needle flashed in and out as she darned one of Papa's thick, gray socks. She smiled as she said, "I can just see Frank's big toe stickin' out through this big hole. To get back to you, young man, when your mouth stays open in a yawn and you need toothpicks to prop open your eyes, it's time for bed."

Fred protested, "But staying up real late is our treat."

"Well, it's gotten to the point where you're punishin' yourself with pleasure," Mama said.

As we started off to bed, Fred said, "I can hardly wait until breakfast in the morning when Papa will tell us about the fair.''

Our eyes were big as saucers as we listened to Papa's news. Papa said, ''I talked with some men last night at the fair. They told me they had been to the New York World's Fair. They saw a demonstration there of television. The demonstration showed how television works. They told me a Du Mont Laboratory is makin' television sets for the public's use.''

''What does television do, Papa?'' Fred asked.

We listened in wide-eyed amazement as he answered, ''I don't know how it works. I understand that a lot of electronic parts are involved. The screen is about three or four inches square. You can see a picture on it. It probably won't be too much longer until lots of people will have television sets in their homes.''

Fred and I became very excited. ''Can we have one, Papa?''

Mama stuck her hands in the pockets of her floral printed apron as she said emphatically, ''Ah sugar, nobody will ever have anything as expensive as a picture box for home use, except maybe rich folks. Why I can't imagine anyone ownin' such a fanciful thing as that!''

I felt suddenly deflated. My mind wandered away from the present conversation.

We didn't have a radio. We did have a portable phonograph that Lawrence and Elena had given to Papa and Mama. Lawrence had paid twelve dollars for it. It was brown. It had a crank handle that wound up the spring motor. We had a total of eight records and Papa's favorite was a song called, ''I'm Headin' For The Last Roundup.'' So often, just as I finished cranking the motor and started reaching out for a record, I would hear Papa's voice call out to me, ''Play 'Roundup' again.'' Sometimes Papa would request the same, old song for the eleventh or so time. As the motor wound down, the record gradually slowed down. I would let the record play until the motor was almost completely unwound and the words of the singer grew slower and slower. Then I would start cranking the motor with the record still playing. This would cause the singer to sound like he was dying one minute, and then the next minute, his voice would begin to speed up like he had drunk a cup of Mama's hot ginger tea. Papa would call out in a tone of voice that needed no answer, ''Rosebud! What in tarnation do you think you're doin'?''

My mind returned to the present as I heard Papa saying, ''You see, it's not intended to project stories like a movie screen. The notice at the fair stated that television is to be used for educational purposes.''

Mama said, ''Well, I've never been in a theater to see a movin' picture, so I don't suppose I'll be missin' anything.'' She got up from the table and that was the signal that it was time to begin the morning chores.

I watched Mama as she hung Papa's suit on a coat hanger. She carried the suit out to the clothesline and brushed it and left it swinging gently in the morning breeze.

Later in the day, she carried the black suit to the bedroom. She wrapped it in the old bedsheet with her wedding skirt and blouse and suspended the hangers from the nail on the back of the bedroom door. Their wedding garments from twenty-eight years ago would hang there together another year. The fair was gone.

13

WHO WANTS TO BE THIRTEEN?

Papa, Fred and I were working in the turnip patch when we heard a car chugging up the road. The turnip patch was far from the house. Rover was presumably at the house, so he had not alerted us that someone was coming. The driver parked the car at the side of the road. A big man introduced himself to Papa as Mr. Whitlock. He introduced his boys by saying, "These boys are my sons, Kenneth and Cameron." He didn't point out which boy was which.

Mr. Whitlock continued, "I heard in town that you have some mighty good turnips for sale, Mr. Clark."

"They're real good this year. Do you want to sample one?" Papa asked.

Papa pulled a turnip and handed it to Mr. Whitlock. The turnip was plump and white with a medium purplish tinge around the bottom half. The color was important. Too much white usually meant a slightly pithy, dry turnip. A dark purple usually meant a strong- flavored, unsweet turnip. These turnips were firm, juicy and mildly sweet.

Mr. Whitlock rubbed the last vestige of earth from the turnip. He pulled out his pocketknife. We watched as curls of turnip peeling were felled by the sharp blade of the knife. He bit into the turnip as he continued his conversation with Papa.

I stood to one side and looked at the boys. They were handsome boys and nicely dressed. My attire left something to be desired. Papa was strongly opposed to females wearing pants. When I worked in the fields, Mama insisted on pants to protect me. They compromised. I could not own or wear any pants made for females, but I could wear his overalls in the fields. That way he could adhere to his belief that pants were men's garments and also quiet Mama's fears that I might chop my unprotected legs with a hoe.

So here I stood today in my adorable outfit. My ruffled bonnet hung down my back, dangling from the ties around my neck. (Mama insisted on my wearing my bonnet to protect me from the sun.) My feet were lost somewhere within a pair of Papa's lace-up, work boots. I had shot up in height this past year to five feet, three inches. I was also skinny. Therefore, I had plenty of excess room in Papa's bib overalls. The overall legs were rolled up a few turns to accommodate the difference in mine and Papa's height. I wore his long sleeved, blue chambray shirt and the tail of it was hitched up and blousing out from the sides of the overalls. Thus I stood, in the presence of these handsome young boys, gloriously attired in baggy shirt, baggy britches, baggy shoes and ruffled sunbonnet. I tried to jam my hands into the pockets of the overalls, but that was rather ineffectual because my hands wouldn't reach the bottom of the pockets. I shifted from one heavy foot to the other. I tried to look elegantly disdainful. The two boys stared solemnly at me. I did not recognize a hint of destiny staring me squarely in the face from the eyes of one of these handsome boys.

At thirteen, I still had enough problems without adding boys to the list. Some days, I felt grown-up and I rejected my dolls and playhouses. On other days, I played as though my life depended on it. Some days, I was exuberantly happy. I sang, whistled, laughed, teased, and thought of life as beautiful. Other days, I wished I had never been born. I had developed new bodily functions that I wanted no part of because they interfered with my tomboy ways. I wished I could be ten years old again and remain ten forever. Other days, I could hardly wait to be sixteen and really grown-up. Some days, I was lost in daydreams. I was soaring down a highway in a yellow Roadster with the top down. I lived in a mansion and showered rich gifts upon my less fortunate family. Boys that looked like Clark Gable flocked around me. I was the belle of the ball. Other days, I felt sad, dull, bossy, and irritable.

Mama said, "You're mighty hard to live with these days, missy, but it's a stage all girls go through. It will pass."

"But Mama, this is my second year of feeling like six different people. I'm tired of this stage. I want to be just one person again. Sometimes I feel like I'm at the end of my rope," I said fretfully.

Mama pumped the sewing machine treadle back and forth,

back and forth. She moved her material dexterously beneath the needle as she answered, "Tie a knot in the end of your rope so you won't slip off, and start climbin' back up again."

"I guess that's more of your 'makin' do' stuff," I said.

"Anybody can see this is not one of your better days," Mama said.

The entire mountain of greenery was turning into a riot of autumn color. Lewis and Carrie came to get me on one of the brilliant October days. Lewis had been transferred to the Covington, Chesapeake and Ohio Railroad Office. They had rented a house in Rayon Terrace. This was the village owned by the Industrial Rayon Plant, of which Carrie was a former employee. Carrie wanted me to help her get settled in and then stay on for an extended visit.

We had such fun being together again. We washed windows and hung fresh curtains, singing as we worked.Some of our favorite songs were "The Beer Barrel Polka," "Over the Rainbow," "Jeepers Creepers" and "The Three Little Fishes." We laughed hilariously when our tongues got all twisted up on the dittum, wattem words of the fish song.

They took me to see lots of movies during these autumn days. I had adored Shirley Temple, but now my fickle affections were transferring fast to Mickey Rooney, star of the Andy Hardy movies. Times were changing. The swing band music of Glen Miller, Tommy Dorsey and others were heard on every radio. Frances and Dorothea referred to dancing as "cutting the rug." I wasn't allowed to attend dances, but I was having loads of exciting good times anyway.

I soon discovered lots of boys and girls my age living in the Terrace. When evening shadows fell, we were free to stroll up and down the street in groups. We could gather on the steps of each other's porches to talk and laugh together. We were not allowed to say we were dating. That rule didn't stop us from falling in love for at least a week at a time with first one boy and then another. The boys were as caught up in this romancing thing as we were. We held hands as we strolled along with a chosen heart throb. Two sweethearts would sneak a kiss in the semidarkness, only to find they had been observed, judging from the giveaway giggles of the others.

I was soon to discover that even this ecstasy, of so called carefree youth, had its measure of pain, too. Sometimes one or the other of us lost a boy's attention to another girl before that particular one was ready to throw the boy aside. The same catastrophe struck the boys at times. These occasions caused horrendous heartbreak that we each felt would never heal. There were tears of agony shed. There were many lovelorn messages sent by proxy to an errant sweetheart. Sometimes one of us even regained the straying sweetheart, only to find by the next week that we didn't really want him anyhow. By that time, someone else's flirty dark eyes had captured our hearts.

On one miserable occasion when I wished I were dead because another girl had stolen my loved one away, Carrie tried to comfort me. She said, "Remember a song we used to sing about a boy who flirted with other girls? His sweetheart dropped him flat because of it. He died with a broken heart and then she died because life wasn't worth shucks to her without him. Someday you'll look back, as we have, and you will think of these as your 'Barbara Allen' days. Only you'll be glad that you didn't really die like she did."

Soon it was Halloween and I decided I didn't want to die after all. The city officials roped off one block on Main Street for a Halloween Square Dance. One could hear the shuffling of many feet as people of all ages danced to the music and the calls of "The Mixers," "The Virginia Reel" and "The Birdie In The Cage." There is something about a square dance that can cause strange things to happen. Many times, one's partner could be a perfect stranger as people came to the dance from West Virginia also.

Now when Virginians and West Virginians get together, it's not unusual for the togetherness to deteriorate into fist fights. The rivalry was traditional and it was a matter of pride to keep it up. The West Virginians were proud of their coal mining heritage. They took pride in their higher mountain range. The Virginians were just as proud of their agricultural background and their broader backed mountains. When Virginians visited on West Virginia turf, the Virginians proclaimed they were from the *original* state of Virginia. When the West Virginians came over the line into Virginia, they retaliated by saying they wre from West (by God) Virginia. Whenever visiting on each other's turf, those two taunting proclamations were enough to start fights among the Virginians and West Virginians, especially the teenagers.

The Main Street Square Dance was an exception. There was a hail-fellow-well-met feeling derived from the exhilarating music. The laughter and joking were shared by all. The rhythm of many feet stepping in time to the music of the fiddlers, guitars and banjos, could not give way to rivalry. We were all good friends as the caller's voice instructed, "Now swing your partner and promenade home."

Much of the friction between Eastern Virginia and Western Virginia was enhanced by the controversial slavery issue. The western region refused to join the eastern region when the eastern region seceded from the Union in 1861. Western Virginia, the region northwest of the Alleghenies, subsequently formed a separate state and was admitted to the Union on June 20, 1863. West Virginia was only a two-year-old state when it abolished slavery.

The city of Charleston became the capital of West Virginia. Charleston is the hub of large coal and gas fields, plus many other industries.

Eastern Virginia remained the state of Virginia. Virginia is bordered on the north by Maryland and on the south by North Carolina and Tennessee. It's bordered on the west by Kentucky and West Virginia.

The city of Richmond is Virginia's capital. Richmond is home to many of the tobacco industries. The famed Jefferson Davis Museum of Confederate relics, etc., is in Richmond.

These two states are known the world over for their respective resort hotels and their healing springs. The Homestead Hotel is located at Hot Springs, Virginia. The Greenbrier Hotel is located at White Sulpher, West Virginia. Douglas Fairbanks, Jr., (in this year of 1939,) has a private vacation home at Warm Springs, Virginia. Franklin D. Roosevelt is a frequent visitor at Warm Springs, because of its reputation for having healing waters. Many movie stars come to each of the resorts to relax from their demanding careers. Noted businessmen and other influential people come to rest. They come for tournaments. They come for conventions. The great Worker's Union in America came to hold memorable meetings. Lewis once noted a sign on a door as he passed by in one of the great halls in the Greenbrier. The sign read, "The President's Meeting Room. Do Not Enter. Meeting in progress."

Covington is only twenty-five miles from White Sulphur

Springs. There were dreams of future super highways that would bring these places minutes closer.

White Sulphur Springs is just across West Virginia's state line and Lewisburg, West Virginia, adjoins White Sulphur Springs. Covington, Virginia borders West Virginia's state line. Young people from these small towns on both sides of the line thought it expedient and a matter of principle to keep the rivalry between these two states alive and well! Just before WWII, this rivalry was the only form of excitement young people could stir up in these sleepy, little towns.

Sometimes Carrie grew irritated with Lewis. In his job with the railroad, he always knew beforehand when movie stars or other famous people were coming through by train. The trains stopped in Covington. Lewis was sworn to secrecy lest the famous passengers be mobbed by autograph seekers. Lewis never once betrayed his trust. Carrie's friends beseeched her to find out these secret times and dates. Lewis was like a rock despite Carrie's pleadings.

Mr. Trumbolte had a long talk with Papa and Mama one day while I was still visiting Carrie. Mama related the conversation to us later.

Mr. Trumbolte had said, "Mr. Clark, this farm is large enough to need constant care. It's too much for you of late. I'm very sorry. I hate to lose you, but you'll have to move. I wish I had other recourse because you are fine people."

Mama had said, "I can start doin' Frank's work."

Mr. Trumbolte had shaken his head as he answered. "No, no. This is man's work. It would be impossible for you to cultivate fields and round up cattle and keep up repairs."

Mama had squared her shoulders as she had implored, "I realize that, but I've been doin' a lot of thinkin'. You could take the cattle to another farm and bring in more sheep. I could care for sheep. I could also raise chickens for market. The sheep would keep the land cleared. The children will help me. I can do it. I know I can if you will only give me a chance."

Mr. Trombolte had dropped his head as he answered, "You don't understand. There's far too much involved. A woman and three children cannot possibly do the work in question. Sheep and chickens would require supplemental feed for winter. Sheep have to be sheared. A much larger building would have to be erected to house the chickens. Besides, I don't want many sheep.

167

They ruin the land for other purposes."

Papa had said, "I can still do a lot. I'll do all I can to help Dora. I have good days when my legs give me no trouble to speak of."

Mr. Trumbolte had said, "The size of the farm needs a younger man now. You can stay here until the end of February. That will give you plenty of time to find something less strenuous without having to rush to do so much."

We went home for Christmas. I stayed. I sorely missed the camaraderie of friends my age. Dorothea had come home, too. She planned to stay for a long visit since she lived so far away now. Mama was usually very talkative when any of the older girls visited, but this time she was preoccupied and worried.

Carrie had brought some material for a birthday present for me. I would be fourteen on the eighth of January. Mama made me a new dress. The material was green and beige checked cotton. Mama used some solid beige material she already had for the trim. The finished dress had wide, pointed, beige cuffs on the short sleeves. The beige collar was wide and ended with narrow points beneath my throat. The pockets were trimmed in a band of beige with the pointed effect also. Mama attached green buttons at each of the points for accent.

Mama had sewn darts into the dress bodice like the women's dresses had to give the bodice more fullness where it was needed. I was thrilled. My bust was finally expanding a little, but I didn't think anyone had noticed. I told Mama it was the prettiest dress she had ever made for me.

I was so excited when Sunday morning came. After the chores were finished, I went to the bedroom and put on my new dress. As I looked at myself in the dresser's mirror, I began to have second thoughts. As usual, my thrifty-minded Mama had left me a little room to grow. I knew the girls would tease. I thought about it for awhile and came up with a solution. I had some tissue paper, saved from rare presents. I got out the box and crumpled some bits of tissue into small wads. I kept adding little wads of paper until my dress was filled out in the right spots. Now the darts complimented my bustline. I didn't have a bra. I had to move cautiously so as not to disturb the tissue paper.

The girls arrived just before dinner time with their families. The men gathered in the living room to talk. The children ran hither and yon. The girls stayed in the kitchen to help Mama finish preparations for the noon meal. They oohed and aahed as they admired my new figure.

Dorothea said, "Maybe that was the problem. You needed darts. Those straight lined dresses you've been wearing made you look flat."

Carrie said, "It's strange that the dress could make that much difference. Rosemary, you look positively grown-up."

Elena said, "It looks as though you blossomed out overnight. You look very pretty, Rosemary. I like your pretty new dress."

Mama told me to go pump a bucket of water. I went to the cistern. I hummed the tune to a popular song titled "Blueberry Hill" as I pumped the clear water until my bucket was full. I carried the filled bucket into the house and lifted the bucket up onto the washstand and turned around. The girls broke into gales of gay laughter. Mama grinned and tried to hide the grin. The girls clasped their arms across their stomachs as though to hold onto something. They rocked back and forth as peals of laughter filled the room.

I stood staring at them, wondering what funny thing I had missed out on. Carrie pointed toward me as Elena mopped at her eyes. Dorothea tried to smother a fresh giggle, and they were off again, dissolving into helpless mirth. I looked down at myself to see why Carrie had pointed. I instinctively looked at the bodice of my dress. The left side of the bodice looked as though it had been vacated. The right side looked as though something was in the process of moving out. I looked down at my feet. Several, forlorn little wads of tissue lay at my feet.

Mama said, "Rosebud."

I interrupted her before she could finish the sentence. I said, "I know, Mama. If I can't learn the easy way, I must learn the hard way."

Carrie laid her head on the table and in a voice crackling with laughter she said, "Remember your philosophy, Mama. She was just trying to 'make do'."

That broke up the other girls again. They grasped their stomachs even tighter as their laughter burst forth anew and tears rolled down their cheeks. I left them in their misery and went off to the bedroom to remove the remaining bits of tissue.

14

MAMA!

It was nice to have Dorothea home again. She and Mama were alike in one way. They were both in constant, quick motion as they went about their work. They were different in most ways though. Mama was a quieter person. She was also shy except among family and close friends. Mama hummed tunes off key as she went about her duties and they were always the tunes of yesteryear.

Dorothea was very talkative and she never met a stranger. She was expressive, using many face and hand movements. She sang the new songs, "Blueberry Hill," "South of the Border," "In An Old Dutch Garden," and "Oh Johnny," in her clear soprano voice. The lilting words filled the little white house with warmth.

She was singing one Monday morning as we helped Mama with the wash. Her voice drifted into silence as she watched Mama, who was reaching up to a shelf above her head for a new cake of Octagen soap. Dorothea was silent a moment longer and then she asked, "Mama, aren't you getting fat?"

Mama had gone back to scrubbing the collar of a shirt up and down over the washboard's metal grooves. She said in answer to Dorothea, "You mean you finally noticed?"

Dorothea said, "I had noticed you looked a little more plump than usual, but just now I thought you almost looked pregnant."

Mama smiled as she said again, "You mean you finally noticed?"

Dorothea squealed, "Mama! Are you pregnant?"

I let the sheet I was wringing out fall back into the rinse water. My mouth fell open as though my jawbones had caved in. We both stared at Mama as she nodded her head yes. Dorothea clapped her tiny hands to her head. We sank down on a bench and sat there dumbfounded, staring at Mama.

Mama squirmed around finally and said, "You girls stop that. I feel like a bug on the end of a straight pen."

Dorothea asked in a weak voice, "When is the baby due?"

"In late March," Mama said.

We were struck dumb again. This was the middle of January.

"Are you two goin' to help get this wash on the line or do you plan to sit their starin' at me the rest of the day?" Mama said.

When we came back from hanging up the load of clothes, Dorothea said, "Mama, I'm almost twenty-four years old. I've had three babies. I can't believe you are almost seven months pregnant and I've been right here with you since Christmas and didn't know it." Dorothea looked startled as a sudden thought struck home. "Mama! Do you realize you are forty-five years old?"

Mama bent over the washboard as she nodded her head yes. "I never really looked pregnant with any of you. I haven't told Mr. Trumbolte about my pregnancy. I've been real worried though, about havin' to move somewhere else this close to my time."

"But, Mama, why did you get pregnant again at your age?"

"Well," Mama said. "Remember last June when you brought Bud home from Knoxville? You stayed here for a two week's visit. Frances came home on vacation, too, so she could spend some time with you. Well, the house was mighty crowded. Frank and I never seemed to have any time alone to talk over things, so one day when he was workin' in the upper cornfield, I took him a fresh jug of water and stayed to talk awhile."

Dorothea grinned at Mama, "That must have been some conversation," Dorothea said.

Papa must have been just as worried as Mama because he talked to Mr. Trumbolte about the situation the next time he came up. He asked Mr. Trumbolte for an extension of time.

Mr. Trumbolte said, "I had hoped to get another man up here for early planting. Of course Mrs. Clark can't move in her condition. I wouldn't want her to do so. I will give you until the end of April."

Papa tried to do as much as he could toward getting the farm ready for spring. He had to spend many days away from the farm as he searched for a job elsewhere.

Dorothea told Mama, "I hadn't planned to stay nearly so long, but I will extend my visit until after the baby is born and you're back on your feet. You've always helped us when we needed you. Now I'll help you.''

The other girls came on Sunday and Dorothea raced out to meet them. She couldn't wait to tell them about Mama. They entered the house looking as goggle-eyed as we had on Monday two weeks previously.

Carrie grinned as she said, ''Mama, have you thought about how many children we girls have? The baby you're expecting will be an aunt or uncle to seven children from the moment it's born.''

A friend told Papa about a man he knew who was looking for a tenant farmer. Papa and Mama went to see the man. He agreed to give Mama a chance. The farm had been vacant for a long time. The man was looking for someone who could put the farm back into shape to become once again, a working farm. The wages would be a minimal amount each month. The house, water and firewood would be theirs to use without cost. They could move in as soon as Mama was able.

The next morning, I found Papa standing in the front yard. He was standing so silently, looking out over the orchard. The fruit trees were barren now. There was no field of golden oat grasses waving gently in a summer's breeze. Up above the orchard lay one huge, barren cornfield. Within my memory, I could envision Papa in past years . . . he was plodding along behind Prince and either the plow or the harrow. He was guiding the implement, his muscles taut and strong as he bore down upon the implement's handles. The spewing earth was giving way to the implement, turning over in great clods as Papa prepared the field for planting.

I was to watch that same field that lay above the orchard in years to come from a vantage point far below and miles away. I was to see its barrenness, remembering again Papa's toil as he had worked to clear it of trees, vines, undergrowth and rocks. I was to remember the six summers that same field had nourished rows and rows of tall, sturdy corn. I was to watch as the force of nature gradually claimed it back as one of its own until, over a period of years, it was no more. Once again it became a part of the forest. How necessary is man's toil upon this earth, and in the end, how futile.

My eyes turned back toward Papa. He had been limping badly

this morning. One could tell that his legs were giving him much discomfort today. He stood there looking out over this farm he had wrested from virgin soil. There was pain and worry in his gray eyes. He turned back toward the house, leaning on his cane. The cold wind of February ruffled his wavy, snowy white hair.

"Come on, Bud. You and Fred can help me put up some new roost poles in the chicken house today," he said.

"Papa, life isn't fair," I said.

Papa answered, "Life itself is fair enough. It's easy to handle life's bonuses. What counts is how you handle the hard knocks."

As I looked at Papa, I thought, no matter if his physical labors came to naught, what my Papa gave to life from his heart and mind would live forever.

Mr. Trumbolte came up on Sunday, March twenty-third. He told Papa to bring Prince to one of the other farms on the Monday to follow. He explained, "You won't be needing Prince this spring. You can keep the two milk cows here until you're ready to move and then bring them down. The other cattle will be all right left here. I'm not sure just when I'll get someone else up here to take your place."

Mama had come out to talk to him also. When she heard his instructions about the milk cows, Mama looked sad for a moment, then her eyes brightened. She said, "Mr. Trumbolte, we have some money saved up. Will you let us buy Lady? We must have a cow and I'd rather have Lady than any other cow I could purchase."

Mr. Trumbolte said that would be fine. They agreed on a price and Mama went to the house and returned with the money. Mama was very happy. She was now the proud owner of her treasured Lady.

Papa curried Prince on Monday morning and turned him loose to run free for awhile. He stood watching as the proud horse raced up a hillside. His golden mane lifted in the briskness of the March wind. His tawny coat glistened in the sunlight. He whinnied as though he were asking, "Master, is this my free day?"

Papa cupped his hands around his mouth as he called out, his voice carrying upon the wind, "Go on, sweetheart. Run!"

Prince reared up. His forelegs lifted high into the air. He looked as though he were posing for a prize winning picture. In a moment his hoofs came down upon the earth. His muscles rippled beneath his shining coat as he raced along the top of the hill, running free.

We stood there, looking toward the top of the hill after Prince had disappeared down the other side. Leafless trees lifted their bare limbs upward, as though entreating the warmth of the still distant sun. Their sturdy roots, embedded deep into the cool earth, held their great height as the strong wind swayed them slightly, back and forth. Their thick barks of browns, whites and blacks stood out in bold contrast against the dark greens of the pine and cedar trees.

Prince came back about midmorning. He stood above the orchard, waiting for a familiar voice.

Papa called him, "Come on, sweetheart. Come on home."

The high spirited horse came thundering down the hillside and slid to a stop when he reached Papa. Papa gave him a lump of sugar. He took Prince to the barn and gave him a brisk rubdown and left him in his stall to cool off gradually.

After dinner, Papa went back to the barn. He put the bridle on the playful horse. They started off down the mountain road. Papa and Prince were making their last trip together.

I went into the house. There was bitterness in my heart. "Mama, you said God looked after us. Why is He letting this happen?"

Mama looked alarmed as she answered, "Rosebud, how many times have I told you, you are not to question God. His ways are not our ways. Sometimes we don't understand why things happen as they do, but God knows what He's doin' and why."

"Then why did He do this?"

"God didn't do it. Your Papa knew from the first that Prince was too high spirited to be a work horse, but he didn't want to give him up. God gives us a mind and heart to listen with. Sometimes we go our way and do what we want to do whether it's best for us or not."

I returned to my perpetual, rebellious question, "If we're too dumb to know what is best for us, why did He put us on this earth in the first place?"

Mama gave me her usual answer. "He did more than just put us here. He gave us freedom of choice. We can choose to seek His wisdom in makin' decisions, or we can abide in our own knowledge, which is not all seein' as His wisdom is. I have told you before. If you would read the Bible, you would learn more about God."

I turned and went outside. I went to the barn and stood looking at Prince's empty stall. My heart felt empty, too.

When I left the barn, I went in search of Fred. He was giving Tommy and Mitty instructions on how to mold bowls from clay mud. He had already carved out wooden knives for them to use in smoothing out the rough spots as the bowls gradually began to dry. When Fred gave his approval on Tommy's bowl, Tommy then set it aside to finish drying while he began to mold another. Fred then began to help seven-year-old Mitty because her bowl was turning out rather lopsided.

The morning of March twenty-sixth dawned. It was one of those deceptive days, the kind of day the month of March loves to pull from its bag of tricks. The sun was beaming a warm good morning to the awakening earth. The birds were flocking from tree to tree. Other birds were running on tiny feet over the ground in search of fattening worms. All around us, we could hear the birds' gay medley of chirps and twitters. There were the tiny, slate gray snowbirds and the brown sparrows. Among spring's early returning birds were the blue jays and the black and white chickadees. There were the most important birds to us, the beautiful, red cardinals, Virginia's state bird. As I listened, I heard a woodpecker boring busily into a tree. He was preparing a sanctuary for himself in anticipation of summer's storms. I thought of a poem I had learned long ago at Mallow School. Dimly, I heard again the sound of children's voices reciting, "When the woodpecker pecks out a little, round hole and makes him a home in the telephone pole..."

Mama had gotten sidetracked yesterday from her rigid routine of washday on Monday. All of us had been rather unsettled about Papa having to take Prince away. Anyway, today being Tuesday, she seemed to be in even more of a hurry than usual to get started. She called out, "Bud, how long does it take you to pump two buckets of water?"

I busily added the sound of the pump to the cheerful songs of the birds. Mama and Dorothea halted the washing process about eleven o'clock a.m., to prepare dinner. Other than that, the washing, rinsing, bluing, starching, hanging and drying rigamarole went on late into the afternoon.

Dorothea and I brought in the last armful of clothes from the clothesline. We laid them on one corner of the table so Mama could reach for separate pieces to sprinkle. She always used a small, wide-mouthed, Mason jar. I marveled at how evenly she could sprinkle the water onto each garment. The girls had to use a Coca Cola bottle with a cork-tipped sprinkler inserted into the opening in order to achieve even sprinkling. Mama folded the big, white cotton cloth around the dampened clothes.

"Some of the things people do don't make much sense," I said.

"Why?" Mama asked.

"Dorothea and I just finished feeling every garment on the clotheslines, to make sure they were all perfectly dry before we brought them in. You have just made sure you dampened every dry piece with water," I said.

After supper, Mama got up from the table without drinking a second cup of coffee. She began to gather up the leftover food. She said, "Frank, with the exception of Fred, I've had our children with only my Mama to help me. I think I had better have a doctor this time."

Papa was lighting his pipe. He looked up and spoke between puffs, "Whatever you think, Dora. You just let me know when you want to go and I will take you to see a doctor."

"I don't mean that, I mean I want you to fetch a doctor."

"All right, you just let me know whenever you think you need him," Papa said.

Mama turned around, "Now," she said.

Papa leaped from his chair. He grabbed his hat with one hand and his cane with the other. As he sailed out the door, Mama called after him, "Frank, now don't you run. There's plenty of time. Don't walk back home. Wait for the doctor and ride back with him."

She may as well have tried talking to the wind. Papa was sailing around the bend before she finished speaking.

Dorothea grabbed a bowl from Mama's hands and said, "You go in the living room and rest. Bud and I will take care of the dishes. You've been working as hard as you could go all day, scrubbing clothes on the board and cooking meals. Mama, why didn't you tell me earlier?"

"There was no need," Mama said.

We sailed through the dishes and Dorothea went to the bedroom to check on Mama. She came back while I was sweeping the floor. She added two more sticks of wood to the fire. She put pots of water on the stove to boil.

Fred and I went out to do the chores. Jersey was dry, so he gathered wood while I milked Lady. I didn't do a very thorough job. Lady kept turning her head, stomping her feet and swishing her tail. She wouldn't eat the oats Fred had brought to her from the barnloft. I quit trying to squeeze the remaining milk from her udder and left. Lady remained right where she was, as though patiently waiting for Mama to come.

There was always one kitchen chair placed near the wall at one end of the stove. It was a very cozy corner to sit in during the wintertime when one came in from the cold and snow. There was no snow tonight, but that corner looked inviting. After I had strained the milk and Fred had filled the woodbox, we pulled two more chairs against the same wall. We seated Mitty in the corner chair and we sat down in the other ones. All of the kitchen chairs were chairs Papa had redone with spare parts. None of the chairs matched in design or color. He had painted them with whatever paint he had leftover from the other projects. Therefore, Mitty sat in a yellow chair with a black leather seat. Fred sat in a green chair and I sat in a white one. The latter two had hand-caned seats that Papa had woven. We sat there and watched the water boiling in the pots for lack of knowing anything else to do.

Tommy knelt on the gray bench and tried to play with my jack rocks upon the table. He spent most of his time chasing the small, bouncing, red ball all over the kitchen. Patsy sat under the table. She was chattering to herself as she played with a group of toys Dorothea had placed on the floor.

Dorothea came in from the bedroom. She checked the fire. She added more wood. She added more water to the stove's tank and left again.

In a short while we heard the sound of a motor. We sighed in relief. The doctor entered the house shortly with Papa right behind him. Dorothea took the doctor's black bag. He removed his coat and handed it to her.

The doctor was laughing heartily as he talked to Dorothea. "Mr. Clark called me on the telephone from a home not far from the foot of the mountain. I told him to wait right there and I would pick him up. As soon as I hung up the telephone, I instructed my nurse to send the remaining evening's patients home and close the office. I picked up my bag and left immediately. When I stopped to pick up Mr. Clark, the man told me Mr. Clark had left and had said for me to pick him up along the road. Mr. Clark must have sprouted wings. I finally caught up with him halfway up the mountain road and I hadn't been losing any time,'' he said. The doctor was still laughing and talking as Dorothea led him toward the bedroom.

Papa looked at us and asked, ''Are you children all right?''

''Yes, sir,'' we answered.

He pulled out a gray chair with a slatted wooden seat and lined it up beside ours.

Dorothea hurried into the kitchen with a handful of gleaming instruments from the doctor's bag. She dropped them carefully into the boiling water.

In memory, I saw again a hospital room. There had been a doctor and lots of nurses. They had all been dressed in white. The operating table had been surrounded by tables filled with gleaming instruments. The doctor and nurses had seemed in a hurry as I had fought against the anesthetic. Coming back to the present, I looked down at the scar and flexed the thumb that had been severed so long ago. The thumb worked fairly well now. I wasn't quite sure why this doctor needed instruments to help Mama.

I sensed there was much about having babies that I should know but didn't know. Mama always turned my questions aside with words, ''I'll tell you grownup things when you grow up.''

Whenever I asked the girls, they just squirmed and said, ''Ask Mama.''

We watched the flickering flame of the kerosene lamp. The lamp was centered upon the table. The yellow flame, flickering above the red and white checked oilcloth was familiar and comforting. Papa sat with a deep frown upon his face. He was staring at the stove as though it were a very interesting object. Mitty had grown squirmy and had begun devising ways to hang upside-down from the seat and also the back of the chair. The black leather squeaked as she moved about. Papa roused from his thoughts and told her to sit still.

The clock on the living room wall began to strike. We counted under our breath. It stopped striking on the count of eight. Surely it must be later than that. Patsy was getting fretful because it was her bedtime. I picked her up and cuddled her on my lap. The clock struck again as Pasty began to doze and the sound caused her to jerk slightly. The clock had struck only once for eight-thirty. A few minutes later we heard the wavering cry of a baby.

Papa's frown smoothed out as his lips parted in a broad grin. Fred and I looked at each other and we grinned, too.

It wasn't long until the doctor came to the doorway and said, "Mr. Clark, you have an eight pound girl. Mrs. Clark and the baby are both doing fine. Dorothea proved to be a very good nurse." He motioned Papa to follow him into the living room.

In Papa's haste, he left the door slightly ajar. We overheard the doctor say, "Mrs. Clark is forty-five years old. She's a strong woman, but this has been pretty hard on her. She told me this was her twelfth pregnancy. I hope it will be her last."

Papa said, "I'm sixty years old. I hope I live to help raise this one. I, too, hope it will be the last child."

As soon as the doctor had gone, Dorothea said we could all come and see Mama and the baby. We thought the baby was beautiful with her black hair, baby blue eyes and reddened face. Except for Fred, that is, he wanted to know why her face was all wrinkled up and why she wasn't a boy.

We were all so excited we had trouble getting settled into sleep. I finally went to sleep only to drift into a nightmare. I dreamed that I was running along a clothesline. A thumb was chasing me along the wire. I tried to run faster, but my entire body felt as heavy as lead. Faster and faster the thumb ran. I strained with all my might, but still I ran in slow motion. I screamed out, "You are not my thumb. You are Tom Thumb. I read about you in a book." The thumb laughed and began to make little hops along the wire. It was gaining on me. I tried to run faster. My feet wouldn't move. I screamed.

I awoke to the sound of Papa's voice. He was saying, "Bud, Bud, wake up. You're all right. You were havin' a bad dream." He lit the lamp and went back to bed. I lay there with a quilt pulled up to my chin. I was too hot under the heavy quilt, but I was shivering. I needed Mama and she couldn't come. I thought back over my life span. I had always been subject to the fearful grip of nightmares. It seemed like I had dreamed my way through every unbelievable subject, every distorted vision there could possibly be. Their horrors would not release me from their grasp even when awakened. I had always needed light and Mama's soothing voice to dispel the effects of nightmares.

Poor Mama. She had always arisen at 5:00 a.m., seven days a week. She had been so in need of sleep as she had fought to stay awake with me in the middle of those nights when I had awakened her with my screams. Sometimes her head had nodded and I had asked in alarm, "Mama, are you awake?"

Her head had jerked up and she had rubbed her eyes as she had answered, "Of course I'm awake. Try to go back to sleep. The lamp is lit and I'm right here."

"But you dozed off, Mama."

"I was just restin' my eyes. I'm awake. There's nothin' to be afraid of."

As I burrowed under the quilt on this lonely night, I held onto those words she had so often spoken.

Mama let us suggest names for the baby. She wasn't thrilled with our individual suggestions of Jane, Penelope, Gloria and Rita. Mama chose Carolyn Ruth. Papa never did learn to pronounce it correctly. He called her "Kerlin."

We were fascinated with the new baby. We watched Dorothea bathe her every morning. Carolyn had such a mop of black hair. Dorothea tried to curl bits of the baby's hair around her fingers while it was still wet. The curls fell out promptly, except what we called the little rooster's comb on top of her perfectly rounded, little head. That lone little curl made her look cute and sassy. We watched Mama nurse her. We ran to the bedroom every time the baby cried.

Papa didn't pay much attention to her. Even after such a parade of his own babies, he still seemed almost afraid of a baby's seeming fragileness. He had taken more interest in each of us after we had grown old enough to follow him around outdoors. There he could share his knowledge and inborn wisdom of nature's world.

The days flew by. It was mid-April. Clarence came to take Dorothea and the children home. Tommy hugged me tightly and asked me to go home with him. Tommy was as special to me as Len was. Tommy had been born at our house, too. He had been born on my eighth birthday, in fact. He, too, had spent much time with us. I had changed his diapers and rocked him to sleep. I had played with him. I had taught him the alphabet. I had long ago taught him two little rhymes. I remembered how he used to recite those rhymes with an angelic smile upon his face. "Here I stand upon the stage, don't I cut a pretty figure? Girls don't like me now, but just wait 'til I get bigger." The second rhyme went thus, "Nary a penny, a beggar I must be. You are the doggy, I am the flea." The recitations had always gained him many hugs and kisses from his adoring audience when he had been a three-year-old.

Tommy was still a handsome boy. He had good body lines. His dark brown hair, dark brown eyes and winning ways captured everybody's heart. He would become a schoolboy next year and Dorothea's visits would be fewer. This would also be their last visit to our beloved mountain home. I hugged Tommy closer as these thoughts passed through my mind. Soon they were off down the mountain road. Clarence blew the air horns wide open. The sound diminished and was swallowed up in distance.

As always, the house seemed strangely silent without the volatile and voluble Dorothea. Mama was up and about now. She was pale and quiet. Her days were crowded with the regular tasks plus caring for Carolyn and packing up to move.

"Mama, how many times have you moved?" I asked.

Mama thought about it and then she said, "Countin' a few moves like from one house to another just down the road a piece, this will make the thirteenth time."

"Thirteen is an unlucky number," I said.

"Only when the thirteenth falls on a Friday," Mama said.

I grinned. I had known she would say that.

I was watching Mama stir sticky, moist cake yeast into a cup of lukewarm potato liquid. That meant we were going to have potato yeast rolls for supper. Fred came in and made a motion of licking his lips in anticipation. In years to come, I was to remember Mama's delectable rolls and long for the tantalizing smell and taste that could not be reproduced with dry yeast that was to obliterate the use of cake yeast. Cake yeast had a very dominate flavor, but it lost its leavening power rather quickly. Dry yeast would remain active for a year without requiring a cool temperature for storage. Women were to become more involved in activities outside the home and they would, therefore, seek less time consuming methods of cooking and housekeeping. It was nice not to know this yet on this beautiful April day as the yeasty smell of rising rolls, made with cake yeast, filled the house and wafted through the open windows to tantalize Papa, too.

Early one morning, John Henry came with his truck. He and Papa had played together in boyhood. They had ridden side by side astride their fathers' horses to their one room schoolhouse. This morning, they talked and laughed in remembrance of many boyhood pranks as they loaded the furniture onto the truck bed.

181

The truck began to pull out of the yard with the first load. Mama came rushing out of the house and ran after the truck. She was waving her arms in the air and calling out to Papa. Her blue-checked apron flapped against her as she ran. The truck screeched to a halt. As Papa alighted from the truck, Mama screeched to a halt, too. Fred looked at me and we grinned as we discovered what the ruckus was all about. John Henry had packed Mama's broom on this first load. He had forgotten Mama's cardinal rule. Her broom must never be moved until the last load was packed on a truck and she had closed the door on a clean swept, empty house.

She told Papa to move the stove on the second load. She wanted him to make sure he had the proper lengths of stovepipe to connect it to the flue in the other house. She wanted her stove ready to use tonight so she could cook supper for John Henry before he started his journey home.

I sat on the bare floor and held Carolyn on my lap while Mama swept the floors for the last time. I watched as she turned her broom sideways to reach into the corners with the narrow side of the broom. I thought about her pet admonition to us. "Never leave any rounded corners in your life," she always said. Mama finished and we went out. She pulled the kitchen door shut behind us. She put her broom on the truck and we all became silent as we gazed about us, each with our own thoughts.

I looked at the little white house. The rooms that had been so small and crowded were large and empty now. I could almost see the pallets crowded upon the floor on weekends, to save the beds for the grownups. I could almost hear the music and the feet tapping out the rhythm on those Saturday nights and holidays. I looked at the unpainted, grayish barn. I saw the red barn and the huge tree that had been my refuge the day I had run away from home. It was springtime now, but I wouldn't be building a playhouse under Crooked Jake for my Annabelle. I was too old now anyway. I saw the ring where Fred, Len and I had shot marbles this past Sunday.

I gazed up at the Allegheny Mountains just beginning to green. I looked at the sloping orchard. The cherry trees were clothed in a waving sea of pale pink blossoms. I looked up at the top of another hill. I saw the unplowed potato patch. I could almost see the bent forms of Mama and Papa working shoulder to shoulder beneath the blazing sun. I looked upward, beyond the flowering cherry trees, and I could have sworn I saw Prince standing above the orchard, his proud head held high, waiting for Papa's call.

Mama turned and Papa helped her over the running board into the truck. I handed Carolyn up to her. Papa got in and seated Mitty on his lap.

Mama said to Fred and me, "You children climb into the truck bed. Frank has fixed a place for you to sit. The sun is sinkin' low and we had best be goin'. Lookin' back is a waste of time."

Mama had always thought thus. So we had always turned to Papa for the stories of bygone days and times. Mama said a body had enough to do to keep up with today and plan for tomorrow. I didn't agree with her and pestered her for stories from her childhood and those of our grandparents. If I coaxed a few sentences from her once in awhile, I considered myself lucky. I firmly believed that there must be a past as well as a present and a future. Else, there could be no whole.

Fred hopped over the side of the truck to shut the gate for the last time. The old truck soon left the hard-packed, dirt road behind and labored along a paved highway. I looked back and our mountaintop home was as one with the majestic mountains.

I settled back against the tailgate of the truck and looked at Fred. "I'm going to visit Carrie as soon as I help Mama get settled. You'll be stuck in that silly, new place," I taunted.

Fred looked at me and grinned. There was devilment in his soft brown eyes. "I'm going to have a bedroom all to myself. You will have to share a room with Ronnie and Priscilla," he said.

"You can have your silly bedroom, see if I care," I said.

"You do so care."

"I do not."

"You do care," Fred shouted.

I shouted back, "I do not. You know what Mama and Papa say when we argue. You'd better hush."

"You're just trying to get in the last word," Fred yelled.

Papa stuck his head out the window as he called, "What in tarnation is goin' on back there?"

"Fred's trying to start an argument and I told him to hush. I'm just trying to set a good example like you always say for me to do, Papa," I said.

Fred looked at me in astonishment. I looked back at him

innocently as the old truck roared on down the highway toward a new adventure.

15

YOUNG LOVE

I strolled through the five spacious rooms in this house. After living in the three-room house on the mountain for the past seven years, this house should have seemed like a mansion to us. Somehow it didn't. There was no time to dwell on that paradox though. It was time for the early spring planting.

We hadn't made much headway yet toward cleaning the overgrown fields to ready them for planting crops. Besides, it was out of the question to spade up fields for corn and potato crops. We had no horse now. We spaded up and began to plant a huge garden. The manual spading resulted in four pairs of blistered, swollen hands.

We struggled along trying to repair the fences. Papa helped all he could, but his legs were giving way beneath him more frequently. Some days, he could only lean on his cane and instruct us. Mama had to be taught how to use the wire stretchers to pull the wire taut. Fred and I knew how, but we soon discovered that without Papa's strength, his hands behind ours on the stretchers, our efforts were feeble. Nailing the new wire to the fence posts was the only part of stringing fences we were good at without Papa's help.

Carolyn was a croupy baby, which added to Mama's weariness as she walked the floor with the fretful baby in the evenings. Mama would mix sugar and a tiny bit of kerosene together. She administered this to Carolyn as Carolyn fought for breath. The mixture helped cut the phlegm gathered in the respiratory passages. The mixture was an old homemade remedy handed down through generations of Mama's family.

We kept hoping for a miraculous recovery for Papa, but it was not to be. He finally gave in to Mama's pleading and went to see a doctor. Following examinations and tests, the doctor talked to Papa and Mama.

"Mr. Clark, the jarring fall you had sometime ago when you fell from the wagon to the hard earth has permanently damaged the nerves in your legs. To put it in layman's terms, you have a creeping paralysis. The paralysis will gradually spread throughout your body as it follows the nervous system," he said.

"You mean to tell me I'm not goin' to get well?" Papa asked.

"You seem like a sensible man. I believe you would prefer to know the truth, so you can learn to deal with it. The paralysis will spread. The pain you already suffer will increase in intensity."

"How about me seein' another doctor?"

"That's up to you of course. You will be wasting your money. There's nothing any doctor can do. The only reason you're doing as well as you are at this point is because you are a determined man. You're pushing yourself to keep going by sheer will power."

The diagnosis of paralysis, though valid, served only to further Papa's distrust of doctors. Papa had been so healthy all his life he had never needed a doctor before. Now he did need one and there was nothing any doctor could do for him.

The sultry days of summer dragged on. They blurred together in never ending, backbreaking toil. The sultry nights were just as bad for me, although in a different way. I lay in my bed at night, my tired body aching with sore muscles, listening to the frogs gathered at the pond. The mournful croaking sounds of their mating calls brought tears of frustration to my eyes. I longed to be with my young friends in Covington, or Clifton Forge, or Staunton, or Knoxville. It didn't matter which town or city, just so long as there was youthful laughter and fun and romance. I clamped my hands over my ears, trying to shut out the lonesome sounds of the frogs. Tears wet my pillow as I thought about the happiness and freedom our mountain home had afforded.

I often tried to decide on which was the hottest place to work on such sultry days. Was it inside the house where a fire was burning in the cookstove, or outside under the blazing sun? Sweat dripped from our foreheads and dampened our armpits as we toiled through the humid days.

Clearing the fish pond was a major undertaking. We found old rusty cans, broken glass, bits of clothing, all manner of debris in the shallow, stagnant water. After we cleaned it out, the owner sent a man with a tractor to return the pond to its long ago depth and dimensions. It was near the end of summer before the rains filled the pond sufficiently for the stocking of fish.

Mama's face was drawn and pale by the end of summer. There were some days now when Papa could not arise from bed. She had to take care of the house, care for him and care for Carolyn. She had to oversee the work that Fred and I tried to do. The garden did not produce very well because we could not keep up with tending it. The owner was not well pleased with our summer's lack of accomplishments, but he said he understood.

Fred and I no longer argued for the fun of it. We argued in earnest because we were so bone weary and because we felt so inadequate to cope with the present situation.

Mr. Trumbolte came to see Mama in late autumn. He talked pleasantries for awhile and then he got down to the purpose of his visit.

"Mrs. Clark, I'm ready to take you up on your former proposition to live on the mountain and raise sheep and chickens."

"Why?" Mama asked.

"Well, the young tenant farmer I hired is just not worth his salt. The farm is going down hill fast. He spends quite a bit of his time engaged in forbidden hunting. I've no idea of the cattle count this autumn. I realize Mr. Clark's health hasn't improved, but you and the children are hardworking and trustworthy. I need you to come back."

"I'm sorry, Mr. Trumbolte. I wish you had been willin' to at least let us try my plan when I pleaded for a chance. It's too late now. The kind owner of this farm has been most understandin'. We'll do our best for him."

Some neighbors, living about three miles distance, came to visit us not long after Mr. Trumbolte's visit. They apologized for their tardiness. "Their crops had kept them tied close to home until all were harvested," they explained. They had a son, Billy, who was about two years my senior. They were a pleasant family and we enjoyed their visit, the first of many through the winter.

The Sunday following the Brown's visit, another family came to visit. They had a son, Jim. He, too, was about two years older than I. Billy, Jim and I quickly became good friends.

As always, Papa had somehow managed to meet more people than the rest of us. When he could, he made trips to the mailbox, since our roles had become somewhat reversed. Therefore, he became acquainted with others coming in from their homes to send or pick up mail. On one such day, he came home and asked me if I would like to work for a lady for a week for wages.

"What would my duties consist of?" I asked.

'She's expectin' a baby.. She already has a four-year-old boy and a two-year-old girl. She says all you'll have to do is look after them, see that they don't get hurt and keep them out of mischief. Her husband will do all the work." Papa said.

"We do need the money. I guess I'll go," I said.

"She says she'll send her husband for you when the time comes. I'll tell her tomorrow that you have accepted her offer," Papa said.

A few weeks later we heard a knock on the door. Mama opened the door. It was the man who had come for me.

I gathered up a week's supply of clothing and toilet articles. I packed those in a large shopping bag. The man did not offer to carry the big bag for me. We started walking into the dusk of evening. When we reached the man's home, he took me into a cluttered kitchen where two small children sat, wide-eyed and alone.

"The youngun's didn't have no supper yet," the man said. "Can you fix up a bite for them?"

He left and went into another room. I searched through the scanty grocery supplies, looking for something to cook quickly for the children. I found a box of Mother's Quaker Oats. I measured some of the oats into a pot of boiling water. While I stirred the oatmeal, the children looked at me, bashfully.

"What are your names?" I asked.

"Me Jackie, she Mary," the boy answered.

The man came back just as I was removing the oatmeal from the stove. He placed several large pots of water on the stove and went outside to draw more water from the well. He came back and sat the filled buckets beside the stove. He looked at me and said, "The doctor ought to have been here by now. Come on in the parlor room and I'll have you meet my wife."

The woman in the tumbled bed looked up. The dampened strands of her long, dark hair spread out across the pillow. She tried to smile, but she winced in pain and drew her knees up.

The man stood looking at her helplessly. "I'll go back to the service station and call that doctor again. When I called him a good while back, he said he would be right along. Rosebud, you stay here with my wife as much as you can, but see to it that the youngun's stay in the kitchen.''

"Just go ahead and put them to bed. Then you can come back to me,'' the lady said.

I went back to the kitchen and asked Jackie to show me where their bedroom was located. He led me down a long, drafty hall. He opened a door to a large room at the end of the hallway. In one corner of the room, sat an iron bedstead with a sagging mattress. A soiled sheet and a ragged quilt formed a tumbled heap upon the mattress. A scarred, cumbersome old chest leaned against one wall as though too weary to hold itself upright. I found the children's sleeping garments in the chest. I helped, 'me Jackie' and 'she Mary,' undress and don their sleepwear. The room was icy cold as the outside temperature had dropped drastically. My fingers felt numb and clumsy as I tried to button their garments. The shivering children dove under the heavy quilt and promptly covered up their heads.

"Goodnight,'' I said.

Receiving no answer, I blew out the flame of the smoky, kerosene lamp and started back up the long, dark hall.

By the time I re-entered the kitchen, the man was back and the doctor was with him. The doctor was acting rather strangely, I thought.

He slurred his words as he asked, "Whosh she? Whur's th' lady? Couldn't find my nursh. Guess she must be out partying.''

He kept laughing as he tried to master the English language. He disappeared into the living room, still talking over his shoulder. We heard him talking to the lady and we heard the lady groan.

"He promised to bring a nurse,'' the man said. "That doctor is half drunk. No wonder he forgot to come when I called him the first time. It's too late to find another doctor now.''

The doctor came out to the kitchen. He looked at me and I shrank back. How I longed to be safe at home.

"Young slady, you'll have to be my nursh. I can't do everything myself,'' he said, staggering slightly as he talked.

"I can't, sir. I know nothing at all about babies. I'm only fourteen years old.''

"You can't take this young girl in there. I'm responsible to her father for her,'' the man said.

"Do you want to help? Not that you'd be any help. Men never

189

are,'' the doctor said, grinning.

"I can't," the man said.

"Come on, young slady. I'll tell you what to do,'' the doctor said.

The next morning, I fed the children and helped them dress. I tried to tidy up the rather hopeless kitchen while the silent children watched. I took them in to see the new baby girl, sleeping soundly within the circle of her mother's arm. The mother said the children could remain with her while I did the washing.

I scrubbed the sheeting from the night before upon the washboard. My throat was so constricted it ached as I tried to fight back my tears. I could hardly bring myself to look at the tinted water. I left the cold back porch where I had washed the clothes and went out to the clothesline. As I pinned the flapping sheets to the line, I longed to run away and go home.

I can't do that, I thought in despair. I ran away from school and have regretted it ever since. I can't run away from unpleasantness again. I can't leave this cold, strange family. The lady is helpless. I must stay.

I turned to go back to the porch to empty the wash water. My eyes were drawn toward the road in wishful thinking. Then my heart leapt with joy! Papa was coming up the road. He was leaning rather heavily on his cane. In my heart, I flew down the road to meet him and leapt into his arms. Papa was not a demonstrative man, physically. I stood still and waited. This beautiful vision of my Papa, coming up the road toward me, was never to leave my memory through the years ahead.

"What are you doin, washin' clothes? You're supposed to be lookin' after the children,'' Papa said.

"The lady said I must because there is no one else to do it.''

"Where is Mr. S.? Mrs. S. told me he would be doin' all this kind of work.''

"He's off in the woods gathering firewood. Papa, have you ever witnessed the birth of a baby?''

"Animal babies, yes. Where were you last night? Didn't you stay with the children?''

"I couldn't. The doctor's nurse didn't come. I had to help the doctor.''

Papa's face looked like a thundercloud. "You go in the house and gather up your clothes. I'll be ready to take you home as soon as I talk to Mr. S.,'' Papa said.

"I can't go, Papa. The washing has to be finished. Mama would not like for me to leave a job unfinished. There's no one else to help Mrs. S.," I said.

"You won't be leavin' a job unfinished. The washin' and helpin' the doctor last night were not your jobs. Your job was to put the children to bed last night and to watch after them the rest of the week. That's all the job you had."

Papa returned shortly with Mr. S. They went into the living room and talked with Mrs. S. When Papa returned to the kitchen, he motioned me to follow him.

As we walked down the road, I said, "I was kind of scared. They are a strange, quiet family. Will they be all right, Papa?"

"They're not out of pocket any. I told Mr. S. he didn't have to pay you for last night and today since you wouldn't be finishin' out the week. I'm to stop up the hollow apiece and get a neighbor lady to come and stay with them the rest of today. Mr. S. says he'll go into town and bring his sister back tonight. She'll stay with them until Mrs. S. is back on her feet.

"I wish I could undo this experience, Bud. I should not have sent you off to a family I knew only as a mailbox acquaintance. I got to thinkin' about that this mornin'. That's why I decided I'd better come and check on you," Papa said.

The winter wore on until it wore itself out. With the warmth of a new spring, Papa seemed to improve. Our hearts soared with hope that the doctor had been wrong in his diagnosis.

Mama said since Papa was doing so well that I could go for a visit with Carrie. My heart raced ahead in anticipation. It was April. I was fifteen years old now. I felt as though my young spirit had been released from bondage.

I soon found out it wasn't going to be all play and no work at Carrie's. She wanted me to help her spring clean. Mama had taught her girls well. They spring cleaned just the way she had brought them up to do, which meant we took one room at a time and there was left not one smidgen of room nor one piece of furniture that had not been cleaned to perfection.

I discovered that Carrie didn't iron her curtains anymore. She had purchased wooden curtain stretchers. The stretchers were adjustable to fit various sizes of curtains. Sharp pointed nails, placed about one inch apart, protruded around the edges of the slender frames. The nails would secure four curtain panels placed one on top of another, holding the curtains to their proper shape and proper measurements while they were drying. This was an impossible feat on a clothesline. Judging from our fingers, often pricked as we pinned the curtains over the sharp pointed nails, I personally thought the advantages of using curtain stretchers were debatable.

Carrie gave me freedom from work in the late afternoons and early evenings to be with my friends. On one such evening, I met a boy who had joined the group since my last visit. I shall call him Ned. He had black hair and the bluest eyes! He was always neatly dressed, usually in navy blue trousers and a white shirt. The evening we first met, I caught him staring at me with those blue, blue eyes. I looked deep into those wonderful eyes and fell head over heels in love with him and he with me.

What fun we had from then on. Some of the older boys had old, beat up cars. Ned and I, along with other couples, could pile into someone's car and ride all over the place. Packed in like sardines, the girls seated on their boyfriends' laps, we were living it up. Riding along up and down Main Street, up and down mountain roads, over into West Virginia, we sang all the popular songs with gusto. We joked and laughed, hugged and kissed, and life was gloriously perfect.

We girls wore hair ribbons, which proved to be a pain in the neck to our mothers. They could not keep us supplied with hair ribbons. The boys snatched our ribbons every night. They hung the ribbons over the rear view mirrors of their cars or took them home and hung them on the posts of their dressers. It was an ongoing contest among the boys to see which one could collect the most hair ribbons.

Early April was still very chilly and we dressed in pleated, plaid skirts and Sloppy Joe sweaters, bobby socks and saddle oxfords. The sweaters must be two sizes too big. The white part of the saddle oxfords must never be really clean. It was a matter of life and death to our group of girls that we be dressed exactly alike. The pleated skirts were a special must. We often rode over to Lewisburg, West Virginia, to a small dance hall I shall call, Jack's Hut. When we danced, the skirts swished and swirled around our legs. The girls with the prettiest legs had the most boys cutting in to dance with them.

When Ned and I danced to the slower, dreamier music, Ned sometimes bent over from his taller height to steal a kiss. Often he would whisper, "I love you, my darling." Ooh, how my heart would turn flip-flops at the sound of his boyishly deep voice whispering those beautiful words as he drew me closer to him.

How Ned and I dreaded the twelve midnight curfew Carrie had set for me. Night after night we stood on Carrie's front porch, or sat in the porch swing, hugging and shyly kissing each other. We whispered pledges of our love to one another, vowing it would endure forever and forever, not stopping to remember there can only be one forever.

Sometimes I couldn't resist flirting with some other cute guy at the dances. Ned would become furiously jealous. He did look so handsome as he stood near the jukebox determinedly pouting. There would appear a cute, little frown between his dark, dark eyebrows and his blue, blue eyes would turn almost black with anger.

If he didn't make up with me and forgive my errant ways by the time we said good night, I would cry myself to sleep. The next night, I always said, "I'm sorry, Ned. I won't hurt you again."

Ned always answered, "You knew I couldn't stay mad at you, my precious." He would gather me close against his heart as we pledged our love anew and vowed there would never be anyone else, forever and forever.

On the tenth of May, Mama said I must come home. It was time to plant the early vegetables, such as leaf lettuce, onions and radishes.

That last night with Ned would be etched in my heart, outlined in red hot pain forever, I thought.

The next morning, I sobbed to my best friend, Elsie, "Oh, Elsie, I can't bear the thought of going home. Ned can't come to the farm to see me because he doesn't have a car. Elsie, we sat in the porch swing last night, our last night together. I'll never forget how handsome Ned looked in the light from the street lamp. There were tears in his deep blue eyes. Oh, Elsie," I blubbered, "We must have said goodbye sixty-five times. Each parting kiss was so beautiful. Elsie, what if some mean, old, flirty girl tries to steal Ned from me while I'm gone? Why, my life would be over! I would just have to kill myself!"

"Oooh," said Elsie. "That sounds so romantic." She put her arms around me as she continued, "Rosemary, please stop crying. You know Ned will wait for you to come back. He's hurting just as much as you are over this parting. You know what he told me last night when I danced with him? He said you were the most beautiful girl he had ever known and the most beautiful thing that had ever happened to him.''

''That's beautiful,'' I breathed softly.

I went home with the pain of my lost love written all over my face. I mourned for my handsome Ned as I planted onions and radishes.

Papa came home one day in June and told me something so startling, it made me gasp out the question, ''You mean Billy asked you for a date?''

Papa grinned, ''He sure did, except he don't want me to go on it. He wants the date with you. He wants you to help him celebrate his graduation from high school, his new job at the Paper Mill and his purchase of a car. He wants you and another couple to go ridin' with him Sunday afternoon. I told him he could pick you up at three o'clock Sunday afternoon.''

''Papa! You can't do that. Billy is a good friend. Girls don't date friends.''

''Well, you've been moonin' around here somethin' fierce over that boy, Ned. It'll do you good to get off with some nice young people for awhile.''

''But you can't make dates for me, Papa. That's old world stuff. I won't go.''

''You'll have to go. I already told him you would. Billy's a nice boy. You wouldn't want to hurt his feelin's now, would you?''

I was still angry with Papa as I dressed on Sunday afternoon to go on what I still referred to as, ''Papa's date.'' How could I remain true to Ned and go on a date with Billy, even if he was just a good friend?

I sat in my bedroom and thought about Ned. I tried to picture his handsome face. That's strange, I thought. I can't envision his face clearly. My thoughts grew panicky when I realized I hadn't thought much about Ned one way or the other these past few days. I promised myself I would think about him all day tomorrow to make up for the lost time.

I heard Billy's voice in the living room and then Mama called me. I sat a little while longer. I looked in the marred mirror on my dresser and fiddled with my curly hair.

It was unethical to be ready when a boy arrived. Ten to fifteen minutes was considered the proper amount of time to keep a boy waiting even when you're dying to rush right out. Since I wasn't eager to go on this date, I waited an extra five minutes for good measure.

When the twenty minutes were up, I entered the living room and smiled sweetly at Billy. I seated myself beside him on the settee while we visited with my family for another ten minutes, which was also the polite thing to do.

I liked Billy's 1938 Chevrolet sedan. I listened attentively as Billy said, "This car is three years old, but at least I can afford it. The payments aren't as rough on a used car as a new one. Since I went to work at the Paper Mill, I have to have a car for transportation to work. I'd been driving my dad's pickup truck to work every day until I could save up enough money for a down payment on this car."

I ran my hand over the fender of the dark green car. "The car is really nice, Billy. I like the color."

"I knew you would. I've known you long enough to know green is your favorite color. In fact, that pale green dress you have on now looks nice in contrast against my dark green car."

"Thanks, Billy," I said dryly.

"Oh, Rosemary, you know what I mean. It just didn't come out right somehow."

"Never mind. I know what you meant."

I seated myself in the front seat and adjusted the full skirt of my pale green dress. I resettled the bow of the white ribbon in my reddish-brown hair as Billy settled himself into the driver's seat.

"Where are we going? Papa said another couple would be going with us."

"Yes. We're going to pick up Johnny and Margaret at her house."

"I don't know them, do I?"

"No, but you'll like them. I met Johnny at work. He's been dating Margaret for about a month. He has a black convertible and I've been out on double dates with them several times. They're a lot of fun."

'Who did you date?"

"None of your business, nosey."

Billy pulled up in front of a house on Hemlock Street and tooted the car horn. A boy and girl came out of the house and walked down the sidewalk, swinging hands. Billy introduced them to me and we each said, "Glad to meetcha."

Johnny said, "Let me drive, Bill. I want to try out this old bus of yours."

Billy and I got out and transferred to the backseat and Johnny and Margaret got in the front seat. The three of them kept up a running conversation as we tooled out into the country. The radio was sounding out with lively music and in spite of myself, I was beginning to enjoy this afternoon.

As we sped up and down the curving roads, a strange thing began to happen. My eyes kept being drawn to the rear view mirror, and every time I looked into it, Johnny's brown eyes were looking back at me.

The steep, winding road and the fast motion of the car kept throwing me over against Billy as we sped around the curves. Margaret was being thrown against Johnny. It was a little game all of us played. The driver of the car was expected to speed on the curving, mountainous roads. We called the little game, joy riding, and there was always much squealing from the girls and laughter from the boys as they were thrown against one another.

This afternoon was different though. Billy was just my good friend. As the frequency of the curves increased, I noticed Margaret may as well have been Johnny's friend for all the attention she was garnering from him.

Although joy riding was turning out to be a dull game today, the brand new game Johnny and I were playing was very interesting. Johnny started slowing down on the curves. That way he didn't have to watch the road as carefully as the driver usually did. The slower driving gave us more chances for our eyes to meet in the rear view mirror.

We stopped off at The Falls, near Falling Springs, Virginia. We stood at the retaining wall and watched the enormous sheet of water falling to depths far below. The roar of the rushing water made conversation difficult.

The waterfall is a favorite spot for young people from surrounding areas and for sightseeing vacationers alike. The beauty of The Falls makes a perfect backdrop for picture taking. The young people and the vacationers swap cameras back and forth. The young people take pictures of the vacationers so they will have something to show to their folks back home. The vacationers take pictures of the dating couples, as several couples pose together. When darkness descends, the comings and goings of the vacationers cease. Then it becomes a romantic spot for young couples to park.

Many, many whispers of love have been uttered, almost unheard by recipients because of the roar of the falling water. Many engagements have been sealed with a kiss within the darkness of individual cars parked there. Many tears of heartbreak have been shed there because of broken engagements. A few pregnancies have taken place there. Then, a couple of months later, those same romantic falls have muffled the sounds of a terrified girl's voice revealing a pregnancy to an equally terrified boy.

Carefree repartee, laughter and songs have been shared there. Yes, the rushing water below this ever popular, ever romantic parking overlook roars on its eternal ways, harboring the sadness and the gaiety of many youthful hearts.

The Falls is not a place to park with your best friend though. We took pictures until the sun began to sink too low and then we left and drove back down the mountain. After it became too dark for Johnny and me to flirt in the mirror, we all settled down to singing along with the music coming in loud and clear through the radio. One of our favorite songs and a very popular one was, "Step It Up And Go, Baby."

Eventually we drove back to town and went to a hot dog stand. The fresh air, dashing in through the car's open windows all afternoon, had made us ravenous. We devoured our hot dogs and Coca Colas. Then Billy took over the driving and we took Margaret home first. Johnny said goodnight there also because he had left his car parked at her house. As Billy and I drove away, Margaret and Johnny stood on the sidewalk, waving gay goodbyes.

When Billy took me to my door, he said, "I had a good time, pal. Thanks for coming along. See you soon. Night."

"Night, Billy. I had a good time, too."

The next week, I tried hard to miss Ned dreadfully much. I reminded myself that Ned and I were in love forever and forever. Even though I knew my heart must still be sore from the pain of being apart from Ned, I kept seeing Johnny's cute face in the rear view mirror. Were Ned's eyes blue or brown? I found it hard to remember. Johnny's eyes were brown. I tried to remember the magic of Ned's arms around me, but somehow, they kept changing into Johnny's arms. What could be the matter with me?

197

16

HEARTACHES

We were setting in the living room. It was Saturday night. Papa and Mama were reading their Bibles. Mitty was playing with her dolls, totally absorbed in her own imaginative world of make believe. It seemed such a different world to me now than when my Bilo baby named Lucille had absorbed my interest. Elena's little girl, Betty, had my Lucille now, what was left of her that is. Betty had dragged Lucille around by one leg until that leg had become dismembered. Betty was working on the other leg of late. Poor Lucille. What a way to have to go.

My attention moved on to Fred. He was sprawled out on the floor. He was lying on his back with his legs hiked up and crossed. He was playing a lively rendition of "Golden Slippers" on his jew's harp. His interest in music was increasing. Lawrence was teaching him to play the guitar and Fred was an apt pupil. His voice had deepened and had acquired a golden, melodious tone. His dreams had changed from his childish dream of being king. His dream now was to become a musician and a singer. One could easily prophesy that he had the talent to make his dream come true.

I wasn't in the mood for music tonight, though. I was just getting ready to ask him to cease and desist when his music voluntarily came to an abrupt halt.

Rover was barking. We knew from the tone of his bark that he wasn't familiar with the sound of the car he heard approaching. Papa got up from his chair, laid his Bible aside and reached for his walking cane. He went out onto the porch to wait. Soon we heard a car pull to a stop at the yard gate. A car door slammed shut and in a few minutes we heard a voice. My heart fluttered excitedly when I recognized Johnny's voice as he introduced himself to Papa.

198

They came in together and Papa introduced Mama, Fred and Mitty to Johnny. I sat demurely silent while Johnny asked Papa if I could go to a movie with him, that is if I had no objection, he added. I had none. Papa said to come straight home after the movie.

I settled down beside Johnny in his convertible. He had the folding, convertible top laid back. I wasn't used to riding in convertibles and had not thought to bring a head scarf to protect my hair from the rush of the night wind.

Johnny threw back his head and laughed when he observed me holding onto my hair with both hands. He said, "You act as though you are afraid your pretty curls will blow away."

Straight hair would have streamed out behind me, creating no problem, but I knew what a tangled, windblown mess my shoulder- length, curly hair would present by the time we arrived in town. I guessed he didn't understand that.

Johnny bought a bag of popcorn at the street stand outside the theater. We sat in the darkened theater and munched on hot, buttered popcorn as Humphry Bogart played a rough and tough guy on the screen. After the popcorn was gone, Johnny's warm hand enveloped mine. We sat shoulder to shoulder in the dimness of the theater. We looked at each other more than we looked at Humphry on the lighted screen.

I wished the movie would never end, even though we were paying the talented Humphry scant attention. Johnny's left hand was holding my right hand. His right arm had crept around my shoulders and he was whispering sweet nothings in my ear. Why would I want the movie to end?

Humphry Bogart and Alan Ladd were actors all the guys were interested in. In each and every movie either of these men starred in, his filmed image always strode across the screen, looking tough and nonchalant, wearing a double-breasted trench coat.

The grown men were quite taken with Bogart's and Ladd's tough guy portrayals, too. It had become a common sight to see the men of Covington all decked out in trench coats this past winter. They were caught up in the Bogart and Ladd image they thought they conveyed while hurrying to their places of business or strolling along Main Street on Saturday nights.

Johnny and I left this particular Bogart movie, never really knowing what it had all been about. Johnny drove to Sam's Place. We ordered two hamburgers and two Coca Colas. Sam's Place was a popular hangout for teenagers. It contained many built-in booths with red tabletops and gaudy yellow seats. Sam could stack a mean hamburger. As he worked, he kept up a running stream of banter. His coarse, booming voice and his roaring laughter endeared him to all of us.

Sam's hamburgers were just what the doctor ordered to appease teenagers' ravenous appetites. Sam would place a sizzling hot, thick, juicy hamburger between two halves of a large, warm bun. On top of the big patty, he would slap a thick slice of onion of a size that could have easily covered the large palm of a man's hand. Sam lavished mustard, ketchup and thick slices of pickle on top of the onion. The finished work of art was so big we had to open our mouths like lumberjacks to take bites of its mouth-watering goodness.

We left Sam's and Johnny drove me home. We talked of many things as we sought to become better acquainted. Seated in his car, parked just outside the yard gate, Johnny's arm around my shoulder helped speed up the getting acquainted process. We leaned our heads back against the leather seat's back and gazed up at the stars. Johnny leaned over and placed a firm kiss upon my lips. Our young hearts quickened their beats as our lips met in our first kiss. Our thoughts concurred that these are the kinds of times when young people in love wish they could live forever.

We noticed a light come on in the living room. I knew that Papa had lit the lamp to signal me that my date time had more than expired. Johnny walked me to the door. He leaned down from his tall height, and, whispering the words against my lipstick-reddened lips, he asked me for a date for Sunday afternoon. I floated into the house and went to bed on a soft cloud with a rainbow for my pillow.

While I was busy falling eternally in love with Johnny, Elena was busy giving birth to another baby. Lawrence came up very early on a Tuesday morning to tell us that Eunice had arrived. Mama couldn't leave Papa now for any length of time, so Lawrence had arranged for a neighbor lady to stay with Elena for the necessary ten days.

"Elena said to tell you she knows you can't stay with her, but if her Papa is feeling all right today, can you please come just for today to visit with her and see baby Eunice? Lewis says he'll drive you back home tonight," Lawrence said.

I begged to go, too. Papa said he would be all right with Fred and Mitty there. Mama hurried to dress Carolyn in a pale yellow dress, pale yellow bonnet and white, high-topped shoes. Lawrence carried Carolyn to the car, tickling her ribs and grinning at the sound of her baby laughter.

Lawrence dropped us off at his house and then he went on to the radio station. He was playing in a band. The band broadcasted over the local station each morning at ten o'clock. He worked the second shift at the Silk Mill. He would have plenty of time after the broadcast to come home and change from his suit to work clothes before reporting for work at the mill.

Mama and Elena were busy talking while I sat in a rocking chair and snuggled the tiny, newborn Eunice.

"I'm glad everything turned out so well. I was real worried when you were only two months pregnant and you contracted German measles. They can prove to be mighty dangerous to the baby in early pregnancy," Mama was saying.

"That's what the doctor said. I was worried, too. Eunice is a fine, healthy baby though. I'm so glad all the worry was unnecessary," Elena answered.

"You had a severe case of the measles. We had plenty of room to be worried," Mama said.

"Mama, turn on the radio. Time has just about slipped up on me. It's time for Lawrence and the band. He made me promise to listen in today. I usually do anyway, but once in awhile I forget."

We sat in contented silence as we listened to Charlie Scott and His Harmonizers. Charlie had formed a great band. He saw to it that the band members met regularly for practice. He wanted nothing but the best performances from his band.

This morning, Charlie was jiving it up on his mandolin. His brother was jiving right along with him on the guitar. Wally had his banjo practically talking. Lester Flatt was playing his guitar as only Lester Flatt could play a guitar. Lawrence was engineering the "Orange Blossom Special" right on down the railroad tracks with the train's whistle wide open on the fiddle. The "Orange Blossom Special" wound down on the instruments as the musicians pulled it into the depot. Then Charlie announced that Lawrence had an announcement to make.

Lawrence's voice came over the air waves. "I want to share with all of you good listeners a bit of good news. I have a spanking new baby daughter, born early this morning. I know she and her mother are listening to this broadcast right now. I want to dedicate this next song, in honor of Eunice Faye Herron.''

With those words, Lawrence led off on the fiddle and the band joined in. Their voices sounded triumphant as they harmonized on the words to the song, ''Rubber Dolly.''

We broke into gales of laughter. Eunice slept on, unperturbed.

Lawrence came home with his billed cap perched at a jaunty angle. He was wearing his perpetual grin. Elena kissed him. She laughed again as she asked, ''Lawrence, why in the world did you pick ''Rubber Dolly''?''

''That's the only song I could think of about a baby,'' he said as he grinned down at the sleeping Eunice.

Johnny and I continued to date as often as Papa would allow. We kept falling deeper and deeper in love.

Upon visiting Carrie, I was still bubbling over with my new found wisdom concerning love. I told her, ''Now I know that being in love with Ned was just puppy love. Being in love with Johnny is the real thing. I'll never love anyone except him for as long as I live.''

''I'm not sold on Johnny and neither is Mama. You're in love with the idea of love. It's only a month since you were in love with Ned for the rest of your life.''

''Oh, you don't understand. You've been married for simply ages. You can't even remember what it's like to be in love. I'll bet when Lewis comes home and kisses you, you don't even see stars and hear fireworks explode anymore.''

''Let's see,'' Carrie mused. ''Lewis always comes in and grabs the coal buckets and takes them out for refilling. He comes back in and goes straight to the bathroom to wash up for supper. He plays with the kids a few minutes and then it's time for supper. He never seems to have time for kissing. Come to think of it, I don't remember the last time Lewis kissed me when he came home. Must have been quite awhile.''

''See there,'' I said.

We had been making up the bed as we talked and Carrie grinned as she started to answer me. I never did find out what she meant to say because we heard a voice at the back door, calling out, ''Yoo hoo!''

''Come on back,'' Carrie answered. ''We're in the bedroom.''

No one anywhere in Covington ever locked their doors.

Neighbors walked in and out of each other's homes with only a pause at the door to herald their presence. If one didn't receive the answer of, "Come on back," they received the alternate answer of, "Have a seat and make yourself at home. I'll be right out."

Today, this particular, "yoo hooing" neighbor came on back to the bedroom per Carrie's instructions to do so. She plopped herself down on the slender vanity seat. Her fat hips spread out over the sides and she kind of spread-eagled her chunky legs to balance herself. She and Carrie chatted while Carrie and I finished making up the bed.

The three of us went out to the kitchen. Carrie invited the neighbor to stay for a cup of coffee. The neighbor accepted Carrie's purely polite invitation. That meant we were going to be late finishing the washing and getting the clothes on the line.

The neighbor had apparently come for a bit of gossip. She had no more than seated herself at the table than she asked, "Why didn't you tell me Douglas Fairbanks, Jr. was coming through on the train this morning? I would have been there at the depot to get his autograph if you had let me know about it."

Carrie's face flushed. "I didn't know he was coming through this morning," she said.

"If I were you, I'd have a talk with Lewis. He shouldn't keep things like this from you. A man should never have secrets from his wife. I know I wouldn't like it one bit if Matthew kept important news from me. I'd give him a piece of my mind and Matthew knows I would."

Carrie's hand moved quickly to grab at Priscilla's hand as Priscilla reached for the cup of hot coffee. Carrie was too late. The spilled coffee spread across the clean tablecloth. As she dabbed at the stains with a dishcloth, she answered the neighbor, "It's part of Lewis' job not to tell. The railroad employees must protect famous people's right to privacy."

"I know that, but he could have told you so you and I could have been there. That's different from letting a whole bunch of nosey people know about it."

"He's not supposed to tell anyone, not even me. Lewis takes his obligations seriously," Carrie said.

I could almost see the wheels turning in Carrie's head as she bade her neighbor goodbye and hurried to finish the wash. Carrie never liked it when a neighbor found out something of interest that she could have known first but didn't. Uh oh, I thought, Lewis is in for trouble tonight.

Carrie picked up a pair of Lewis' work pants from the washer and started guiding them through the wringer. The wringer made a sound kind of like "squrank," then it jammed. Carrie released the pressure from the wringer's rollers by lifting the appropriate lever. She pulled the pants back from the wringer.

She looked at the bulge in one pocket. She ran her hand down into the dripping wet pocket and brought forth a buckeye. Lewis always carried a buckeye in his pants pocket. He firmly believed the old wive's tale that carrying a buckeye upon one's person at all times warded off rheumatism. Apparently, in his haste to get to work early and double check on the security precautions for Douglas Fairbanks Jr., he had forgotten to switch his buckeye from yesterday's pants pocket to the fresh pair he had donned this morning.

The forgotten buckeye should have been of minor importance. The needling by the neighbor, the stained tablecloth, her burned hand from the scalding coffee, all added to the nuisance the buckeye had created and altered Carrie's frame of mind. All these things, plus the fact it was nearing lunchtime and the washing was still not finished, made the handwriting on the wall plain to see. The lowly buckeye had just become Carrie's battle cry. She would use it to wage war on Lewis at suppertime.

Just as Carrie was getting Priscilla settled down for a nap shortly after lunch, we heard a car drive up. Carrie tiptoed her way from Priscilla's bedroom. She came into the kitchen and smiled at Elena. Elena had come in and seated herself on a kitchen chair with Eunice on her lap. Lawrence was still outside in the driveway. He was talking to Carrie's next door neighbor, Tom.

"This is a surprise," Carrie said, "Sorry you caught me with the house in such a mess. Today has been Blue Monday all the way. Too many interruptions."

Elena looked at Carrie and burst into tears.

"Wait a minute now. I didn't mean you. Your dropping by had nothing to do with it. I was complaining about the frustrations of this morning."

Elena didn't seem to hear Carrie's apology. She checked her tears and began to speak in a monotone, like a recording. "Lawrence and I just came from the doctor's office. We took Eunice to an ophthalmologist because she doesn't respond when we hold up toys for her to see. The doctors says she has cataracts on both eyes. The German measles I contracted when I was pregnant has caused her to be blind.''

Carrie slumped down into a chair. ''Elena, is the doctor positive? Perhaps you should get a second opinion.''

''He did all kinds of tests. There's no doubt. Carrie, I feel like it's my fault. Carrie, Eunice is blind! My baby can't see!'' With that agonizing cry, Elena gathered Eunice close against her breast and dissolved into a torrent of heartrending sobs.

Oh, God. How does one comfort a mother, grieving for her child? Carrie and I were both fighting back tears. Carrie stood by Elena's chair, helplessly patting Elena's shoulder. Carrie leaned over and gently took the baby from Elena. She handed Eunice to me.

She said, ''Let me make you a cup of hot tea, Elena. You must not let this get you down. It's not your fault. You had no control over contracting German measles, you know. You'll handle this because you must. You're made of sturdy stuff. Eunice will need you now more than ever. Please, Elena, you've got to pull yourself together.''

As Carrie talked, Elena's sobs gradually subsided. She finally took a sip of the strong tea. Though her breathing was still ragged, she was in control of herself now. She sat silently for a time and then she said, ''That's not all. Lawrence was laid off from the Silk Mill yesterday. Orders for their goods are very low. There is only a slim chance he'll be called back to work.''

Carrie whistled softly. ''As Mama will say when she hears about all of this, 'When it rains, it pours'.''

''Yes. Lawrence plans to leave the first of this coming week with a friend who was also laid off. A friend of a friend's is working in Washington as a cab driver. He thinks he can get them both a job with his company.''

''Are you going with him?''

''He can't take us with him. We'll just have to wait and see how things work out. I don't know how we'll get along without him. I need him with me right now especially.''

''Now don't you start crying again. We'll be here and we'll help you all we can,'' Carrie said as she put her arms around Elena.

I was glad when Johnny and a carload of friends came for me that night. I could put aside Elena's troubles for awhile and pretend they didn't exist. We thought we had a lot of troubles of our own. The group grew volatile when I told them about Lawrence's plan to go to Washington to hunt for a job.

"Well, good for him. Wish we could get out of this hick town."

"Yeah, there's nothing to do here. This town is as withered up as my great, great grandmother."

"This town is as dumb as West Virginia."

"It's as dull as my history class."

"Man, it's worse than that. It's as dull and plain as my old maid history teacher." This remark was followed by giggles.

Then Johnny swerved the convertible a little in a teasing fashion when he spotted a pretty girl swinging along down the street. Emitting his mock wolf's whistle, he said, "Hey, guys! Wook at the wegs on that wabbit!"

This remark was followed by playful slaps from the girl friends of the swivel-headed guys.

"Hey, I'm hungry. Let's go over to Sam's Place for hamburgers," somebody said.

"On your mark, get set, let's go!" everybody chorused.

I went home at the end of the week. To my surprise, I found that Dorothea had arrived the previous day for a surprise visit. She had brought Papa several boxes of Prince Albert pipe tobacco. Fred and I immediately began to vie for the future ownership of the boxes when they would become empty. The red metal boxes with Prince Albert's picture on the front were great little boxes to store tiny keepsakes in.

Dorothea drove us to Clarks Gap while she was home. We visited Papa's relatives. Then we drove to the family cemetery to pay our respects to those who had gone on to their just rewards.

Papa's sister-in-law, Elizabeth, had passed away in the year, 1938, three months after Aunt Nanny had died. Elizabeth's husband, Papa's brother, Luther, had followed her in 1940.

We met Lilbourn and Dena at the cemetery. They were visiting Dena's father's grave. Dena's late father was our Uncle Albert Christian Clark. He had also been a half brother to Uncle Henry. Lilbourn was one of Uncle Henry's sons, therefore, Lilbourn and Dena were half first cousins.

They had fallen in love and had married, despite family objections. They had decided never to have children because of the blood kinship between them. Lilbourn and Dena were two wonderful people. They were kind and friendly toward everyone. Their love for each other had grown stronger with each passing year.

As the tall, slender, dark-haired Lilbourn and my gray-haired Papa stood near Uncle Albert's grave, they were speaking of the fact that only two of Grandma Margaret's six children were still living. Lilbourn's dad, my Uncle Henry, was Grandma Margaret's oldest son. Lilbourn' uncle, my papa, was the youngest of her children.

These observations must have started Papa thinking. He began the very next day to have long talks with Mama about what to do and how to handle things thus and so after he was gone. On the days when his legs would not support him at all, he could think of bundles of things to give her instructions about for the future.

"I don't want to talk about these things, Frank. It sounds like we've made up our minds that you won't get well."

"We both know I won't, Dora. You have never had to be the head of the house. I took you from your Pa and Ma when you were only fifteen years old. I took over with you where they left off. It will be different for you in the future. I have to prepare you, Dora, the best I can. You can do it if you kind of know what to expect. It won't be easy, but you're a strong woman."

That same month, Mitty became ill. Mama tried her home remedies to no avail. Mitty's illness continued to worsen. She kept on vomiting and complaining of pain near her navel. Her fever became high. Mama walked the long distance to town. She carried Mitty in her arms. Mitty, though very small for her age, would be nine years old this coming October. Mama had to stop sometimes along the way to rest because the small child was still a load for our five-foot-two-inch Mama to carry such a long distance.

When Mama finally reached the doctor's office, the nurse took one look at Mitty and ushered her past a waiting room filled to overflowing with people waiting to see the doctor. Mama followed Mitty and the nurse to the doctor's examining room.

The doctor examined Mitty and told Mama, "This child has acute appendicitis. She must be admitted to the hospital and an appendectomy must be performed at once."

Mama left his office with Mitty and walked several blocks to the hospital. Mama explained to personnel at the admitting desk why she was there. They said the doctor had called ahead and they were expecting Mitty. When personnel discovered that Mama did not have the $50.00, admittance fee, they refused to admit Mitty.

The exhausted Mama walked back to the doctor's office, half carrying, half dragging the ill Mitty. The doctor became very angry upon hearing that Mitty had not been admitted. He told Mama to go to the Red Cross office. He said the Red Cross would help Mitty.

Mama walked several blocks to the Red Cross office, stopping twice while Mitty retched violently. She held Mitty's feverish head and Mama's face blanched with apprehension.

A Red Cross worker asked Mama the necessary questions and filled out the necessary forms. She told Mama to wait while she made some necessary telephone calls to verify the information Mama had given her. The Red Cross worker presented the information to her superiors and they mulled it over in order to decide if Mama's need necessitated their help. The entire process took about three hours. When the case worker received the necessary go-ahead, she called an ambulance and they rushed Mitty to the hospital.

By the time the appendectomy was begun, Mitty's appendix had ruptured and poison was seeping into her system. Following the operation,the attending surgeon told Mama,"If we had been just a few minutes later performing the surgery,it would have been too late to have saved your daughter's life."

Apparently, even in matters of life or death, bureaucracies must abide by due process.

In August, Mama let me spend two weeks with Carrie, so I could spend some time with my friends. On quite a few of these sultry August evenings, several carloads of us would motor deep into the woods surrounding Covington. We would locate a small, suitable clearing and there we would build a fire and have a wiener roast. After we had eaten our fill of hot dogs and had further stuffed ourselves with toasted marshmallows, we would engage in dog fights.

The dog fights were much on the order of snowball fights. Using the leftover wieners for weapons, our battles were fast and furious. Our weapons often missed dodging targets and, falling to the ground, gradually became embedded with particles of sand and bits of leaves. After the wieners became somewhat like dirty, limp noodles, we would call off our cold war.

Whenever a dog fight was in progress, we girls would leap and whirl as we dodged or threw wieners at our opponents. Our striped, broomstick skirts would balloon out around our legs like brightly colored umbrellas. The elasticized waistbands on the skirts emphasized our tiny waists. Our white, peasant-style blouses with their many gathers complimented our youthful bustlines. The inevitable hair ribbons kept our faces free from our bouncing, shoulder-length hair. The squeaky leather hurraches upon our feet were absolute musts in our opinions.

The boys were equally as stereotyped in their solid color pants of tan, green or blue. Their striped Polo shirts emphasized the rippling muscles in their chests and arms as they drew back their arms to hurl wieners at us. The sounds of their deepening voices, filled with laughter, contrasted with the shriller tones of the girls laughter and squeals of protests.

We always made our peace with one another once the dog fights had ended. Each boy would grasp his girl friend in his arms and lift her high into the air. The girl's broomstick skirts would swirl in colorful array as the boys pivoted upon their feet, twirling the girls 'round and 'round. Ah, on these fun-filled summer afternoons, we wished we could live forever right here in a little glade.

I returned home from my two weeks of fun and frolic. Not long afterward, my love life began to fall apart again. The reason was humiliating this time. Johnny began making dates for Thursday nights only. He had become mysteriously busy on the weekends.

A dateless Sunday night wasn't so dramatic, but a dateless Saturday was devastating. Any girl in our group who was caught without a Saturday night date became the groups' object for pity the following week.

I pined away my weekends, alone. My healthy appetite was gone. The music from Freds jew's harp brought easy tears to my eyes. The melancholy ribbit ribbits of the pond frogs became unbearable.

Elsie came to see me in October. She said a friend of hers had told her that a friend of the friends' had told her that Johnny was seeing a pretty, blond-haired girl. The grapevine had it that the girl had come to live with Johnny's cousin, Maude. Johnny had apparently become smitten with this new girl's charm. The new girl had a job babysitting on Thursday nights, which was why Johnny could spare those for me.

Carrie, who had brought Elsie to see me, said, "I tried to tell you that boy is a rat."

Elsie said, "Mrs. Mahaney is right, Rosemary. Johnny is pretending to go steady with you and he is pretending to go steady with the blond. He's a rat."

Mama joined in with, "I won't say I told you so, but there is somethin' about that boy a body can't quite put their finger on. He never looks a body straight in the eye. That kind of person is usually sneaky."

"I don't care what anyone says," I said in my best anguished tone of voice. "I still love Johnny and I always will."

After two more weeks of misery, Johnny stopped coming on Thursday nights even. My world became a blur of lonesome sobs and heartaches.

17

PAPA

Papa was confined to bed now. Mama set up a cot in the living room for him. The living room opened off the kitchen and we could minister to his needs more efficiently.

Mama's work load increased with Papa bedridden, so it became my job to change bedsheets on washday. The top sheet must be turned down to form a protective flap over the blanket or quilt. The flap was then pinned securely to the blanket or quilt with large safety pins. As a young bride, Mama had begun this practice so Papa's growth of whiskers wouldn't fray the softer fabric of the covers. Alas, the habit had spilled over to include the top sheets' flaps on all her children's beds, too, irregardless of our whiskerless chins. The indisputable fact that pinned flaps stayed securely in place on a restless youngster's bed was a fact that tidy-minded Mama could not resist.

Papa's pain intensified at night. Many nights Mama was up with him most of the time. He tried to roll himself from side to side as he sought to relieve the excruciating pain. He could no longer turn himself. He was completely paralyzed from the waist down. Often, one or the other of us stood by his cot by the hour, turning him whenever he tried to turn himself. Often through the night, he cried out in pain, "Lord, have mercy, Lord, have mercy."

So many times after Mama had shooed us off to bed, I heard the soothing tones of her voice, trying to comfort him. I buried my head under the pillow as I sought to retreat from his voice pleading with God. I still resisted God's call to me whenever I sensed He was calling. I still could not reconcile a loving God, whom Papa and Mama had so much faith in, with the injustices of life in this world. Questions often tumbled about in my heart, as on these nights of Papa's agonizing pain. Why would not a loving God answer Papa? Why had He not prevented Papa's fall in the first place? Why was hardworking Mama called upon to go almost beyond human endurance? I did not accept Mama's answers to me. My heart was too cold to hear God's answers.

We had to lift Papa to a chair several times a day as we fought a losing battle against his bedsores. His reed-thin body afforded no protection against them. Papa still had use of his upper torso, arms, neck, etc. He could pull himself onto a chair. He also had become incontinent, which was a source of humiliation to him.

Papa began to beg Mama to bring a Baptist preacher to him. Papa wanted to be baptized in the fish pond. Somehow he had never gotten around to joining a church and being baptized. Now he felt this unconquerable need to follow the ordinance of baptism. Mama tried to reason with him. She told him he was in no condition for such an undertaking. Papa only became more persistent in his driving need.

Mama visited a Baptist minister. He promised to come and talk with Papa. After several weeks and upon a third request from Mama, he finally came to see Papa. He brought a doctor with him. The doctor tried to explain to Papa that he could not allow Papa to be baptized.

He said, "Mr. Clark, your resistance is too low to fight infections. The water is too cold. You are a prime candidate for pneumonia if you are exposed to cold and wetness."

Papa remained adamant that he be baptized. He turned to the preacher and renewed his plea.

The preacher shook his head as he replied, "Mr. Clark, I cannot immerse you in your condition and against the doctor's orders. Baptism is needful in order to follow the Bible's instructions, but only when your physical health permits it. It isn't necessary to your salvation. The thief on the cross was not baptized. He could not be, yet his faith in the living God was accepted by Christ."

"Well then, please just sprinkle me with warm water, so I can prove my intentions."

"I cannot do that. The Baptist doctrine is that of immersion. You can contact a Presbyterian minister if you would like to be sprinkled."

"I am of the Baptist doctrine. Since you yourself said God accepted a man without baptism, I believe He would have accepted a sprinklin' of me by a Baptist minister," Papa said wearily.

212

The doctor and the preacher left after a round of shaking hands and a prayer, uttered by the preacher. The preacher promised to come back to visit Papa.

He never came back. I added the preacher to my doubts about Christianity.

I was very despondent about life in general. I was bored with all work and worry and no play. On a Monday, as I sat alone in the kitchen I spied a partial pack of Lawrence's forgotten cigarettes. He had left them behind yesterday and Mama had placed them upon the kitchen shelf.

Mama was out in the woods this afternoon. She was helping Fred and Mitty gather black walnuts. She had taken Carolyn with her. I remained in the house to listen out for Papa. Papa was taking a nap. I had propped my kitchen chair against the wall. I leaned my head against the wall and watched Papa's face, drawn and lined with pain even in his sleep.

The longer I sat, the more bored I became. I reached over to the shelf and picked up Lawrence's cigarettes and matches. I drew out a cigarette and lit it. Papa couldn't smoke his pipe anymore. I thought about that as I puffed on a cigarette and tried to blow smoke rings as I had seen Papa do with pipe smoke in days gone by. I became caught up in my endeavor and forgot about being in view of Papa. All of a sudden, I heard his sharp rebuke.

''Now ain't you a pretty sight?'' Papa said.

The legs of my chair hit the floor and I streaked for the stove, lifted the lid and dropped the remains of the cigarette into the fire. It wasn't the end of experimenting with cigarettes, but never again did I experiment in view of Papa.

Fred and I sneaked cigarettes every chance we got lately, from Lawrence, or from Dorothea on her visits. Mama had caught us smoking just last week. We were supposedly repairing fences. We hadn't heard her approaching to check on our work. The roll of new wire had lain at our feet. We had been propped back against the broken fence, puffing on cigarettes. Mama had reprimanded us severely, but she hadn't burdened Papa with our misdemeanor.

Fred and I both were becoming rather devious in our efforts to break the monotony of work-weary day following work-weary day. There were many of these work-weary days when Mama kept going with only two or three hours sleep in every twenty-four. She never once complained. Once again, I wished I were more like my enduring Mama. I had once heard someone say, "If a wish is to come true, the wisher must make footprints." I was making no footprints leaning against a broken fence.

Papa couldn't play his banjo anymore. He must have missed playing and singing dreadfully, because he began to entreat me to sing to him. The older girls could sing. I took after Mama's side of the family. Very reluctantly, I sang to him his favorite songs, "Precious Jewels," "Bringing In The Sheaves," and his favorite of favorites, "Beyond The Sunset." I would sit in a kitchen chair, tilted back against the wall on many an afternoon and sing my very best. Fred always assumed a pained expression and left the house on some pretense or other, even if it were pouring down rain outside. When I finished each singing session though, Papa always said, "That was real pretty, Bud."

About the middle of October, Papa seemed to be having a respite from the terrible pains that had so often racked his body from the waist down. Lewis and Carrie came to visit. When she heard how Papa was feeling, she asked Mama if I could be spared for a week.

Mama said, "I think I can get by for two weeks without you, Bud. I know it's hard on a young girl bein' isolated like this from young people. If I need you back sooner than two weeks, I'll get Billy to come for you."

Most of my friends were back in high school for the fall semester, but they would be free in evenings. When they talked of school events, I grew quiet. This was one experience I couldn't share with them.

I was glad today was Saturday. My friends wouldn't have as early a curfew as they had on school nights. As soon as I hopped out of the car in Carrie's driveway, I asked Carrie's permission to go see Elsie. I ran up the street and dashed into Elsie's house, calling out the regulation, "Yoo hoo."

I didn't know until I entered the living room that Elsie's mom and dad had visitors from Florida. These friends of theirs had decided to take a leisurely trip to the mountains in order to enjoy the beautiful autumn foliage. They had dropped in on Elsie's folks unexpectedly. Their son, Hank, was with them.

Elsie drew me aside and whispered, "I'm so glad to see you. I've got a date with Dick tonight. I can't just go off and leave Hank here. Mother would kill me afterwards. Will you please go along as a date for Hank?''

I looked at the tall boy. His face was very bumpy, (from eating too many sweets probably). His clothes sort of hung on his skinny frame. He had a nervous twitch to one eye.

''Elsie! I thought we were friends,'' I practically shouted in protest.

''Shh. He'll hear you. It's because we are friends that I can ask this favor of you. A whole bunch of us are driving over to Lewisburg, West Virginia. We're going dancing at Jack's. Please, Rosemary. You won't have to dance with Hank all the time.''

''Dance? He probably thinks two-stepping means stepping on both my feet at the same time.''

''Rosemary. I'm simply crushed that you would let me down like this.''

''Oh, all right. I'll go, but remember, friend, you'll owe me one for this.''

I went back to Carrie's and changed clothes. This autumn, we were wearing black ballerina skirts for dancing. We wore dainty white blouses with Peter Pan collars. Black ribbon bows were primly pinned at the throat of the rounded, white collars. Black ballerina slippers completed these fetching ensembles. Our ballerina skirts would swirl magnificently when our dance partners swung us around the dance floor, often drawing a gasp from the onlookers.

It was still a matter of utmost importance to us that we girls dress exactly alike. The boys still had the same set of rules for their attire. Why would any young person want to be classed as an individual or different? Perish the thought.

Dick and Elsie came by Carrie's for me when it was time to go. Two other couples were already squeezed into the back seat of Dick's car. Elsie, myself and Hank squeezed into the front seat, almost shoving poor Dick out of the driver's seat.

Dick sped around the curves on our way to West-by-God-Virginia. The girls were squealing in mock modesty as they were slung against the boys. The boys were laughing as they put protective arms around their girls. All but me, that is.I was hanging onto Elsie's arm for dear life. The boring Hank was ignoring the frivolity of the others anyway. He was talking about his five foxhounds.

I looked at him in astonishment. ''Do you hunt foxes in Florida?'' I asked.

"I don't hunt at all. I just like foxhounds. I have a large pen and runways for them. They're my pets."

"The foxhound is Virginia's state dog. Did you know that?"

"No, I didn't."

"Foxhounds are born with the instinct to hunt. If they aren't used for hunting foxes, all they're good for is to eat you out of house and home. Fox hunting is a great sport in Virginia. Did you know that?"

"No, I didn't."

I was so relieved when we skidded into the crowded parking lot at Jake's. What a stimulating conversation we had engaged in. I could have had more fun at home arguing with Fred.

My earlier prediction proved to be correct. What Hank called dancing was stomping all over my black ballerina slippers. None of the boys dared cut in. Their dates didn't want to get stuck with Hank as an exchange partner.

I was totally miserable by the time another group of laughing young people entered the crowded dance hall. I looked up and noticed one of them in particular. A sandy-haired, freckled-faced boy was making his way to the jukebox. My interest in the evening began to pick up. Perhaps all was not lost after all.

Pretty soon, the cute stranger tapped Hank on the shoulder. The new boy and I glided smoothly in step, except when jostled by other crowded dancers.

"Let's get out of this mob. Let's go get a Coca Cola and get better acquainted," the boy suggested.

We sat down at a small ringside table and introduced ourselves. "I'm Russell," he said.

"I'm Rosemary," I said.

"Russell and Rosemary kind of go together, don't they?"

"Maybe," I answered.

The remainder of the evening flew by. Russell and I sat and talked. Hank leaned on the jukebox. When it was time for my party to leave, I stood up. Russell stood up, too. He asked me for a date for Sunday afternoon. We agreed on a time, then I gathered up nice Hank from the corner of the jukebox. Bless his heart. He had been good for something after all. If it hadn't been for him, I wouldn't have met Russell.

During the lovely drive back to Falling Springs on Sunday afternoon, I decided to call Russell, Rusty. It went better with his cute freckles. Before the evening ended, I had fallen in love

216

again.

My two weeks of vacation flew by, but when they had ended, it didn't matter. Rusty came to the farm several nights a week. He also came Saturdays and Sundays. We went to movies. We went for long drives. We went dancing. Sometimes we didn't go anywhere. We just sat in his car, parked near the pond, and cuddled. The frogs had a different sound now. As we held each other close and talked about our futures, the frogs made hauntingly beautiful sounds. The night Rusty asked me to marry him and I said yes, the ribbits, ribbits, ribbits became a song of love.

When Carrie found out that Rusty and I were engaged, she shook her head in dismay. "You don't really love Rusty. He's a nice boy, but you'll want and expect more in the man you marry.

"You want to learn many things. Deep inside you, there's an inner urge to improve your mind. Rusty is satisfied to remain just as he is, a nice boy."

"You find something wrong every time I fall in love. This time, you're wrong. This time it's for real."

"How many times have you said that before?"

"Only twice."

"Those aren't counting Charles when you were ten years old and Pete when you were thirteen. You also had a solid crush on Mr. Trumbolte's chauffeur somewhere along in there. Oh, and what about Lucious in the first grade?"

"Those don't count. You know they had to be puppy loves. Come to think of it, Ned and Johnny must have been puppy loves, too."

"Me thinks the puppy in you is still there. Just don't rush into a marriage before the puppy grows up."

I wouldn't have admitted it to Carrie under any circumstances, but I knew she had a point. Somewhere, deep down in my heart and deep down in my mind, there were tiny, nagging doubts. It had been so with Ned and Johnny. It was so with Rusty. How was one supposed to know beyond a doubt the difference between puppy love and the real thing? No one seemed able to enlighten me.

Clarence and Dorothea came home for Thanksgiving. Young Tommy was worried. His school teacher had already assigned parts for the coming Christmas play. Tommy was to play the part of the littlest angel.

"I'm supposed to kind of float across the stage. I don't want to be an angel. What if I trip and fall down? Why can't I be Joseph? All Joseph has to do is stand beside the manger and look down at the dollbaby.''

Playfully, I chucked him under the chin as I said, ''The teacher won't be angry if you mess up, Tommy. What she expects from you is that you do your best. I remember when I was in a school play in the second grade. The star of the play was to be a dancing doll. I was chosen for that part. I didn't get to be the dancing doll though. Another girl had been chosen to be a vocalist. She was to hide behind an empty radio cabinet and sing while the dancing doll danced.

"The other girl cried because she didn't want to be hidden behind the radio's cabinet. The teacher switched me to the singing part and the crybaby got to be the dancing doll. It didn't work out too well. The crybaby could have danced just fine, except I couldn't carry a tune very well. I sounded as though I had just swallowed a porcupine.''

Tommy giggled at the story. He asked, ''Was that the only play you were ever in?''

"No. When I was in the third grade, I played the part of a dancing duck. I had to flap my wings and dance across the stage. As I danced, I had to keep saying, quack, quack, quack, quack, all the way across the stage. I wasn't the star in that play either, but I sure did make a fine duck.''

By this time, both Tommy and Mitty were giggling. Tommy would probably worry again later, but right now the worry was forgotten. Mitty was singing, ''I wouldn't be a girl with a little old curl. I'd rather be a duck, wouldn't you?''

Clarence, Dorothea, Tommy and Patsy returned to Knoxville, Tennessee, after the Thanksgiving Holidays. I returned to Carrie's. Everything was quite as usual until December 7. That day, many, many people's lives began to change, although most of us didn't realize it for quite some time. When the news first came to us over the radio, it was only an announcer's voice. He gave the news in a staccato voice. The Japanese had bombed Hawaii's defense port, Pearl Harbor. As the day wore on, we began to realize the enormity of what they had done.

In Pearl Harbor, the Sunday morning had begun as usual. People were going to church. People were playing tennis. People were working. People were sleeping. Tourists were strolling about. Women were giving birth. Couples were making love. Children were playing. It was a normal Sunday morning.

Then came the surprise attack. Japanese bombers roared across the blue sky, high above the blue sea. Bombs, triggered by Japanese hands, came hurtling from those planes. Those screeching bombs exploded upon Pearl Harbor. The Japanese bomber planes circled and came back again and again.

Men were running to man defense arms. Men and women, boys and girls, children and babies were screaming as they sought shelter from the bombs. Mothers were screaming their children's names and children were screaming their mothers' names. Already it was too late for many of them. There were those who could not answer.

What had been a beautiful Hawaiian haven was now a smoldering shamble. The Japanese had turned Pearl Harbor into a crumbling, fiery hell on earth.

Our gang was riding around town that Sunday afternoon. We kept the car radio turned on, but there were no bands playing music to sing to. We listened to the news of the sneak attack on Pearl Harbor. We were too young to grasp the enormity of the horror that was ahead, that, in fact, had already begun. It was something we were hearing about, but it seemed far away from us. Covington had not changed. We had not changed.

We didn't see the event that was so very noteworthy. We heard about it. It was such an important event that it would go down in history, just as Pearl Harbor would go down in history. The event was a televised newscast. CBS presented the very first televised newscast on December 7, 1941, televising the events at Pearl Harbor.*

The gang dropped me off that night and as I was coming in the door, I heard the voice of President Franklin Delano Roosevelt making the announcement. Japan had declared war on the United States of America. Japan was a little late declaring. They had already started the war that morning when they bombed Pearl Harbor.

Lewis and Carrie were seated right in front of the radio, straining to hear every word our President uttered. Their faces looked drawn with worry. Carrie looked up as I paused near her.

---

*Encyclopedia Americana. Vol. 26 Page 421.

"Did you hear what he said?" she asked.

"Sure. Don't worry. We'll beat the socks off Japan in no time."

"It's not that easy. You don't realize how serious this is."

"Oh, Japan is acting too big for their britches. They're just a little country. America can handle them."

"You've got a lot to learn, Rosemary."

On Monday evening we were riding around again when we heard the President's voice over the radio. The U.S. Congress had officially recognized a state of war on Japan. A great shout of jubilation went up from us. Now we'd show Japan they couldn't push us around. The boys began to laugh and to talk about joining up in the armed forces. "Now we'll get away from this hick town and see a little excitement," they said.

"What about us? What are we supposed to do while you all are away having exciting things happen? We'll still be stuck here in this dull town," we girls protested.

"You can still be our sweethearts. You can write to us and wait for us to come back," they answered.

I looked at Rusty. I could envision him wearing a snappy uniform and fighting bravely for his country. He would look cute in a jaunty cap, tilted over his smiling, hazel eyes and freckled face. It was all kind of thrilling.

Carrie took me home the following Sunday. We were in for a surprise. Somehow, it hadn't dawned on either of us that Papa, Mama and Fred would not know we were at war. They had no radio. They received no newspaper. No one had come to see them during this past week. They were stunned and very worried because of the news we brought. They were upset about the fact they had not been aware that the American people had been forced to strike back against another country.

Gradually, we young people began to realize that war changes everything. Even the movies changed. The plots were still about young people and about love, but now those plots were also about war, about parting, death, fear and loneliness.

Before the beginning of any movie we, the audience, stood at attention in the darkened theater with our right hands placed over our hearts. We heard the triumphant music of "The Star Spangled Banner." We saw the printed words to our national anthem as they moved across the screen. Everyone remained at attention and sang the words with gusto and patriotism. We saw the American flag waving bravely over fields of golden grain upon the screen. We saw ships at sea and airplanes flying high beneath a blue sky.

Then President Roosevelt would be shown, seated in his chair beside a flickering fire. He would talk to us as a father would have talked to his adult children, elaborating on important issues such as the role of American people in wartime. He emphasized the need of Americans pulling together as a team on the battle front and on the home front. These messages were called his fireside chats. I thought he was the greatest man that had ever been elected President. He was our thirty-second President and the only one to be elected to a third term.

We were proud of Virginia as a patriotic state. Virginia is known as The Mother of Presidents having brought forth eight Presidents. Those eight were Presidents Washington, Jefferson, Madison, Monroe, Harrison, Tyler, Taylor and Wilson.

Virginia is also named, by order of Elizabeth, virgin queen of England. Virginia was the first permanent English settlement in America. Here, also, was the first representative assembly in the new world.

From her original territory, eight states came into being. Pennsylvania became the second state in the new world in 1787. In 1788, Maryland became the seventh state and in 1788, South Carolina became the eighth state. In 1788, Virginia became the tenth state. Then in 1789, North Carolina became the twelfth state. In 1792, Kentucky became the fifteenth state and in 1796, Tennessee became the sixteenth state. In 1863, West Virginia became the thirty-fifth state. Since these states were a part of Virginia's original territory, Virginia is acknowledged as The Proud Mother of States.

There was a flaw in Virginia's proud heritage. She was also the first state who accepted slave labor when Negroes were brought in on a Dutch trading vessel in 1619. True, Virginia was in the throes of economic poverty at the time, but that doesn't excuse using people as slaves.

Perhaps, in part, Virginia was trying to rectify that error in judgement when she adopted her state seal in 1930. The standing figure of the seal represents Virtue. She is dressed as a woman warrior. She stands triumphant over tyranny, the fallen figure.

We were beginning to realize more and more how war affects everyday living. Food items such as sugar were rationed.

Cigarettes were rationed. Gasoline was rationed. The War Department came out with ration books to be issued to each family. The ration stamp quotas varied according to how many members and the ages of the members in each family. Without those ration stamps, one could not purchase items that were in short supply.

Plants and other industries were rationed on supplies, especially steel, rubber, etc. Supplies had to be poured into industries making items with which to fight a gigantic war. Anyone and anything engaged in the war effort had top priority on all products. Priorities and rations became familiar household words.

More countries had joined Japan in fighting to take over America. Rusty and many of the other boys enlisted in the Armed Forces. They became Marines, Sailors, Soldiers and Airmen. They went away to Norfolk, Virginia. They went away to South Carolina, North Carolina, New Jersey, Maryland and California. They engaged in various types of boot training on land and sea.

There were already parents, wives, children and sweethearts across our land, grieving for sons, husbands, fathers and sweethearts, killed or missing in action. There were others in government hospitals, fighting now for their sanity. (Sanity that had fled from them because of the horrors they had witnessed and been involved in.)

Laughter could still be heard in our land because Americans were an optimistic people. Letters written with humor and optimism poured back and forth between our precious loved ones on the battle fields and their families at home. Often, in the darkness of night, pillows of those at home were dampened with their tears as they prayed to God, entreating Him for the safety in mind and body of our men, and of our boys who had become men overnight.

No doubt, there were pillows, or rocks, or the ground in trench holes, that were sometimes dampened with tears of men.

For a long time, a lot of us hated all Japanese for what they had done to human beings and to our country. It was quite awhile before we began to realize that we couldn't lump all Japanese into one hideous pile. There were some Japanese who hated what their country was doing as much as we did. It was their country though, and they were not allowed to be traitors to their heritage. For the Japanese leaders who had deliberately planned and instigated such a monster as war upon another country, what can we say of them?

Preachers all across our land were proclaiming from their pulpits, "Jesus Christ prayed for his murderers, 'Father, forgive them for they know not what they do.' Luke 23:34.

"These Japanese leaders do know what they have done, what they are still doing. What can we, as Americans, pray?

"Father, help us to win this war and to restore peace for all countries."

It was now July 1942, and we young people had long since learned that war and hate throw up walls. Peace and forgiveness build bridges.

We still went dancing with the few boys left in Covington. Some of these boys were waiting to be drafted. Some were exempt because of physical disabilities, others because of deliberate gimmicks falsifying physical disabilities.

Our boy friends who had enlisted had been gallant in instructing us not to sit at home while we waited for their return. We no longer danced to peppy songs like "Step It Up and Go, Baby." We danced instead to the haunting strains of songs like "I'm Walking The Floor Over You," and "No Letter Today." Many patriotic songs had burst into prominence also. Yes, the war had changed even our music.

Lewis would not be drafted into the armed services even if Uncle Sam came to the point of drafting married men with children. Lewis was listed at the War Department by the Chesapeake and Ohio Railroad as a Key Man. This meant his job was essential to the railroad's war effort in transporting war personnel and war supplies.

Lawrence went to work for Bethlehem Steel in Maryland. He, too, was exempt because Bethlehem Steel made parts and units for warships. Lawrence was making good money in the refrigeration unit at the shipyards. When he came home to move Elena and the children to Glen Burnie, Maryland, he had good news.

"John Hopkins Hospital is close," Lawrence said. "The doctors there are very advanced in newer techniques. They may well be able to help Eunice."

Elena didn't even wait to get her house in order properly before she took Eunice to John Hopkins for tests. When the tests were completed, one of the doctors talked to Lawrence and Elena.

"We cannot guarantee exactly how much we can help Eunice's vision, but we know we can help her to some extent. It will take a series of operations on the cataracts over a period of several years. We believe we can get her to the point that, by wearing very strong lenses, she will be able to see shadows of people and objects. She may always be legally blind, but seeing shadows even will be a great improvement over total blindness."

Elena went home to write Mama a letter heralding the hopeful diagnosis.

Dorothea came home in late July to visit Papa. For the past month, Papa had often mixed our identities with one another's. Sometimes he didn't know us at all. He was more alert the day Dorothea arrived. He knew her name and he was very glad to see her. He drifted back to her baby nickname for the following days, the one his mother, Grandma Margaret, had given her. He called "Dutch" to his bedside several times that day.

Dorothea's visit seemed to have a healing effect upon Papa. By the end of the week he seemed so much better and a glad smile lightened the look of anxiety that had been so obvious in Mama's soft brown eyes.

Mama said, "Frank seems so much better since you came, Dorothea. When you leave tomorrow, I want you to take Bud home with you. I think I can manage for a week or two without her help."

"Mama, are you sure?" Dorothea asked.

"Yes. Bud, I want you to go home with Dorothea. I'll give you money to pay for your bus fare back home. You can return on a Greyhound bus."

Before I consented, I, too, asked Mama if she was sure she wanted me to go.

Mama said, "Bud, you've stayed here at home for seven months. You need to be with young people. Fred is only fourteen years old. He's not interested in datin' yet. You're sixteen and you are interested. Yes, I'm sure I want you to go."

Before I left, Papa called me to his bedside and he said he wanted to talk to me.

"What do you want to talk about, pop?" I asked. I had begun calling him Pop in conversation months ago.

Papa grinned. He said, "I think you call me, Pop, because I wouldn't agree to you callin' me, dad. I kind of like it though. You're the only one who calls me that."

"Is that what you wanted to tell me?"

"No. I've been meanin' to talk to you about somethin' else for a good while. I just never seemed to get around to it. What I wanted to talk about is this. You have to go off somewhere else sometimes to be with people your own age. I know you're always with family even then, but if anything ever happens, Bud, this is your home. What I mean is, no matter where you might go, no matter what you might do, bein' young and all, this is your home. I don't mean we don't trust you, bein' young and all, but sometimes things happen you didn't mean to get caught up in. If you ever need me, I'll be here. You'll always be welcome here."

My throat was all choked up by the time Papa finished speaking. It was hard for Papa to express his innermost feelings, to say what was in his heart. Sometimes we could only guess at what he thought or felt. I knew this had been very hard for him.

"Thanks, Pop," I said. I turned and fled.

A little later, Papa called Dorothea to his bedside. I never knew what he talked to her about.

We left on Wednesday, August 5, for Knoxville, Tennessee. Dorothea had driven home in their car. The drive back to Knoxville was pleasant. The weather was hot and humid, but the trip was much shorter than it would be going back on the Greyhound bus. I had traveled by Greyhound before from Knoxville to Covington. I had had to change buses at Elizabeth City, Tennessee, on those trips. The bus always stopped all along the highway to drop off or pick up passengers. It stopped at several bus terminals for short periods of time. All these interruptions had made the trip by bus long and drawn out.

Clarence was so happy to have Dorothea and the children home again. He was glad I had come, too.

Thursday, I helped Dorothea catch up on a backlog of chores and details. I went to the city on Friday and helped Clarence in the shoe repair shop. I couldn't repair shoes, but I could work at the front counter waiting on customers. The conversational exchanges with the customers was interesting, or irksome, depending on the dispositions of the varied customers.

When Saturday came, Clarence told Dorothea he would keep the children and she could take me shopping and to a movie. What fun we had. We strolled up and down the streets in the busy, downtown section of the beautiful city. We went in and out of shops, looking at many lovely clothes and trinkets. We didn't have money to spend, but we had a great time looking and wishing. We went to a little sandwich shop and ate our lunch. We went to the afternoon matinee at a theater and stopped at a doughnut shop on the way home. Dorothea bought a dozen glazed doughnuts, still warm from the oven.

We arrived home late in the afternoon. Clarence stacked a pot of coffee and put it on the stove to boil. As soon as the coffee was ready, we each poured ourselves a cup. We dunked doughnuts in the hot coffee and had ourselves a treat. We lingered around the table, laughing, talking, eating and drinking. Clarence finally stood up and said, "When are you two going to start supper?"

Dorothea squealed "Supper? Clarence! Where are we going to put it? I'm simply stuffed with doughnuts."

A lock of Clarence's pale blond hair had fallen across his forehead. He ran his slender fingers through his hair to push the errant strands back. His blue eyes twinkled as he grinned down at Dorothea. "The kids haven't eaten, Dorie, my girl, and I can probably find room for a tad of meat and vegetables myself."

Dorothea laughed up at him as she nodded her curly head, "Now the truth comes out, me lad."

Dorothea emitted a mock groan as she went to the sink and started peeling potatoes to fry. I began to clear the table so I could set it for supper. In a few minutes, Dorothea began singing in her clear soprano, ". . . from the halls of Montezuma . . ."

We sprawled out in the living room chairs after breakfast on Sunday morning. We passed the comic section of the newspaper back and forth and then we traded off other sections. Once the newspaper was sufficiently scattered over the living room floor, we got up and began to do the morning chores. We made short work of those and then prepared a big Sunday dinner of chicken and all the trimmings.

Clarence's helper, Archie, came over for dinner and to visit with me. After dinner, Clarence took us all for a long, leisurely drive in his big car. Archie didn't own a car. He had a wooden, right leg and could not drive. He was cute though and a lot of fun.

Dorothea and I spent most of Monday and Tuesday doing laundry and ironing. We also experimented with creating new hair styles for each other. We laughed uproariously at our creations and ended up with each of us redoing her hair to its original style.

Wednesday morning dawned, hot and clear. Clarence left for work and Dorothea and I started on Wednesday's conglomeration of chores. About 10:00 a.m., Clarence walked in the door. He wasn't smiling and his face, always pale, looked somewhat paler.

Alarmed,Dorothea asked, "What are you doing home in the middle of the morning?"

"Carrie called me at the shop a little while ago. You all hurry and get packed. We must leave as quickly as possible for the farm."

"Is it Papa? Is he worse?" Dorothea asked anxiously.

Clarence hesitated, "I don't know any easy way to tell you. Mr. Clark died this morning."

Dorothea screamed. Clarence reached out and gathered her in his arms. I stood alone and trembling.

"He can't be gone," Dorothea sobbed against Clarence's chest. "He was better when we left last Wednesday, Clarence. It's only been a week!"

"Carrie said he grew worse almost as soon as you left. She said he was calling your name this morning. He was calling for "Dutch" just before he passed away."

Dorothea whimpered and Clarence gathered her closer to him.

We were mostly silent as Clarence sped along the highway. The drive seemed to take as long as a Greyhound bus would have. When we pulled up to the yard, Lawrence and Uncle Sam came toward the car in the darkness. Mama came running out of the house and put her arms around both of us.

The house was filled to overflowing when we entered. Grandma and Euna had come with Sam. Upon inquiring, Grandma said Grandpa had been feeling poorly and couldn't make the trip. What that really meant was that Grandma had come away and left gentle Grandpa behind again. True, Grandpa was ninety-three years old now. Yet in the future, he would celebrate his one hundred and fourth birthday by dancing a jig for his cheering guests at his birthday party.

Mama led us through the crowd of relatives and friends spilling out into the yard. She led us through the crowded kitchen and on into the living room. She led us across the room.

There in front of the windows sat the gray casket. I stood, looking down at Papa. He still had his shock of beautiful, wavy, snow white hair. The lines of pain were gone from his face. I

227

looked at his thin body clothed in his wedding suit.

Dorothea reached under the thin veiling to touch his thin cheek in caress.

I did not touch him. I had never touched anyone after life had passed from them. I did not cry. As I looked at my papa, I saw him in his wedding picture, (still hanging on the wall in this very room), dressed in his black, three-piece wedding suit. In my mind's eye, I saw him, dressed in his wedding suit, attending the funerals of his brothers. I saw him, dressed in his wedding suit, visiting Carrie in Craigsville, dancing Ronnie and baby Priscilla on his knees. I saw him, dressed in his wedding suit, happy and excited going down the side of the mountain to the county fair. Now, he was dressed in his wedding suit again, but he was lying so still and silent. My pain went too deep for tears.

Papa had been born on Friday, April 12, 1878. He died Wednesday, August 1, 1942, at sixty-four years of age. That's all his tombstone would say about this man. Only we would know.

There would be no papa to tell us stories about Sweet Kate or Old Joe Clark. There would be no papa with a repertoire of mountain music to teach us. There would be no papa toiling behind a plow, ten hours a day, in order to feed and clothe eight children. There would be no papa to teach us great truths from the small things of nature. There would be no papa, teaching us that if one is upright, one doesn't need the false security of pride. There would be no papa saying, "This is your home. You'll always be welcome."

That night we sat around the kitchen table and spilled over into every available chair crowded into the large kitchen. We were subdued. Mama came in and looked at our gloomy faces.

She said, "A body could hear a coin drop in here. You're not actin' like Frank's girls and sons-in-law. He loved the clatter of all of you talkin' at once and pickin' on each other. He loved the laughter and the reminiscin'. He would be right in the middle of it as always if he could. He would not want you to gather at home and act like you're actin' now. He would be the first to say to you right now, 'What's the matter? You youngsters are actin' like a passel of cats when somebody steps on their tails. Then they creep into the corner to lick their wounds.'

"Now, I'm goin' to lie down for awhile. I want it to sound in here like Frank liked it to sound. I'll be listenin'." Mama turned and went through the living room and on into her bedroom.

We sat, looking at each other, and slowly we nodded our heads at one another. Mama looked so terribly exhausted. Her face was lined with grief and fatigue. Her eyes were bloodshot from lack of sleep. She didn't need this. She needed it to sound like days of old. Happy days with Papa right in the middle of his big, boisterous family. Slowly we began to talk and after awhile to laugh.

About an hour later, Mama came back into the kitchen. She poured herself a cup of coffee. "I couldn't sleep, but I feel better now," she said.

Grandma began telling Elena about a relative of hers who had died in the late 1800s. "He was my Uncle Eugene, in fact, I named my boy, Eugene, after him. Uncle Eugene suffered something terrible before he died. He died of gravel."

We all burst into hilarious laughter. Elena mopped at her eyes as she said, "Ah, Grandma. You must have made that up. There's no such thing as Gravel." Elena dissolved into laughter again.

Mama said, "Mama is tellin' you the truth. A long time ago, a lot of people died from kidney stones. People used to rely on home remedies to cure their ailments. They didn't understand exactly what kidney stones were, or that kidney stones could prove deadly without proper treatment from a doctor. Whenever a person sufferin' from stones passed small bits of stone, they called it 'passin' gravel.' Whenever the kidney stones caused death, it was said that the person died of gravel."

Elena smothered a grin as she said, "I'm sorry, Grandma. I had never heard that expression before."

The rest of us dutifully wiped the grins from our faces, too, and nodded respectfully at Grandma.

I went back into the living room in the wee small hours and stood beside the casket. I wanted to be alone with Papa for just a little while. My mind began to drift back to the years spent on the mountain.

I remembered the long days we had worked together rounding up cattle or cutting firewood. I thought about the hours Fred and I had spent with him out in the woods. Sometimes when we heard a shot, we'd walk though the woods in search of an errant hunter who had strayed or sneaked onto land posted against hunting. Those trips through the woods were philosophical times when Papa would teach us great truths from the simple things of nature. It seemed I could almost hear his deep, slow voice speaking. I thought about one of his most impressive lessons.

"Now you take this tree. It spreads its roots deep into the soil. It draws its strength from the earth, the sun, and the rain. This tree gives back shelter, warmth and beauty. It helps prevent soil erosion. So you see, children, it gives more than it takes. A tree is hardworkin', honest and honorable.

"Now you take this mistletoe. It looks real pretty, way up there in the tree. It looks innocent with its little white berries. It's used by some foolhardy folks for Christmas decorations. This mistletoe has no roots. It's a parasite livin' off the tree. Its pretty berries are poisonous. Mistletoe is a taker, not a giver. Children, don't try to travel through life ridin' high on somebody else's shoulders, like the mistletoe. Build your own roots, like the tree. Do you understand what I'm sayin'?"

"Yes, Papa."

I stood here now in the hour just before dawn and looked down on Papa's familiar face, so still. How vast the silence seemed.

18

THE FUNERAL

The long line of cars left the Blue Ridge Parkway at Clarks Gap and wound down into a hollow. Then the cars ascended almost straight up the steep, private road leading to the family cemetery. We gathered around the gravesite. Papa's resting place would be between those of his mother and his sister, Carrie. On the other side of Carrie's, were the graves of his brother, Luther, Luther's wife, Elizabeth, and his brother Henry's wife, Nanny, in that order.

The casket had to be opened at the gravesite, another tradition of the Clarks, Masons and Fairfields. This was done so that any who had not been able to travel long distances to the homes of those who had moved away, could come to the cemetery to pay their respects to the departed one.

The cemetery was on top of a steep knoll with open fields sloping away from it on all sides. The knoll was always like a frozen icecap in the winter and like a red hot furnace in the summer.

As the long line of relatives and friends filed past the open casket, we stood to one side, waiting. The August sun was blazing down upon us. Sweat was pouring down our bodies. The hordes of houseflies, drawn by our sweat were lighting on our sticky flesh. The stinging pain from nipping horseflies and the sounds of swarming bees added to our total misery. All of a sudden, Mama slumped to the ground. She had fainted for the first time in her life.

Those long, hard days and nights of toil, in the fields, in the house and taking care of Papa had taken their toll on her. I thought about all those many, many nights when she had said, "It's 3:00 a.m., you two go on to bed. You've got a hard day ahead tomorrow. I'll keep turnin' Frank.''

"But, Mama, you know how tired and cramped our arms get from turning him. You can't do it alone.''

"I'll be fine. Go on now. Do as I say.''

"But you won't sleep or rest tomorrow, either.''

"Well, I'll make do the best I can. The good Lord will give me the strength I need. Don't worry.''

I thought about last week when she had sent me off for a vacation and she and Fred had managed all alone. I looked back over the past two days when she had stayed on her feet, trying to make sure everyone had something to eat, that everyone lay down at one time or another to sleep awhile. She had endured right up to these last rites, but now, for a brief moment, she could endure no more.

In just a moment, she was back on her feet assuring everyone gathered around her that she was, "just fine.''

At long last they closed the casket and the church choir gathered to sing. The words of the hymn were lifted into the hot, still air and hung there. "What A Friend We Have In Jesus...''

A friend? Why did Mama and Papa believe so wholeheartedly that He was a friend. What about those days and nights that sometimes blurred together as one when Papa's pain would not stop? What about the sound of Papa's tortured voice, (ringing in my ears even now), as he pleaded, "Lord, have mercy, have mercy.''

Whenever I had protested in my disbelief, Mama and Papa had rebuked me.

"The Lord does have mercy. I could not get through the bad times if He weren't right here helpin' me. He understands my pain,'' Papa had said.

"How do you know that?'' I had asked.

"He died in torture. He died for His enemies. I am dyin' only for myself.''

Mama had said, "Rosebud, you keep runnin' away from God. That's why you question Him so. If you didn't care, you wouldn't bother to question.''

"Why doesn't He heal you, Papa?''

"The body is not meant to last because of sin. He has healed my soul forever. Now is not as important as eternity.''

I looked at Mama's weary, grief-stricken face. I looked at the closed casket. I still did not understand. I turned away in rebellion with questions still raging in my heart.

19

AFTER TOMORROW

After a funeral is over, everyone disappears back into the busyness of life. You are left alone in a void. The void swallows you up into its silent emptiness. It's then you face reality. It comes to you in the lonely void. It greets you with a hard slap across your heart. It's then you either cower in a corner or you stand to fight against the void. I knew which way Mama would choose.

"I need you to stay with me for while, Bud, until I rest some and kind of get my bearin's. Then we'll start makin' plans for the future."

We were seated on the front porch steps when Mama spoke these words. It was the night after the funeral. Rover came up to Mama and laid his head in her lap. He looked at her with his big, brown eyes. He whimpered deep in his throat. Mama patted his head as she comforted him. Rover raised his head and looked at the door. He wanted to see Papa. Mama and I looked at each other.

After Papa had become bedridden, Rover would scratch on the door to signal that he wanted to be let in to visit Papa. Mama would let him in. Always he went straight to Papa. He would squat beside the cot and lick Papa's hand or lay his head on Papa's chest. In a short while, he would go to the door of his own accord and wait for Mama to let him out. Every day for many months Rover had been faithful in his daily visits to Papa.

During the wake, Rover had not been allowed to enter the house despite his pleading, and now, tonight, he was pleading again for permission.

Mama spoke to him in a soothing voice, "No, Rover."

The next day, Rover kept begging from early morning. He finally became so agitated, he was scratching and banging against the screened door every little while.

Mama tried to talk to him, "Frank's not in here, Rover. He's gone." Rover only whimpered and scratched and banged that much harder.

Mama said, "All I know to do is let him in. That's not goin' to solve anything though. He still won't understand."

She opened the door and Rover bounded in with his curly tail held high. He ran to the living room. He stopped and looked at the spot where the cot had sat. He turned and looked at Mama with the saddest look in his soft, brown eyes. He turned and went to the door. He stood there with his tail drooping, waiting for Mama to let him out. Never once after that did Rover scratch at the door to be let in.

I straightened up the living room the following day. Papa's walking cane, that he had carved for himself, was propped up in the corner near where his cot had been. It reminded me of a song he used to sing to us when we were children, "...Hand me down my walking cane, I'll be leavin'......sins are taken away." Papa's walking cane...was it symbolic of a larger meaning? Papa had said God had healed him for eternity. Papa didn't need his cane anymore. Papa's walking cane, propped in a corner...

The owner of the farm came up the following week to talk to Mama. "Mrs. Clark, I'm very sorry about Mr. Clark. He was a fine man."

"Thank you, sir."

"I don't mean to upset you. It's just that you and I both know that you and the children can't run this big farm on a profitable basis. It's just too much for a woman, even of your caliber. I hadn't said anything before because you already had more problems than you could handle. I assure you, you've got a home here until you can make other arrangements."

"I can't tell you how much I appreciate your understandin'. I'll try not to hold you up very long, sir. I just need a little time to rest first."

"I know you do. You know, of course, that my father is a successful business man. Well, he gave me this farm and he said, 'The place needs of lot of work, son. I've neglected to oversee its tenants for years now because of other business interests. It's good land though. I'll be waiting to see if you can make something of it. If you can't, that's all the help you'll get from me.'

"That's why I tried to be tough at first. I had to try to prove myself to my father. When I agreed to let you come, I didn't realize that Mr. Clark's condition would worsen so rapidly. I could see the problems very soon, but I couldn't bring myself to demand that you leave with nowhere to go." He grinned ruefully and then went on, "I guess my father thinks I'm a failure."

"I know your father. I expect he knows more about this than you think he does. I don't think he's thinkin' of you as a failure."

Those next two weeks were strange. Mama took care of the necessary things, but that's all. She rested and slept and slept and slept. She was very silent. At night, she would ask me to sit on the front porch with her. She didn't sit in her rocker. Papa's rocker still sat right beside hers. Neither rocker had been used for a long time. So now, we sat on the steps. She was still and silent.

I didn't want her to be alone, but by the beginning of the third week, I was going crazy. The sounds of the frogs were hauntingly lonesome. I felt I could not stand to listen to them for another night. I was sixteen. I craved to be with young people. I craved to have someone to talk to. I longed to hear laughter, to do fun things. I never wanted to hear another frog again as long as I lived. I thought I had my feelings well hidden from Mama until one night, she broke her silence and began to talk.

"Bud, I'm rested now. I'm goin' to start lookin' for a house tomorrow. I'll have to go to the welfare office to find out if they will help us until I can find out what I can do to make a livin'. It's always been a matter of honor to Frank and me that no matter how hard times got, we never had to ask for charity. Frank took out insurance on you children when you were still small. No matter how hard times got, he was determined to pay the premiums on those policies and somehow, he did. He never would take out insurance on himself though. I wish now he had."

"Maybe I can find a job. I doubt if anyone will want to hire me with so little education," I said.

"I don't have much formal education, either. I have two other strikes against me you don't have. I'll be forty-eight years

236

old in November. Many changes have taken place in these modern times that I haven't been able to keep up with. Yes, it will be hard for either of us to find work.''

''What are we going to do, Mama?''

''I don't know yet. It used to be that a widow just took her children and went home to her parents. I don't want to do that. I want us to make it on our own.''

''I'll be glad when we can move,'' I said.

''That's what I started off to talk about. I got sidetracked onto other things somehow. You've been real good about stayin' with me and you haven't complained. I know it's been hard on you, especially at night. I know how you hate to hear those frogs. I can tell it in your face. You always have thought frogs made everything seem lonesome most of the time.

''I like to hear frogs croakin'. I've always liked the country best. I like nature's sounds and I like the privacy. I like to be where I can get outside and work in the good earth. I like to see things growin'.

''You like to be where things are goin' on. You're young and you're still full of 'whys.' You want to be where you can find the answers to your many questions. When Carrie comes up this weekend, I want you to go home with her.''

''You'll be too lonesome, Mama. I know how much you miss Papa. Fred doesn't talk to you very much, and Mitty and Carolyn are still little.''

''I thank you for stayin' when I needed you. I've rested. I'll be fine now.''

Two weeks later, Mama found a house to rent. The welfare said they would help until she got on her feet. Was I ever surprised when Mama first told me where we were moving. We were moving diagonally across the road from the house on Clifton Forge Road where we had lived when I was eight years old!

The house was a two-story house. It had four large rooms downstairs and three large bedrooms upstairs. In a way, it was ironic that we had more room now than we had ever had before, yet our family was much smaller now.

I could stand in the yard of this house and look up, up to the top of the mountain where we had spent so many happy years. I could see the barren fields above the orchard. Fields Papa had wrested from the forest with backbreaking toil and sweat. I could see the large expanse that had been the potato patch, where we had built our cornstalk teepees. I could see the barren cornfield where row upon row of tall corn had once proudly waved with silky plumes. In my mind's eye, I could see Prince. He was standing with his proud head high. His silky mane was flowing in the wind. He was listening to a familiar voice calling, "Come on home, Prince, come on home, sweetheart."

As I stood there looking up, up to the top of the mountain, I heard the voice of my heart calling, "Papa!"

Mr. and Mrs. Joseph F. Whitlock lived right next door, although the houses were some distance apart. They lived in a white stuccoed house, built in a Spanish style. Mama said she had met the Whitlocks when she had gone to their house to inquire about this rental house next door to them.

"Mr. Whitlock said he had been up on the mountain when we lived there. He said he used to come up there and buy turnips from Frank. He also told me he used to bring his sons with him and that he and his sons had met some of my children. That must have been you and Fred. Do you remember meetin' him?"

I thought for a moment. Then the light dawned. Oh yes, I remembered. I remembered two handsome boys, nicely dressed. I remembered me standing there in the turnip patch, attired in Papa's overalls, his big work boots and my ruffled bonnet!

I said, "I had forgotten about it. It was a long time ago. We were helping Papa in the turnip patch. Yes, now that you mention it, I remember."

"Mr. Whitlock seems very nice. Mrs. Whitlock is, too. They told me if I needed help, just to let them know. I didn't meet the boys. Mrs. Whitlock says there is only twenty months difference between the ages of the two boys. The older boy, Ken, is away attendin' a National Youth Administration Trainin' School at the VPI Airport in Blacksburg. He is expected to return home this week because his draft number will soon be reached. His younger brother, Cameron, is in his senior year in high school."

During the next two weeks, Mama talked to the Whitlocks just about every evening. She still had her milk cow, Lady. The Whitlocks had a cow, too. Their cows' pastures met at a dividing fence. They often stood at the fence and talked awhile when they met near it to milk their respective cows.

Mama was always full of chatter about how nice the Whitlocks were. She had met the boys by now and thought they were nice, polite boys. Fred and I were always busy feeding the chickens and gathering in firewood for the next day while she did the milking. Therefore, we hadn't been near the pasture to meet any of the Whitlocks.

The following Saturday, Mama said, ''Bud, I want you to go next door. The Whitlocks have a telephone and Mrs. Whitlock said I was welcome to come use it anytime. I want you to call Carrie. I'm not sure of her plans for tomorrow, but tell her to be sure and stop by here. I have some business details I need to ask her about.''

''Well, if Mrs. Whitlock said you could use her phone, why don't you go?''

''You know I've never used a telephone. I don't know how and you do.''

''You know Mrs. Whitlock though, and I don't.''

''You can tell her who you are.''

''I don't want to go.''

''You have to, so the matter is settled.''

I was wearing an old, faded brown skirt and an old, faded yellow blouse because I was polishing the cookstove for Mama. I put the lid on the can of stove black and went to wash my hands. Some of the stove black clung tenaciously around my fingernails. No amount of washing would remove it.

I donned an old, red jacket and set off to go next door. Mama had said the Whitlocks usually used their back door to come and go and I should go to that door, too. I knocked on the back door. Then I stuck my stained hands in my jacket pockets. Mrs. Whitlock opened the door and invited me in.

''Hello,'' I said. ''I'm Rosemary Clark from next door. I think you've met my mother.''

''Yes. Your mother is a fine woman. I enjoy talking with her. Oh, I'm Zelva Whitlock.''

Mrs. Whitlock was about Mama's size, except taller. Her salt and pepper hair was cut in a very short and casual style. It curled around her rather broad face. She was holding a very tiny, black, terrier dog in her arms. He was about the size of a wiener. She smiled as she noticed me looking at him. ''This little fellow is Winky,'' she said.

The reason I was looking at him was because he was growling at me.

''Mama wanted me to ask you if I could use your telephone to make a call for her?'' I said.

''Indeed you can. I'm very busy here in the kitchen. I'm in the middle of cooking dinner. I picked up Winky when you knocked because he sometimes nips at strangers. Just go on into the dining room and then through the door to your left. The telephone is in the living room. My son is in there. He'll show you the phone.''

''Thank you, Mrs. Whitlock. I'll only be a minute.''

I entered the living room. There, on the couch, sprawled a boy. He was longer than the couch. His head was propped on one couch arm and his feet dangled over the other couch arm. He was reading a comic book. He looked up when I came in, but he didn't rise.

''Hi,'' I said. ''I'm Rosemary Clark.''

''Hi,'' he said.

''Mrs. Whitlock said I could use your phone.''

He stuck up an arm and pointed over his head to a small table. The telephone was on the table. ''It's right there,'' he said.

I looked at the telephone. How was I going to get to it without leaning over his head? I stood in the middle of the room and shifted from one foot to the other. He kept on reading as though whatever was in that comic book was of momentous importance.

After a moment, he looked up again and said, ''Oh, do you want me to move?'' He swung his feet around to the floor and sat up about midways of the couch seat. A lock of his light brown hair dangled over his forehead. He kept on reading even while he was shifting his position.

I went over to the couch and sat down near the end. The telephone was shaped like a long, black stem with a flat bottom. A long, slender receiver hung from the side by resting in a curved hook attached to the stem. I peeped sideways at the boy. He was still reading. I slipped my hands out of my pockets.

I picked up the phone and holding it in one hand, lifted the receiver free with the other. I put the receiver close to my ear and waited for the operator to ask what number I wanted. The operator didn't say anything. I hung up the receiver, lifted it again and waited. No operator.

I sat there in misery. I wished I were in Alaska. I felt like kicking the boy. He kept on reading, letting me stew in my own discomfiture. And Mama thought he was polite!

I picked up the receiver again. Still no operator. Finally, the guy looked up from his comic book.

"You don't know how to use the telephone?" he asked.

"I know how to use a telephone. The operator isn't answering."

"I didn't hear the bell ring. Did you ring her?"

"What do you mean, ring her?"

"Have you never used a country telephone?"

"What's the difference between a country telephone and a town telephone?"

"You must be used to town telephones. You see, in town when you pick up the receiver, it automatically rings the operator and she answers. The country telephone doesn't work that way. Just picking up the receiver doesn't open the line. You have to ring her yourself."

I looked at the telephone. How was I supposed to ring her?

I saw him glance at my stained hands as he asked, "Would you like for me to ring her for you?"

I hated to say it, but I had to. "Yes, please," I said.

The boy got up and came to stand in front of me. He reached up to a contraption that looked like an oblong box on the wall. I hadn't even noticed the box and wouldn't have known it had anything to do with the telephone if I had. He reached for a little handle on the side of the box and started cranking it. The bell rang.

He handed me the receiver and said, "The operator is on the line now. You can tell her what number you want."

I told the operator Carrie's number. She rang it. I gave Carrie my brief message when she answered her ring and then I hung up the receiver and set the telephone back on the table. I stood up to leave. The boy had reseated himself on the couch and was reading the comic book again.

"Thank you," I said.

He looked up and smiled. I stood there a moment looking into his hazel eyes while he looked into my greenish eyes. He was dressed in a pair of gray tweed slacks. His long-sleeved, white dress shirt was open at the throat. I still didn't know which one of the Whitlock boys this was. He hadn't bothered to tell me his name.

As we looked at each other, it was as though I were being transported back to the turnip patch. Once again, here I stood in all my tattered glory. Once again, I was at a disadvantage. Was this to be my fate, meeting this boy again and again in circumstances awkward to me? Once again, I was unaware that I was looking into the face of my destiny.

But then, that's another story.